# Literary Translation

*Literary Translation* introduces students to the components of the discipline and models the practice. Three concise chapters help to familiarize students with:

- what motivates the act of translation
- how to read and critique literary translations
- how to read for translation.

A range of sustained case studies, both from existing sources and the author's own research, are provided along with a selection of relevant tasks and activities and a detailed glossary. The book is also complemented by a feature entitled 'How to get started in literary translation' on the Routledge Translation Studies Portal (http://cw.routledge.com/textbooks/translationstudies/).

*Literary Translation* is an essential guidebook for all students of literary translation within advanced undergraduate and postgraduate/graduate programmes in translation studies, comparative literature and modern languages.

**Chantal Wright** Associate Professor of Translation as a Literary Practice at the University of Warwick, UK, is a translation theorist as well as a translator from German and French. She is the author of *Yoko Tawada's 'Portrait of a Tongue': An Experimental Translation* (2013).

# Routledge Translation Guides

*Routledge Translation Guides* cover the key translation text types and genres and equip translators and students of translation with the skills needed to translate them. Concise, accessible and written by leading authorities, they include examples from existing translations, activities, further reading suggestions and a glossary of key terms.

**Literary Translation**
*Chantal Wright*

**Scientific and Technical Translation**
*Maeve Olohan*

# Literary Translation

## Chantal Wright

LONDON AND NEW YORK

First published 2016
by Routledge
2 Park Square, Milton Park, Abingdon, Oxon OX14 4RN

and by Routledge
711 Third Avenue, New York, NY 10017

*Routledge is an imprint of the Taylor & Francis Group, an informa business*

©2016 Chantal Wright

The right of Chantal Wright to be identified as author of this work has been asserted by him/her in accordance with sections 77 and 78 of the Copyright, Designs and Patents Act 1988.

All rights reserved. No part of this book may be reprinted or reproduced or utilised in any form or by any electronic, mechanical, or other means, now known or hereafter invented, including photocopying and recording, or in any information storage or retrieval system, without permission in writing from the publishers.

*Trademark notice:* Product or corporate names may be trademarks or registered trademarks, and are used only for identification and explanation without intent
to infringe.

*British Library Cataloguing-in-Publication Data*
*A catalogue record for this book is available from the British Library*

*Library of Congress Cataloging-in-Publication Data*
Names: Wright, Chantal, author. Title: Literary translation/
by Chantal Wright. Description: Milton Park, Abingdon, Oxon;
New York, NY: Routledge, [2016] | Series: Routledge Translation
Guides | Includes bibliographical references and index.
Identifiers: LCCN 2015039255 | ISBN 9780415745314 (hbk) |
ISBN 9780415745321 (pbk) | ISBN 9781315643694 (ebk)
Subjects: LCSH: Translating and interpreting–Study and teaching. |
Translating and interpreting–Handbooks, manuals, etc. | Translating
and interpreting–Theory, etc. Classification: LCC P306.5.W75 2016 |
DDC 418/.04–dc23LC record available at http://lccn.loc.gov/
2015039255

ISBN: 978-0-415-74531-4 (hbk)
ISBN: 978-0-415-74532-1 (pbk)
ISBN: 978-1-3156-4369-4 (ebk)

Typeset in Sabon
by Sunrise Setting Ltd, Paignton, UK

**For Dan**

# Contents

| | | |
|---|---|---|
| | *Acknowledgements* | viii |
| | Introduction | 1 |
| 1 | Why do we translate? | 13 |
| 2 | How do we read translations? | 81 |
| 3 | How do translators read? | 120 |
| | Conclusion | 162 |
| | Appendix: Tzveta Sofronieva's German-language poems | 164 |
| | *Glossary* | 167 |
| | *Index* | 175 |

# Acknowledgements

I owe a debt of gratitude to several institutions and many individuals whose help over the course of writing this book was invaluable.

I would like to begin by thanking the School of Modern Languages and Cultures and the Centre for Intercultural Mediation at Durham University, and the School of Translation and Interpretation at the University of Ottawa for hosting me as a Visiting Fellow during the writing of this book. Special thanks are due to Federico Federici, Francis Jones and Luise von Flotow for their practical and moral support in 2013–14.

Sincere thanks are due to those translators who shared their work, their stories and, on occasion, their righteous outrage: Rohini Chowdhury, Peter Filkins, Hana Linhartová, Trista Selous, Maja Soljan, Lorena Terando, Helen Wang and other members of the Translators Association who very kindly responded to my enquiry on the TA e-mail list about translation reviews.

Many thanks to the writers Pankaj Mishra, J. Mark Smith and Tzveta Sofronieva for their willingness to discuss and share their work.

Gratitude is also due to my academic colleagues, many of whom are also translators, for sharing work in advance of its publication date, discussing their approach to teaching, patiently answering queries, pointing me in the direction of interesting material and offering expertise in languages beyond my ken: Kathryn Batchelor, Jean Boase-Beier, Michelle Bolduc, Patrick Gray, Daniel Hahn, Shengchi Hsu, Jason Jones, Gerard McGowan, Leah Leone, A.H. Merrills, Loredana Polezzi, Karen Seago, the members of the children's literature reading group at the University of Warwick, and finally the Translation Studies academic community at large, without whose work this book would not have been possible.

Thank you to my students at the University of Alberta, Mount Allison University, the University of Wisconsin–Milwaukee and the University of Warwick. This book benefitted immensely from our classroom discussions.

Many thanks to Susan Harris and *Words Without Borders* for waiving the need for formal copyright permission for material borrowed from their publication.

# Acknowledgements ix

I would also like to thank my very patient editors at Routledge, Laura Sandford and Louise Semlyen, and Kelly Washbourne for his careful reading of the manuscript and thoughtful comments.

Finally, my particular thanks go to Professor Emeritus Jean Boase-Beier and Professor Emeritus Clive Scott of the University of East Anglia, who showed me that intellectual example need not exclude kindness and grace; to my former colleagues in Translation and Interpreting Studies at the University of Wisconsin–Milwaukee – Lorena Terando, Kathryn Scholz and Leah Leone – models of professionalism in translator education during a dark political age; and to Dan Vyleta, for everything.

The author gratefully acknowledges the permission granted to reproduce the copyright material in this book:

Excerpts from *If This Be Treason* by Gregory Rabassa. Copyright © 2005 by Gregory Rabassa. Reproduced by permission of New Directions Publishing Corp.

Excerpts from *On Translator Ethics* by Anthony Pym. Translated by Heike Walker. Copyright © 2012 by John Benjamins B.V. Reproduced by permission of John Benjamins B.V.

Excerpts from *Translation as Literary Criticism* by Marilyn Gaddis Rose. Copyright © 1997 by Marilyn Gaddis Rose. Published by St. Jerome Publishing. Reproduced by permission of Taylor and Francis.

Excerpts from *Why Translation Matters* by Edith Grossman. Copyright © 2010 by Edith Grossman. Reproduced by permission of Yale University Press.

Excerpts from 'The Magic Mountain' and 'The Lives of a Flaneur' from THE BOOK OF MY LIVES. Copyright © 2014 by Aleksandar Hemon. Reproduced by permission of Farrar, Straus and Giroux, LLC. and Macmillan Publishers Ltd.

Excerpts from *Orientalism* by Edward W. Said. Copyright © 1978 by Edward W. Said. Reproduced by permission of Pantheon Books, an imprint of the Knopf Doubleday Publishing Group, a division of Penguin Random House LLC. All rights reserved. Any third party use of this material, outside of this publication, is prohibited. Interested parties must apply directly to Penguin Random House LLC for permission.

Excerpts from 'After Strachey' by Adam Phillips. Copyright © 2007 by Adam Phillips. Published by *London Review of Books*, www.lrb.co.uk. Reproduced by permission of the author.

Excerpts from *Demons* by Fyodor Dostoevsky. Translated by Richard Pevear and Larissa Volokhonsky. Published by Vintage Classics. Reproduced by permission of The Random House Group Ltd. and Random House USA.

Excerpts from 'Fairy Tale, Fantasy and Folklore'. Copyright © 2011 by *New Books in German*. Reproduced by permission of *New Books in German*, www.new-books-in-german.com.

# Acknowledgements

Excerpts from *A Grain of Truth* by Zygmunt Miłoszewski. Translated by Antonia Lloyd-Jones. Copyright © 2011 by Wydawnictwo W.A.B. English translation copyright © 2012 by Antonia Lloyd-Jones. Reproduced by permission of Bitter Lemon Press.

Excerpts from *Der Zauberberg* by Thomas Mann. Copyright © 1924 by S. Fischer Verlag, Berlin. Reproduced by permission of S. Fischer Verlag GmbH, Frankfurt am Main.

Excerpts from *Revenge* by Yoko Ogawa. Translated by Stephen Snyder. Copyright © 1998 by Yoko Ogawa. English translation copyright © 2013 by Stephen Snyder. Published by Harvill Secker. Reproduced by permission of The Random House Group Ltd.

Excerpts from *Revenge: Eleven Dark Tales* by Yoko Ogawa. Translated by Stephen Snyder. Copyright © 2013 by Yoko Ogawa. Reproduced by permission of St. Martin's Press. All rights reserved.

Excerpt from pp. 359–61 (288 words) from *The Good Soldier Švejk* by Jaroslav Hašek. Translated by Cecil Parrott. English translation copyright © 1973 by Cecil Parrott. Reproduced by permission of HarperCollins Publishers and Johnson & Alcock Ltd.

Excerpt from pp. 359–61 of *The Good Soldier Švejk and his Fortunes in the World War* by Jaroslav Hašek. Translated by Cecil Parrott. Copyright © the Estate of Sir Cecil Parrott, New York, Thomas Y. Crowell Company, 1973. Reproduced with permission of Johnson & Alcock Ltd.

Excerpts from *A Critical Introduction to Translation Studies* by Jean Boase-Beier. Copyright © 2011 by Jean Boase-Beier, Continuum Publishing. Reproduced by permission of Bloomsbury Publishing Plc.

Excerpts from 'Die Aufgabe des Übersetzers' by Walter Benjamin. Copyright © 1972 by Suhrkamp Verlag, Frankfurt am Main. Reproduced by permission of Suhrkamp Verlag AG, Berlin.

'Germans' by J. Mark Smith. Copyright © 2007 by J. Mark Smith. Originally published in *Notes for a Rescue Narrative* (Oolichan Books, 2007). Reproduced by permission of Oolichan Books and the author.

Excerpt from 'The Task of the Translator' from ILLUMINATIONS by Walter Benjamin. Translated by Harry Zohn. Copyright © 1955 by Suhrkamp Verlag, Frankfurt am Main. English translation copyright © 1968 and renewed 1996 by Houghton Mifflin Harcourt Publishing Company. Reproduced by permission of Houghton Mifflin Harcourt Publishing Company. All rights reserved.

Excerpt from 'The Task of the Translator' from ILLUMINATIONS by Walter Benjamin. Published by Jonathan Cape. Reproduced by permission of The Random House Group Ltd.

Excerpts from 'The Translator's Task' by Walter Benjamin. Translated by Steven Rendall. Copyright © 2012 by Steven Rendall. Reproduced by permission of the translator.

# Acknowledgements

37 words from ONE WAY STREET AND OTHER WRITINGS by Walter Benjamin. Translated by J.A. Underwood (Penguin Books 2009). Translation copyright © 2009 by J.A. Underwood. Reproduced by permission of Penguin Random House and the translator.

Excerpts from *Sir Gawain and the Green Knight*. Translated by Simon Armitage. Copyright © 2007 by Simon Armitage. Reproduced by permission of Faber and Faber Ltd.

Excerpts from *The Inferno of Dante Alighieri*. Translated by Ciaran Carson. Translation copyright © 2002 by Ciaran Carson. First published in Great Britain by Granta Books. Reproduced by permission of Granta and the author.

Excerpts from 'Faun's Way' by A.N. Wilson. Copyright © 2014 by A.N. Wilson. Published by *The Times Literary Supplement*. Reproduced by permission of News Syndication.

Excerpts from THE FIVE BOOKS OF MOSES: A TRANSLATION WITH COMMENTARY. Translated by Robert Alter. Copyright © 2004 by Robert Alter. Reproduced by permission of W.W. Norton & Company, Inc.

Excerpts from IGNORANCE by Milan Kundera. Copyright © 2000 by Milan Kundera. Translation copyright © 2002 by Linda Asher. Reproduced by permission of HarperCollins Publishers and Faber and Faber Ltd.

Excerpts from 'Sniffle' by Sheng Yun. Copyright © 2014 by Sheng Yun. Published by *London Review of Books*, www.lrb.co.uk. Reproduced by permission of the author.

Excerpts from Translator's Afterword to *The Tin Drum* by Breon Mitchell. Copyright © 2009 by Breon Mitchell. Published by Houghton Mifflin Harcourt. Reproduced by permission of the author.

Excerpts from *The Tin Drum*. Translated by Ralph Manheim. English translation copyright © 1961 by Pantheon Books. Published by Harvill Secker. Reproduced by permission of The Random House Group Ltd and Steidl Verlag GmbH, Göttingen.

Excerpts from THE TIN DRUM: A New Translation by Günter Grass. Translated by Breon Mitchell. Copyright © 1959 by Hermann Luchterhand Verlag GmbH. English translation copyright © 2009 by Breon Mitchell. Reproduced by permission of Houghton Mifflin Publishing Company and Steidl Verlag GmbH, Göttingen.

Excerpts from *Käpten Knitterbart und seine Bande* by Cornelia Funke. Copyright © 2003 by Verlag Friedrich Oetinger, Hamburg. Reproduced by permission of the publisher.

Excerpts from *Prinzessin Isabella* by Cornelia Funke. Copyright © 1997 by Verlag Friedriech Oetinger, Hamburg. Reproduced by permission of the publisher.

Excerpts from *Pirate Girl* by Cornelia Funke. Translated by Chantal Wright. Copyright © 2005 by Cornelia Funke. Reproduced by permission of Andrew Nurnberg Associates.

## Acknowledgements

Excerpts from *Princess Pigsty* by Cornelia Funke. Translated by Chantal Wright. Copyright © 2007 by Cornelia Funke. Reproduced by permission of Andrew Nurnberg Associates.

Excerpts from *The Pasta Detectives* by Andreas Steinhöfel. Translated by Chantal Wright. Copyright © 2008 by Carlsen Verlag GmbH, Hamburg. English translation copyright © 2010 by Chantal Wright. Reproduced by permission of Chicken House Ltd. All rights reserved.

Excerpts from *Anton taucht ab* by Milena Baisch. Copyright © 2010 by Beltz & Gelberg in der Verlagsgruppe Beltz, Weinheim/Basel. Reproduced by permission of the publisher.

Excerpts from *Anton and Piranha* by Milena Baisch. Translated by Chantal Wright. Copyright © 2013 by Andersen Press. Reproduced by permission of Andersen Press and Beltz & Gelberg in der Verlagsgruppe Beltz, Weinheim/Basel.

Excerpts from *Rico, Oskar und die Tieferschatten* by Andreas Steinhöfel. Copyright © 2008 by Carlsen Verlag GmbH, Hamburg. Reproduced by permission of the publisher.

Excerpts from *Rico, Oskar a přízraky* by Milena Baisch. Translated by Hana Linhartová. Czech translation copyright © 2012 by Nakladatelství Mladá fronta, Prague. Reproduced by permission of the publisher.

Excerpts from *Dirk und ich* by Andreas Steinhöfel. Copyright © 2002 by Carlsen Verlag GmbH, Hamburg. Reproduced by permission of the publisher.

Excerpts from *My Brother and I* by Andreas Steinhöfel. Translated by Chantal Wright. Copyright © 2011 by Carlsen Verlag GmbH, Hamburg. Reproduced by permission of the publisher.

Excerpts from *Landschaften, Ufer* by Tzveta Sofronieva. Copyright © 2013 by Carl Hanser Verlag GmbH. Reproduced by permission of the publisher.

Excerpts from *A Hand Full of Water* by Tzveta Sofronieva. Translated by Chantal Wright. English translation copyright © 2012 by Chantal Wright. Published by White Pine Press. Reproduced by permission of the publisher and the translator.

Every effort has been made to contact copyright-holders. Please advise the publisher of any errors or omissions, and these will be corrected in subsequent editions.

# Introduction

> In order to bring in their babies' bread most translators must have an academic connection and must toil in those insidious groves where translation, along with the rest of literature, has fallen into the hands of the big kids, who like to take things apart to see how they work. I remember the big kids as the spoilers, always ruining what the more imaginative little kids were up to.
> Gregory Rabassa, *If This Be Treason* (2005:42)

Before his retirement, Gregory Rabassa, distinguished US translator of Nobel-prizewinning authors Gabriel García Márquez and Mario Vargas Llosa, among many other Latin American luminaries, was himself a toiler in the insidious groves of academia. He held a PhD and taught Hispanic Languages and Literatures at Queens College, an institution within the City University of New York system. Rabassa's grumble that a position in or affiliation with academia was an unavoidable evil for translators, prompted by financial necessity, no longer holds true, if indeed it was ever really the case. Nonetheless, literary translation remains an inadequately compensated practice and its practitioners almost inevitably rely on additional forms of employment, of which academia remains one, to earn their living. What I am interested in here, however, is Rabassa's true complaint, namely that academics have no business dissecting works of art, which are 'unutterable even when the creation is made up of words' (Rabassa 2005:42). Clearly, a book about literary translation that is conceived as an introduction to literary translation both as a practice and as the academic discipline that it has now become will be a dissection of sorts. I make no apologies for that, being a firm believer that a theorization of artistic practice is necessary because theory 'provid[es] a new view of the world, changing its reader's perceptions, broadening the mind' (Boase-Beier 2006a:56). Jean Boase-Beier, a translator and an academic, has written extensively and in very accessible language about the usefulness of theory for literary translators (Boase-Beier 2006a, 2006b, 2010, 2011) and I will offer only a brief summary of her arguments here. Since a theory of any activity arises from observation of practice or 'a segment of perceived reality' (Boase-Beier 2010:26), theory is, by nature, descriptive rather than prescriptive. In other words, it offers an account of how something appears to operate, but it does not tell us how something should be done, although it can certainly influence how things *are* done. Since theories are based on observation and experience of phenomena, they are partial and subject to refinement as further observation and experience of new phenomena highlight their strengths and weaknesses. In other words, theory is a 'creatively constructed (and shifting) view of practice' (Boase-Beier 2006a:48). Practice can become less intuitive and more considered, less in thrall to convention and more open to innovation, if it is informed by a theoretical understanding of what is taking place. It is for these reasons that Boase-Beier argues for theory as 'an aid to creativity' (ibid:47) that can 'act as a counterbalance to the constraints of the ST [source text]' (ibid:56).

Translation theory and the notion of formal education in literary translation are often still regarded with scepticism by practitioners who work outside ivory towers and red-brick halls and even by some within academia who view translation as a made-up subject. Some practitioners who have undertaken formal study of literary translation find translation theory off-putting and fail to see its relevance for practice. It is obviously perfectly possible to be an accomplished translator without a postgraduate education in literary translation; before the advent of Translation Studies in the 1970s, this was the norm rather than the exception. Thus one can maintain, quite justifiably, that 'I got along perfectly well without theory'. But theory can be a powerful tool when correctly understood and channelled, as Boase-Beier has argued. And, as Antoine Berman reminds us, reflection on translation is not a new invention ushered in by Translation Studies but has existed 'at least since Cicero, Horace, and Saint Jerome' (1992:1). Gaddis Rose goes even further, arguing that 'it is difficult and probably futile to separate the history of translation from the history of translation studies' since 'conceptual issues arise almost automatically. Translations are needed; translations are criticized; translators are advised; finally, translations change lives' (1997:15).

The twentieth-century emergence of translation as an 'autonomous practice' – a field of academic enquiry independent of literary studies, linguistics, theology and philosophy – means that it is now 'capable of defining and situating itself, and consequently to be communicated, shared, and taught' (Berman 1992:1). As a profession, translation of the literary and non-literary varieties continues to be undervalued (Gouadec 2010 [2007]; PETRA 2012), with attendant problems of low pay, lack of recognition and – in the literary field – under-dissemination of translation products. However, there have been significant and ongoing improvements within the realm of Anglophone literary translation in recent years, as noted by Daniel Hahn, former national programme director of the British Centre for Literary Translation (BCLT), in a 2013 editorial piece for *In Other Words*, the journal of the BCLT (Hahn 2013:1). Literary translation's establishment within academia and the increasing number of theoretically schooled practitioners who have emerged from it have contributed in no small way to these changes. The fruits of formal reflection on translation – theorization of the translator as a subjective presence in the target text; a better understanding of translation's role as a mediator of foreign cultures; the conceptualization of translation as a mode of reading and writing – have all had 'impact', to use a phrase currently much in vogue in UK academia, in the 'real world'. As Esther Allen and Susan Bernofsky have recently argued, 'There is a generational move toward an image of the translator as an intellectual figure empowered with agency and sensibility who produces knowledge by curating cultural encounters' (2013:xix).

Translators have certainly become more visible. In the UK, for example, they are involved in readings, panel discussions and other events as literary experts (the London Review Bookshop's Live Translation and World Literature events are a prominent example of this); they engage the school-age public through the Translators in Schools project, working with the cultural riches of a diverse population; they are generally given credit for their work in newspapers and journals and are articulate in their protest when they are not. The academic autonomy of the practice has played an important part in this; a resurgence in engaged, small and medium-sized publishing houses such as And Other Stories and Pushkin Press, staffed by well-travelled, multilingual editors, has also helped, as has the commitment of dedicated international online journals such as *Words Without Borders* and *Asymptote*. Literary translation is also undergoing a florescence beyond the Anglophone world. In a sign that literary translation in Germany has been consolidating its position since the landmark 1997 establishment of the Deutsche Übersetzerfonds, the German President, Joachim Gauck, hosted an evening event in honour of literary translators at his official residence in Berlin in May 2015. In Taiwan, the Taiwan Literary Translation Center, a division of the National Museum of Taiwan Literature, was established in 2012 to promote the visibility of Taiwanese literature abroad, and in August 2014, Taiwan's Word Wave Festival (Huawen Langdu Jie) featured its first Translation Across Frontiers forum, sponsored by the Taiwan Cultural and Creative Platform Foundation, with several panels taking place across four days. There has also been a recent significant increase in the number of works of German literature being translated into Chinese in Taiwan (Deutsche Welle 2015).

If students of literary translation struggle with theory, this may be because abstraction is challenging, particularly for those who are drawn to translation precisely because of its concrete qualities as a practice;

but it may also have something to do with the way theory is taught, and indeed with how a formal education in literary translation is structured, and perhaps with a confusion as to what a theory of translation is trying to account for. Masters students tend to encounter theory and practice as separate pedagogical entities. MA programmes will typically offer a core module on translation theory and a 'hands-on' translation workshop in which participants critique the translations of their fellow students, or some variation of this pedagogical constellation. This separation means that the nature of the relationship between theory and practice is often unclear and might in part be responsible for the commonly held but erroneous view that theory is something to be 'applied', the way one applies a can opener to a tin of baked beans or implements a new skincare regime. There are ways to counteract this tendency: by making sure that theory classes include a substantial element of activity based around the production and analysis of translations and by encouraging students in workshops to reflect on their motivations for translating a particular text and how these motivations influence what happens on the page. There is also a need for students of literary translation to read outside the boundaries of the discipline, to think of themselves as literary scholars and as 'translating writers' (Scott 2012a:180), and for literary translation to discover 'its true and fruitful affinities with life-writing and creative writing' (Scott 2012b:10). Some of this can be achieved by strengthening the ties between programmes in literary studies, creative writing and literary translation – as is the case both at the University of Warwick and the University of East Anglia, for example – which might also result in literary translation being incorporated into the methodologies of other disciplines. Translation's 'theory problem' can also be counteracted by, as Boase-Beier suggests, 'tak[ing] on peripheral theories: of the text, the context, the reader, the effects of history, the nature of literature' (2010:36).

The 'theory problem' is one of the reasons why none of the chapter titles in this book contain the word 'theory', although there is much discussion of theory within its pages. It is more helpful, I believe, to frame the approach to literary translation in other terms. Antoine Berman argued that a modern theory of translation, which involves 'know[ing] what translation must mean in our cultural setting today' (1992:3), requires the construction of a history of translation, an ethics of translation and an analytic of translation (ibid:9). This is because we cannot hope to comprehend our own translational efforts without contextualizing them historically; because we should understand what we are translating for; and because we also require an analytic of translation to make translational practice – good and bad – more conscious, to realize the forces that work on the translator and the textual effects thereof. This book will not offer a history of translation, as this lies beyond its scope, but it will work towards an ethics and an analytic of translation by asking and offering answers to the following three questions, which will also function as chapter headings:

- Why do we translate?
- How do we read translations?
- How do translators read?

Readers may wonder why the obvious and seemingly the most useful question, namely 'How do translators translate?', does not feature on this list. Translators translate on the basis of how they read, and how they read has much to do with why they translate, with their motivations for pursuing the practice of translation and with how they experience literature. If we are able to account for why translators translate and how they read, the 'how' of translation will emerge organically.

Before proceeding to outline the content of each of these three chapters, it is worth re-iterating that this book is about *literary* translation. My definition of a literary text is wide-ranging and encompasses fiction, poetry, children's literature, life writing, philosophical writing and Freud's psychoanalytic writings. (There is no discussion of dramatic texts for reasons which have to do with my own current areas of expertise as a translator and the nature of these texts as works intended for performance, an area that is beyond the scope of this book.) This understanding of the literary is clearly not confined to the fictional, and there is nothing unusual about this position (Boase-Beier 2011:35–46). The quality of literariness is not dependent upon a lack of propositional or truth-bearing content. If this were the case then a text such as James Rebanks' *The Shepherd's Life* (2015), which is a blend of life and nature writing, would not be considered literary, and nor would most travel writing. Literariness has much to do with the style of a text, with its marked and distinct use of features such as voice, metaphor, ambiguity, repetition and defamiliarization, to give but a few examples. With the cognitive turn in literary studies, literary texts are also increasingly being seen as 'embody[ing] a state of mind' (Boase-Beier 2011:46). This is not to say that non-literary texts are entirely without an individual style, nor that they do not embody a state of mind, but that these features are more prominent in literary texts. This is the understanding of the literary that guides my approach in this book.

In the first chapter, I will consider the issue of the ethics of translation by asking why we translate. It is possible to answer this question synchronically and diachronically, for our own time and place and for earlier epochs and traditions. I am primarily concerned with answering it for a contemporary setting, and my focus will be on the English-speaking world, broadly defined (mainly the UK, the US and Canada), in full awareness of the fact that this transnational entity has separate national and subnational faces and concerns. I have adopted this transnational focus because English-language publishing is a transnational industry – literary translators produce work across national borders – and because academia in the English-speaking world is very much in cross-border dialogue, a fact reflected in the business of academic publishing. In broadly addressing and drawing on the experiences of the literary translation community in the UK and North America, it is not my intention to slight the Republic of Ireland, India, Australia, New Zealand or Anglophone countries in Africa and the Caribbean, all of which have their distinct (and postcolonial) Englishes, but rather to focus on those countries where I have spent extended periods of time living and working, and hence with which I am more familiar. The differing national contexts and global positions of the UK, the US and Canada have a significant effect on the why and the how of translation in each one. The UK is a member, albeit frequently a reluctant one, of the political and cultural unit known as the EU, which currently has 28 members and at least as many languages. The UK is a former colonial power and has been involved in several wars in the Middle East in the last few decades. The US is a global political and economic power, whose supremacy has been challenged of late by financial crisis and a changing world order; it has a history of involvement in the affairs of its Latin American neighbours and, like the UK, has been involved in conflict in the Middle East. The US is an immigrant country and is de facto bilingual (Spanish–English) in many of its states. Canada too is an immigrant country; it has two official languages, English and French, with English numerically the more dominant of the two, and this status means that there is a long-standing Canadian Translation Studies tradition (Mezei *et al.* 2014). Canada has a significant Aboriginal population and continues to deal with the legacy of colonialism within its own borders. It pursues a policy of cultural protectionism against its neighbour to the south and attempts to overcome what has been called *les deux solitudes* via a generous system of state support for translation between English and French, among other measures. Canada has also seen its military deployed to the Middle East and elsewhere. When I address the transnational entity that is the English-speaking world, I do so with an awareness of these immense differences and in the hope that this book may also be of interest to English-speaking practitioners of translation elsewhere in the world, and perhaps even more widely than that.

Why, then, do we translate? We translate as individuals and as cultures. We translate for other people and for ourselves. We translate for humanistic reasons: to create a world literature, an ideal that dates back to the early nineteenth century and Goethe's concept of *Weltliteratur* (Eckermann 1982 [1836/1848]:198), to expose ourselves to difference and other ways of seeing, to allow ideas to circulate because we believe in their greatness or their power or because they are unable to circulate in their home culture. We translate for ideological reasons: to assimilate and to exert control, to seek confirmation of our own viewpoint, to persuade and manipulate and to make money. Translation is also an encounter with literature, a mode of reading and writing: we translate as a form of literary criticism or commentary; we translate out of a creative impulse, because we are curious to see, for example, 'what Baudelaire sounds like in my voice, what my voice sounds like in Baudelaire' (Scott 2000:1); we translate because we enjoy playing with words; we translate because translation is the most intense form of reading available to us, an experience that is quite literally mind-altering, and we wish to allow others the opportunity to experience these cognitive effects through our translations. Finally, in one interpretation of Walter Benjamin's mystical essay, 'The Task of the Translator' (2012), we translate because translation is a spiritual endeavour: as we practice translation we strive for the divine. The first chapter of this book will examine these differing and intersecting motivations, giving concrete examples of their implications for translation practice and for the reading of translations.

The second chapter will consider how we read translations, or how we should read translations, and how the nature of our engagement with translations varies according to whether we read for pleasure, for study or in order to produce a book review. Most discerning readers will encounter a text-in-translation at some point in their reading lives and many of those readers will be guided by the reviews they read in newspapers and magazines. In the US many undergraduates in liberal-arts programmes will take a course in world literature in which they will read literature-in-translation; and in literary translation programmes on both sides of the Atlantic students are often asked to assess the 'success' of a target text in relation to its source or to compare several translations of the same source text either in relation to that source or independently of it. Reading a translation is like reading any other literary text, but simultaneously a completely different kettle of fish, and it is this fact that can make readers nervous and leave reviewers floundering. A translation is a text that has originated in a culture other than the reader's own, but which has now entered a new *Kulturkreis* and as such is operating outside the boundaries of the context in which it was created. It is the work of not one writer, but two, and the exact role played by both of these writers within the translation is often a cause for anxiety. Over the past ten years, a number of contributions have addressed the reading anxiety caused by translations. Lawrence Venuti (2004), David Damrosch (2009), Carol Maier and Françoise Massardier-Kenney (2010) and Esther Allen (2014) have all written on the topics of reading, selecting and reviewing translations, with audiences of general readers, students and teachers of world literature and book reviewers in mind. The online literary journal *Words Without Borders* has an occasional series entitled 'On Reviewing Translations'. In an excellent example of modern academia's public-engagement activities, the BCLT has produced a guide for International Fiction Reading Groups (BCLT 2014), and is involved in the running of several such reading groups in Norfolk, where the BCLT is based. I will be drawing on many of these resources to discuss the theoretical issues surrounding the reading of translations, and I will offer a number of case studies to illustrate how reading translations can work in practice.

The third chapter will draw on my own practice as a translator and demonstrate how my reading encounters with texts shape the translations that I produce. This chapter will have a dual focus, reflecting upon two of my areas of specialization: the first section will look at my reading encounters with books written for children and young adults, considering in particular issues specific to that genre; the second section will reflect upon my translations of a number of poems by Tzveta Sofronieva, a native speaker of Bulgarian who has adopted German as an additional literary language, and look at how the wider context of exophony – non-native-speaker writing – as a post-war phenomenon in Germany influences my approach to these texts. The reason that I have chosen this approach to illustrate how translators read and hence how they go on to translate is because literary translation is not a mechanical endeavour but an artistic practice – a performance of sorts – and each translator works idiosyncratically. There is no simple 'how to' with literary translation: the translator's linguistic knowledge combines with their sense of artistic and ethical purpose and their intellectual preparation, which involves knowing which questions to ask and which phenomena to look out for, and all of this is then brought to bear on the translation of a particular text. This third chapter enables the reader to shadow the translator, to look over her shoulder as she performs this task.

Each of the three chapters conclude with exercises and suggestions for further reading. The book ends with an appendix containing a short glossary of key terms that are essential for any meta-discussion of translation within an academic context, and it is complemented by a feature in the Routledge Translation Studies Portal entitled 'How to get started in literary translation'. This contains practical advice for emerging practitioners on getting started in literary translation and includes sections in which I share some of my own experiences and collate existing sources of information.

The author of this book does indeed toil in the insidious groves of academia, but she is also, and no less, a literary translator, mindful of the need to break down the unhelpful boundaries between theory and practice, theoreticians and practitioners. In my own translation practice I have found a theoretical foundation to be invaluable and believe that it has made me a better translator, more confident in my choices. Conversely, I would never have entered academia had I not had a practitioner's relationship to my field of enquiry. It is my sincere hope that this relationship makes itself felt in the pages that follow.

## How to use this book

This book has been written with students of literary translation in mind but also for anybody who has an interest in literary translation as a practice, in the reading of literary translations and in translation as a mode of reading. As such it speaks to emerging and established practitioners but also to students of literature, regardless of whether they find themselves in departments of English, Literary Studies, Classics, Modern Languages, Comparative or World Literatures.

The book is designed to be read cover to cover. It does not offer a straightforward set of instructions for how to translate literary texts, nor is it a synthetic work that summarizes and updates the contents of a corpus of textbooks, for the simple reason that no such corpus exists. What it offers is a snapshot of the current state of the discipline, and hopefully a fresh approach to issues of theory and practice. Throughout it endeavours to open up literary translation as a process and a product, from the underlying motivations of the act, and the implications thereof for the practice, to the process of reading a text in order to translate it. It also models ways of reading translations and of writing about translation both as a process and a product. It aspires to make a contribution to the teaching of literary translation, particularly on Masters and PhD programmes, by providing students with a vocabulary and a structure for the type of tasks and writing assignments typically demanded at this level: theorization of the practice and its products, case studies of existing translations, stylistic analyses of source texts in preparation for translation and critical reflection on and contextualization of one's own translation practice in the form of the commentary. Students of literature will find a framework for approaching and using texts-in-translation, be those texts literary fiction, poetry, critical theory or another genre altogether: the book contains a range of sustained case studies which aim to provide a model of how critical textual engagement with translations may be conducted.

*Literary Translation* is a personal statement on literary translation by a practitioner and a theorist. My goal was not a spurious neutrality of presentation but an engagement – from a position of personal experience and commitment – with issues that have occupied translators and readers for centuries. Like all scholarly works it is best read as part of a programme of much wider reading.

## Further reading: learning more about Translation Studies

For the student seeking introductory texts and reference works, the following titles are extremely useful. A detailed overview of terminology is offered by Mark Shuttleworth and Moira Cowie's *Dictionary of Translation Studies* (1997), although readers should bear in mind that Translation Studies has seen tremendous developments since this book was published close to two decades ago. The *Routledge Encyclopedia of Translation Studies* (2011), edited by Mona Baker and Gabriela Saldanha, and now in its second edition, offers an encyclopaedic overview of terms, issues, topics, sub-fields and national translation traditions, all written by experts in their fields. There are a number of excellent readers in translation history and theory, including *The Translation Studies Reader* (2012), edited by Lawrence Venuti, now in its third, revised edition (a note to students purchasing second-hand copies: the selection of texts varies between the different editions), *Translation – Theory and Practice* (2006), edited by Daniel Weissbort and Astradur Eysteinsson, and *Translation/History/Culture: A Sourcebook* (1992), edited by André Lefevere, which features shorter extracts from a more eclectic selection of texts. *The Oxford Guide to Literature in English Translation* (2001), edited by Peter France, is a very useful reference work for those who wish to trace the history of a particular author or national literary tradition in translation, although it obviously cannot provide a guide to the most recent literary translations on the market. Katie Wales' *Dictionary of Stylistics* (2011), now in its third edition, gives detailed explanations of terminology relating to the meta-language of stylistics (also referred to as poetics or literary linguistics) and is an invaluable reference work for the student of literary translation. For background reading on the discipline of Translation Studies, see Holmes' seminal essay 'The Name and Nature of Translation Studies' (1998 [1972]), Edwin Gentzler's *Contemporary Translation Theories* (2001) and Mary Snell-Hornby's *The Turns of Translation Studies* (2006). Jeremy Munday's *Introducing Translation Studies* (2012), now in its third edition, is a very useful and accessible overview of translation theory and Translation Studies.

## Bibliography

*A note on the bibliography.* Where there is a discrepancy between the publication date of the cited edition and the date of a text's first publication, the date in square brackets indicates the original publication date (and is included in the text). In the case of translations, the date in square brackets refers to the original publication date of the foreign-language source text (and is not included in the text). Some references therefore have two sets of square bracket: the first indicates the date of the translation's first publication in English and the second the original publication date of the foreign-language text.

Allen, E., 2014. Lost in the Book Review. *In Other Words* 44, pp. 26–33.
Allen, E. and Bernofsky, S., 2013. Introduction: A Culture of Translation. In: E. Allen and S. Bernofsky, eds. *In Translation: Translators on Their Work and What It Means*. New York: Columbia University Press. pp. xiii–xxiii.
Baker, M. and Saldanha, G., eds. 2011. *Routledge Encylopedia of Translation Studies*. 2nd ed. New York: Routledge.
Benjamin, W., 2012 [1923]. The Task of the Translator. Translated from German by S. Rendall. In: L. Venuti, ed. *The Translation Studies Reader*. 3rd ed. New York: Routledge. pp. 75–83.
Berman, A., 1992 [1984]. *The Experience of the Foreign: Culture and Translation in Romantic Germany*. Translated from French by S. Heyvaert. Albany, NY: State University of New York Press.
Boase-Beier, J., 2006a. Loosening the Grip of the Text: Theory as an Aid to Creativity. In: E. Loffredo and M. Perteghella, eds. *Translation and Creativity. Perspectives on Creative Writing and Translation Studies*. London: Continuum. pp. 47–56.
Boase-Beier, J., 2006b. *Stylistic Approaches to Translation*. Manchester: St. Jerome.
Boase-Beier, J., 2010. Who Needs Theory? In: A. Fawcett, K.L. Guadarrama García and R. Hyde Parker, eds. *Translation: Theory and Practice in Dialogue*. London: Continuum. pp. 25–38.
Boase-Beier, J., 2011. *A Critical Introduction to Translation Studies*. London: Continuum.
British Centre for Literary Translation, 2014. *International Fiction Reading Group Guide*. Available at: www.bclt.org.uk/events/international-fiction-reading-group/ [accessed 4 February 2015].
Damrosch, D., 2009. *How to Read World Literature*. Chichester: Wiley-Blackwell.
Deutsche Welle, 2015. *Leseboom in Taiwan*. Available at: www.dw.com/de/leseboom-in-taiwan/a-18500808?maca=de-rss-de-cul-buch-3330-rdf [accessed 1 August 2015].
Eckermann, J, P., 1982 [1836/1848]. *Gespräche mit Goethe in den letzten Jahren seines Lebens*. Berlin/Weimar: Aufbau.
France, P., ed. 2001. *The Oxford Guide to Literature in English Translation*. Oxford: Oxford University Press.
Gaddis Rose, M., 1997. *Translation and Literary Criticism*. Manchester: St. Jerome.
Gentzler, E., 2001. *Contemporary Translation Theories*. 2nd ed. Clevedon: Multilingual Matters.
Gouadec, D., 2010 [2007]. *Translation as a Profession*. Amsterdam/Philadelphia: John Benjamins.
Hahn, D., 2013. Editorial. *In Other Words* 41, pp. 1–4.
Holmes, J., 1998 [1972]. The Name and Nature of Translation Studies. In: J. Holmes. *Translated: Papers on Literary Translation and Translation Studies*. 2nd ed. Amsterdam: Rodopi. pp. 67–80.
Lefevere, A., ed. 1992. *Translation/History/Culture: A Sourcebook*. New York: Routledge.
Maier, C. and Massardier-Kenney, F. eds., 2010. *Literature in Translation: Teaching Issues and Reading Practices*. Kent, Ohio: Kent State University Press.

Mezei, K., Simon, S. and von Flotow, L. eds., 2014. *Translation Effects: The Shaping of Modern Canadian Culture*. Montreal and Kingston: McGill-Queen's University Press.
Munday, J., 2012. *Introducing Translation Studies*. 3rd ed. New York: Routledge.
PETRA, 2012. Towards New Conditions for Literary Translation in Europe. Brussels: PETRA. Available at: www.muforditok.hu/docs/PETRA12.pdf [accessed 30 July 2015].
Rabassa, G., 2005. *If This Be Treason: Translation and Its Discontents*. New York: New Directions.
Scott, C., 2000. *Translating Baudelaire*. Exeter: University of Exeter Press.
Scott, C., 2012a. *Translating the Perception of Text*. London: Legenda.
Scott, C., 2012b. *Literary Translation and the Rediscovery of Reading*. Cambridge: Cambridge University Press.
Shuttleworth, M. and Cowie, M., 1997. *Dictionary of Translation Studies*. New York: Routledge.
Snell-Hornby, M., 2006. *The Turns of Translation Studies*. Amsterdam/Philadelphia: John Benjamins.
Venuti, L., 2004. How to Read a Translation. *Words Without Borders*, July. Available at: http://wordswithoutborders.org/article/how-to-read-a-translation [accessed 8 April 2015].
Venuti, L., ed. 2012. *The Translation Studies Reader*. 3rd ed. New York: Routledge.
Wales, K., 2011. *A Dictionary of Stylistics*. 3rd ed. Harlow: Pearson.
Weissbort, D. and Eysteinsson, A., eds. 2006. *Translation Theory and Practice: A Reader*. Oxford: Oxford University Press.

# 1 Why do we translate?

> Translations do not happen easily, anywhere or anytime. It is rarely a question of someone simply wanting to translate. Every translation ensues from a context where someone finds themselves in the presence of a series of necessary elements: something to translate, a social reason to do so, ideas about the nature of translation, and the necessary time, space, money, and intellectual skills. Together all of that can produce a translation.
>
> Anthony Pym, *On Translator Ethics* (2012:100)

> Literature must have been translated for enhancing one group's cultural heritage at the expense of another's. Perhaps a kind of imperialism where the 'text' supported or solidified a territorial or lineal claim. Or perhaps a benign looting to bolster what was felt to be an inferior native patrimony. Or, less benignly, literature could have been translated as a pleasure commodity with a price; life in the case of Scheherazade, but minstrels, story-tellers must have been human trophies all along. [...] All in all, millennia later, the motives for translating literature may not be all that different.
>
> Marilyn Gaddis Rose, *Translation and Literary Criticism* (1997:15–16)

## Why do I translate? A personal response

In his book *On Translator Ethics*, Anthony Pym levels the criticism that much theoretical writing on translation assumes an unspecified translator and a set of universal behaviours, and does not show enough consideration for the particulars of a given context (2012:4–5). In order to avoid this pitfall, and so that the discussion in this chapter might unfold from a place of subjectivity, I will begin by reframing, in the first person, the question of why we translate, offering a personal answer to the broader question of why we, as individuals and by extension as cultures, undertake this activity. Once I have done this, I will proceed to investigate whether my own sentiments and experiences find external resonances. Why, then, do I translate literature? What is it about literary translation as a process and as a product that draws my interest?

First things first, for the sake of honesty: I do not translate to earn my living and I am not always paid for the translations that I produce. There are translations that I would not produce without being paid for the work involved and translations for which, conversely, I do not expect to be paid and where non-financial rewards – 'symbolic (prestige), social (the contacts), and cultural (the learning process)' (Pym 2012:125) – take the place of payment in hard cash. I earn my living as an academic, specifically as an academic working in the fields of Translation Studies and Comparative Literary Studies, and many of the non-financial rewards of the translations I produce, whether I receive payment for them or not, have to do with my career. In my particular corner of Translation Studies – the theory and practice of literary translation – being a translation practitioner adds legitimacy to the theoretical and methodological claims I make in the classroom and in print. My status as a practitioner also legitimizes my existence as an academic on a personal level: I do not think I would be an academic if my research were not practice-based. The purpose of this disclosure is to be honest about the freedoms accorded me by my day job: I can, and indeed, for reasons of time, need to be selective about what I translate. This puts me in a different position to a translator who is self-employed and operating under financial pressure and heightened temporal constraints. I do, however, also work 'commercially', which is to say that I have produced and will hopefully continue to produce translations for which I am paid by publishers whose goal it is to make a profit on their books.

I stated earlier that there are translations that I would not produce without being paid for my labour, and translations for which I do not expect to be paid. It is worth explaining this distinction as it brings me closer to my motivations for translating in the first place. Not all of the translations I have produced have come about as a result of my own initiative. Most translators in the Anglophone context, with the exception of very well-established translators who have name recognition, combine pitching and catching. They pitch translation projects to publishers, taking on an agent-like function (but sadly without the percentage cut that agents charge), and they receive translation commissions from publishers who have purchased the rights to a foreign text and are in need of a translator to render it into English. I too pitch and catch. It makes sense that I am often more committed to the texts that I pitch than to the texts that I catch, but I nonetheless have become very fond of the majority of the texts that I have translated on commission. Commissions are financially remunerated; but although many of the pitches I have made have also been compensated, some have not. Two of the translations I have produced that were not paid in the conventional sense were a collection of poetry by Bulgarian-German poet Tzveta Sofronieva entitled *A Hand Full of Water* (2012) and a prose text by Japanese-German writer Yoko Tawada entitled 'Portrait of a Tongue' (2013). In the former case I was 'paid' for the translation in the form of a grant from the PEN/Heim Translation Fund. When I applied for the grant, I did not have a publisher for the poems and there was no guarantee that I would find one. PEN invested its money to compensate me – and a number of other translators working on a range of projects – for the time spent producing the translation and in order that I would have a complete text to show potential publishers, thus increasing the text's chances of publication. I was lucky enough to receive further payment for the project in the form of a prize, which brought with it a cheque and a publishing contract with White Pine Press. PEN's investment had paid off and I was amply compensated for my work, but through a subvention economy rather than through the marketplace. It is a curious irony that I am likely to have earned more money translating Tzveta Sofronieva's poems than the poet herself made writing the originals. In the case of the second text, Yoko Tawada's 'Portrait of a Tongue', I received no payment at all for my translation. The Canadian publisher, University of Ottawa Press, relied on a grant from the Canadian Federation for the Humanities and Social Sciences' Aid to Scholarly Publications Program to cover its publishing costs. Why was I moved to translate these texts? Why do organizations such as PEN subsidize such projects, and why do small non-profit-making publishers and university presses publish them?

For my own part, I can answer that I was attracted to Sofronieva's and Tawada's work both as an academic and a translator. My doctoral research investigated the translation of German exophonic texts – that is, German literary texts written by non-native speakers of German. I was fascinated by the phenomenon of writers changing their language: by the life circumstances that might lead one to take such a step, by the personal and professional costs of such a decision, the implications that this might have for the writer's style in the adopted language and the effects on the society whose language has been adopted – Germany, in this case. A significant proportion of contemporary exophonic writers in Germany has struggled to find acceptance by the publishing industry. Many exophonic writers have published in part or entirely with small, niche houses, e.g. Yoko Tawada with konkursbuch Verlag Claudia Gehrke and Tzveta Sofronieva with Hans Schiler. In some cases writers have taken to self-publishing, e.g. Italian-German writer Franco Biondi, who now uses Book on Demand after years with the small publisher Brandes & Apsel. Where Tzveta Sofronieva was concerned, the act of translating her poetry contained an element of witnessing to it as literature and of witnessing to her as a friend; we had met quite randomly on a train travelling to the Frankfurt Book Fair when I was a doctoral student and were surprised to discover a common bond in exophony. Friendship, I have since discovered, is not an uncommon impetus for the establishment of a working translator–author relationship: Maureen Freely became Orhan Pamuk's translator because of their long-standing acquaintance, for example (Freely 2013:118). The opportunity to translate poetry for the first time, contemplating how to render its formal features and elliptical narratives in English, also intrigued me. In Tawada's case, my decision to translate 'Portrait of a Tongue' was sparked by the desire to make translatable a text that mused on linguistic equivalence in German and English, a text seemingly locked in to a particular linguistic relationship, to render it accessible to an English-speaking readership with little or no knowledge of German. From this premise grew an experimental translation that embedded the translator in the text by splitting each page into two columns and allowing the translator to fill the right-hand column with her commentary, thus opening up the translation process and making the translator visible to the reader. My motivations for translating in these two instances were 'genre'-specific rather than global: exophonic writing was a political act and a literary phenomenon that raised certain intellectual questions; translating exophonic texts also had the potential to be a political act and was certainly an engaging literary endeavour. Translation would hopefully widen the audience that might be reached by Tzveta Sofronieva's poetry, which had not been translated into English before, allowing her text to travel and her ideas to circulate. Tawada's writing, on the other hand, had already been brought to the attention of the US reading public through the efforts of translators Susan Bernofsky, Margaret Mitsutani and Yumi Selden; my engagement with her text was primarily an intellectual and a creative experiment.

Although a very particular set of circumstances led me to translate *A Hand Full of Water*, the involvement of the PEN/Heim Translation Fund, which now bears the name of its previously anonymous donors – translator and scholar Michael Henry Heim, who passed away in 2012, and his wife Priscilla Heim – was motivated by more global, humanistic concerns. The fund was set up in 2003 'in response to the dismayingly low number of literary translations currently appearing in English' and with the aim of promoting 'the publication and reception of translated world literature in English' (PEN America 2015). The lack of foreign literature available in English was and continues to be seen as a cause for concern in Anglophone intellectual circles. Encounters with the foreign are considered beneficial; isolationism and parochialism can have dangerous consequences. White Pine Press, the University of Ottawa Press and indeed many university presses and publishing houses share in this belief.

I too have global motives for translating, irrespective of the degree to which I am enamoured of a particular text. I have already stated that I feel affection for most of the books that I have translated on commission. *The Pasta Detectives* (2010), written for the 8–11 age group by German author Andreas Steinhöfel, is one such book. It tells the story of Rico and his friend Oscar, two small boys who live in Berlin. Rico has learning difficulties and attends a school for children with special needs. He loves animals, is extremely attuned to people's emotions and adores his mother, who is bringing him up by herself. Oscar is a highly gifted child who is less than socially competent and has a tendency to cause offence with his bluntly honest remarks. His mother has left the family home and he is being brought up by his father, who suffers from depression, is emotionally distant and often neglectful of his son. *The Pasta Detectives* is the first in a trilogy of books about Rico and Oscar, and in it the two friends solve a series of kidnappings. The book manages to be highly entertaining and sensitive in its account of how Rico and Oscar negotiate their differences and work to overcome their respective difficulties. Its contribution to highlighting special-needs issues was recognized by NASEN, an organization based in the UK that advocates on behalf of people with special needs, which honoured *The Pasta Detectives* with its Inclusive Book Award in 2011. The fact that such an award went to a translated text, which was not necessarily perceived as a translated text by the judges, suggests that target cultures can benefit from the fresh ideas and insights and the different world views brought in by translations – and the book's offerings are not limited to its depiction of the life of a child with special needs. The form of childhood depicted in Andreas Steinhöfel's book is very different from contemporary modes of childhood in the UK and in North America. Rico is a latchkey kid who wanders around his block of flats and his *Kiez* – the area of Berlin where he lives – by himself. The very fact that he lives in a block of flats, a typical feature of life in a continental European city and one that does not imply anything about a person's class status, may be disorientating to an English-speaking middle-class child but is perhaps less so to a child who has grown up in social housing in the inner city. The social mix depicted in the book – rich and poor, gay and straight, German and non-German – reflects the fact that it is more usual for people of different income levels and social backgrounds to live in the same building and in the same area in German cities. This social mix is unusual in contemporary Anglophone children's literature, as is the freedom of movement that Rico enjoys, unthinkable among the suburban North American middle class, and curtailed but not yet entirely absent from a child's life in the UK. A child reading this book will encounter this very different world and the possibility of otherness. The claims that I make for *The Pasta Detectives* hold true for many translated texts. Even if a book is not a great book, or for that matter a 'Great Book' in the canonical sense, it can still expose its readers to difference.

My global reasons for translating, then, include giving other readers the opportunity to experience the same enjoyment I get from reading, being intellectually stimulated, entertained and challenged. I am keen to extend the audience for certain texts and authors, and for foreign literature more generally, and I believe that translation is an act of witnessing to literary value and a means of spreading ideas. Books from other cultures can alter our way of seeing the world. This is not to say that books from within our culture cannot also have this effect, or that all books from other cultures have the potential to effect a shift in our perception, but simply that certain books from outside our cultural circle may be particularly potent in this respect and that translation is the prerequisite for them to unleash these effects on an audience outside their source culture. There is certainly something political or ideological in this set of motivations, in the sense that I am clearly a xenophile but also in the sense that this is indicative of a belief that the ideas and forms found in foreign literature can challenge but also make a contribution to domestic cultural products and values.

The 'how' of translation – and I am speaking in basic, practical terms here rather than in terms of the long-standing dualist vision of translation as a positioning towards a source or a target language, text and/or culture – is a further part of the 'why'. Translation presents a linguistic and intellectual challenge: how do I apply my knowledge of the two languages in question and my familiarity with the source and target cultures to the process of producing a translation?

I am increasingly attracted, too, to translation as an intense form of reading that might be described as a type of literary criticism. Translators are the only readers to weigh every single word in a text. We are typically the ones who discover the typos and logical errors in source texts that several pairs of editorial eyes have failed to spot; but our reading goes much further and deeper than this. In my translation of Yoko Tawada's 'Portrait of a Tongue' I experimented with translation as commentary, and although this was somewhat of an academic's privilege, the intention was, in part, to illustrate the textual expertise of translators, their status as skilled readers.

Finally, I would not translate if I did not enjoy the process, and much of this enjoyment stems from the creative nature of the beast: translation is a form of writing and hence a mode of self-expression; in translating, the translator's voice inevitably becomes part of the target text (Schiavi 1996; Hermans 1996, 2014). Translation can also be a meditative practice not unlike yoga – it involves a significant, regular investment of time spent alone in contemplation and the discipline to do this – and hence it has a spiritual dimension too. What I would like to extrapolate from these reflections is a set of motivations for translating that may find resonance in the experiences of other translators and in how our society conceptualizes the translation endeavour. I am going to propose that we translate for some or all of the following reasons, and in this chapter I will be examining each of these reasons in further detail with reference to their contemporary, and in some cases historical, proponents.

First, we translate for what I will call humanistic reasons, which is not to say that translators and those cultures where translation is considered a significant cultural good are necessarily humanist in the strict ideological sense of the term, i.e. secular, guided by rational principles, prioritizing the human over the divine, simply that much translation comes about because practitioners and cultures believe that access to foreign literature and thought has the potential to improve the lives of individual human beings and of humankind. We translate so that others can read good books (some of which we choose to call 'Great Books'); to encounter other cultures and expose ourselves to difference; to allow ideas to circulate; and to bear witness. We also translate for political or ideological reasons (the humanistic motivations I have just outlined also stem from a particular ideological outlook): translation can be a way of assimilating and exerting control, a tool of persuasion, manipulation and evangelization and in the case of a bestselling book a way of making money. We translate to seek confirmation of our own viewpoint, but also to resist and agitate, to confront readers with difference. Further, we translate because we enjoy reading: we want to make our reading experiences available to others so that they too can experience a range of cognitive effects similar to ours and to those of the original audience. Translation is also a mode of reading. It has long enjoyed a close relationship to commentary and is once again being taken up as a form of literary criticism and intense textual engagement (see, for instance, Cohen and Legault 2012; Franzen 2013). Translation is a mode of writing, too: it is a creative endeavour and a cognitive challenge; it is something we do for ourselves as well as for other readers. Finally, there is a school of thought that views translation more esoterically, as a metaphysical enterprise, spiritual endeavour and a dynamic practice that gives us an insight into the nature of language and thought. I will begin with the humanist case.

## Why do we translate? The humanist response

> Translation not only plays its important traditional role as the means that allows us access to literature originally written in one of the countless languages we cannot read, but it also represents a concrete literary presence with the crucial capacity to ease and make more meaningful our relationships to those with whom we may not have had a connection before. Translation always helps us to know, to see from a different angle, to attribute new value to what once may have been unfamiliar.
> Edith Grossman, *Why Translation Matters* (2010:x–xi)

Edith Grossman, distinguished translator of Cervantes and García Márquez, succinctly argues the humanist case for translation. First and foremost, it is translation that makes world literature possible, in the sense of reading beyond the borders of our mother tongue. For those of us in the English-speaking world who do not speak Russian, translation brings us Akhmatova, Dostoevsky and Tolstoy, but also any number of contemporary Russian authors such as Boris Akunin, Victor Pelevin and Tatyana Tolstaya. The most basic rationale for literary translation must be that it expands the range of literary texts available to us, whether canonical, populist, contemporary or temporally distant. By facilitating a world literature, translation also builds bridges between cultures, as Grossman points out, bringing us closer to those we do not know and with whom we would otherwise be unable to communicate. Finally, Grossman argues that translation helps us to see differently, shifting our perception of ourselves and others. It therefore has cognitive value and the potential to effect change in individuals and perhaps also in society.

David Damrosch has defined world literature as 'all literary works that circulate beyond their culture of origin, either in translation or in their original language' (2003:4). Literature written in dominant colonial languages such as English, French and Spanish has the ability to cross borders without leaving its original language of composition, but literature written in smaller languages is dependent upon translation to help it circulate. The term 'world literature', a calque of the German term *Weltliteratur*, can be traced back to a statement made by Goethe in 1827 in which he predicted an end to the era of national literatures and the dawn of a new world literary age (Eckermann 1982 [1836/1848]:198). Today, *Weltliteratur* and its English counterpart function as a 'discursive paradigm' (Pfizer 2006:85). In the English-speaking world and particularly in the US, 'world literature' also denotes a 'pedagogical practice' (ibid), which is generally understood to involve the teaching of a body of literature that extends beyond the purely domestic. It should be noted, however, that world literature, as a field of intellectual enquiry, as a body of texts and as a classroom practice, is ideologically charged and can range from efforts to extend literary studies beyond a focus on the traditional Western literary canon to a radical questioning of the very nature and organization of contemporary literary studies (Warwick Research Collective 2015).

Although it was Goethe who coined the term *Weltliteratur*, the ideas it represents were already in circulation in nineteenth-century Germany. In 1813, Schleiermacher delivered a lecture entitled 'On the Different Methods of Translating', which French translation theorist Antoine Berman has suggested may be the seminal nineteenth-century text on translation (2008:17). Schleiermacher proposed that there were two basic methods of translating: 'Either the translator leaves the writer in peace as much as possible and moves the reader toward him; or he leaves the reader in peace as much as possible and moves the writer toward him' (2012:49). Schleiermacher's preference was for the former method – a foreignizing approach to translation – and his reasoning was that the German reader would thus be exposed to the foreign and that German culture would be enriched by these literary meetings. Schleiermacher went so far as to suggest that German would act as a sort of library, a repository for the literary wealth of nations (ibid:62). Goethe's enthusiasm for *Weltliteratur* was similarly characterized by this 'imperial acquisitiveness' (Damrosch 2003:10). Pym argues that, despite appearances to the contrary, the nineteenth-century German translation project was an attempt to keep languages and national identities distinct, 'since the alternative to translation is the mixing of languages, territories, and allegiances' (2012:29). Such a mélange would have undermined attempts to forge a pan-German national identity at a time when the German nation state did not yet exist. Domesticating the foreign would lead to its assimilation and result in a watering down of any proto-national culture; translation was 'mobilized to keep each language in its place' (ibid). The humanist ideal of *Weltliteratur* therefore contains a nationalist, ideological strand; our contemporary 'humanist' understanding of the value of world literature grows out of this complex heritage.

What might be the concrete benefits of exposure to world literature? In other words, is our belief in the humanist value of translation justified? Goethe's 'imperial acquisitiveness' was counterbalanced in part, Damrosch argues, by his 'provincial anxiety' (2003:10). Writing from his small corner of a Germany that did not yet exist, there was a yearning to feel part of a larger entity. Then, as now, world literature functioned as 'multiple *windows on the world*' (ibid:15).

This belief in the capacity of literature to put us in touch with other worlds is illustrated by elements of the academic curriculum at West Point, the US's military academy. In EN302, an Advanced Composition course taken by approximately 2,000 students between 2012 and 2014, cadets hone their writing skills through an engagement with the topic of Revolutionary Egypt. The reading list for EN302 comprises prominent Egyptian authors to be read in English translation, including Naguib Mafouz, Egypt's Nobel laureate. In an introductory letter to cadets, Course Director Gerard McGowan, who redesigned this long-standing course in its current format, outlines his pedagogical vision:

> We all make and know ourselves through what one might call *the circuits of the other*. To grow as people and professionals we need to make connections, with the familiar, sure, but especially with the unfamiliar. [. . .] If we can or should ever *know* a distant culture [. . .] we certainly cannot *know* another culture by way of country

briefings, timelines, and amassed data-points alone. In short, the texture of real, un-exoticized Egyptian life in time – from its smells, sights, and sounds, to its individual and communal sufferings and delights – will remain just out of reach to you without your patient commitment to these authors and works. However, with your commitment to the hard, college-level work at hand, you might just come to terms with something true about Egypt, its people, and even yourself.

(McGowan 2012)

Similarly, in the blurb for the EP351 World Literature course, the Department of English and Philosophy at West Point urges cadets to 'take this course before you find yourself a lieutenant in a foreign land' (United States Military Academy West Point 2015). The pedagogical rationale for both of these courses is that engaging with literature from other places, and, furthermore, from radically different places, is a way of developing an appreciation for the 'other' that goes beyond facts and figures and gives a nuanced, contextualized, human face to the foreign, reflecting 'the need to extend the American imagination' (Appiah 2012 [1993]:342). By exposing cadets to difference, these courses aim to prepare US officers for deployment to unfamiliar cultural environments where they will interact with local populations, having learned to interpret their foreign surroundings in a culturally sensitive manner. This approach is an alliance of humanism and ideology, where knowledge of the other, acquired through observation, can be used to consolidate control. It represents a complication of the relationship between knowledge and power described in Edward Said's seminal book *Orientalism* (2003 [1978]), since the knowledge in question is produced by the 'Orient' rather than by the West, but is appropriated – in and through translation – by its US readers for their own purposes. Given the history of US intervention overseas, the continued presence of the US military in Iraq and Afghanistan and the current volatility of so many areas in the Middle East, future deployment of US troops to this area is not unlikely. Of course, as the instructor of Revolutionary Egypt points out, engaging with literature-in-translation in a profitable manner requires a commitment on the part of the student reader, but the rewards extend not only to the acquisition of knowledge – factual and cultural – but to greater self-knowledge.

Can interaction with the culturally other really affect self-perception and change our way of seeing the world more generally, as McGowan hopes? Are we genuinely altered by our encounter with the foreign? We should perhaps beware of accepting this claim too easily. If Pym's reading of Schleiermacher is correct, then the point of encouraging world literary encounters in nineteenth-century Germany was not to affect change but to confirm and bolster the very notion of German-ness.

In a similar vein, Damrosch argues that the nineteenth-century reception of the Mesopotamian *Epic of Gilgamesh* was focused on its ability to 'confirm' the Biblical story of the flood at a time when biblical accounts had been called into question (2003:52), i.e. the foreign was very much approached through the lens of the translating culture and harnessed for domestic needs. Nonetheless, there are good reasons to believe that an encounter with the foreign can be mind-altering, bringing with it 'cognitive gains', to use the language of cognitive linguistics (Sperber and Wilson 1995:263–6), and that cultural exchange through translation is more than mere appropriation.

What, then, are concrete examples of the ways in which the foreign can shift our *Selbstverortung* – our personal GPS – calling into question what we know and giving us a new set of windows upon our own world? Let us consider the implications of the proliferation of translated Scandinavian noir in Anglophone culture within this context, both on page and on screen. Nordic, or Scandinavian, noir has developed into a phenomenon in the English-speaking world over the last fifteen years. Forshaw credits the English translation of Danish writer Peter Høeg's *Miss Smilla's Feeling for Snow* with kickstarting the Nordic invasion of an Anglophone genre, with Swedish writer Henning Mankell's Wallander novels following on as 'standard bearer' in the late 1990s, and Swedish 'all-flattening juggernaut', the Millennium trilogy, written by the late Stieg Larsson, breaking sales records in the late 2010s (Forshaw 2012:5). More recently, Danish television series *The Killing*, which was shown on the BBC with English subtitles in 2011 and 2012, achieved cult status in the UK. The commercial success of Scandinavian noir has had several concrete effects: the market for foreign noir literature has expanded considerably, with several smaller presses such as Bitter Lemon, Europa's World Noir and MacLehose Press dedicated in whole or in part to the genre, and larger, established presses also staking a claim, with Penguin currently engaged in publishing all 75 of Georges Simenon's Maigret novels, a proportion of which will appear in new translations. One of the most interesting phenomena to have emerged in the wake of the success of Scandinavian noir abroad is a Welsh television series called *Y Gwyll*, or *Hinterland*, which screened on Welsh-language channel S4C in 2013 and on the BBC in 2014. This television series, which the media has overtly connected to Scandinavian noir with slogans such as 'Welsh Wallander' (Frost 2014a) and 'Welcome piece of Welsh noir is set to make a killing' (Gilbert 2014), follows police detective Tom Mathias and his team as they investigate murders in and around the Welsh town of Aberystwyth. The series was filmed twice, in Welsh and in English, and a hybrid Welsh-English version with English subtitles was also created. These different versions were destined for different audiences: the Welsh version was screened in Wales, the English version was exported and the bilingual version was the one seen by the majority of UK viewers on the BBC. According to director Ed Thomas, the UK audience had been primed for the 'foreign-ness' of Welsh by exposure to Nordic noir: 'People were already used to subtitles, and even enjoying them, it seemed', further arguing that 'I think there's a hunger for discovering something authentic' (Frost 2014b). *Y Gwyll* has been a critical and a commercial success, with a further series being screened in 2015 and rights sold abroad. The UK's embrace of Nordic noir, both in literature and on screen, appears to have created an environment where homegrown subtitled noir could meet with an open-minded audience and remind Britons that 'our own islands are not linguistically homogenous' (Gilbert 2014). Engagement with the foreign has affected a perceptual shift, creating a space for the UK to perceive and embrace the foreign within, and perhaps also forging a new transnational Nordic cultural identity for the island. But one might argue that what is taking place here is a wresting back of an originally Anglophone genre, a process of re-domestication facilitated by the fact that its audience is so familiar with the underlying noir template. All too often Nordic noir has been stripped of its foreignness by giving it a domestic face: there has, after all, been a US television version of *The Killing*, a UK Wallander and a Hollywood adaptation of Larsson's *The Girl with the Dragon Tattoo*, the latter two following on from earlier Swedish adaptations.

If the humanist premise that translated literature can help us 'see from a different angle' (Grossman 2010:x) has its problematic aspects, it nonetheless expresses the experience of countless individuals. Writers in particular stress the importance of the effects of their encounters with foreign literature. Indeed, without translation, Grossman argues, 'a worldwide community of writers would be inconceivable' (ibid:22). Goethe's promotion of *Weltliteratur* stemmed from his 'extraordinary writerly receptivity' (Damrosch 2003:10): Eckermann recounts Goethe's enthusiastic engagement with a Chinese novel (Eckermann 1982 [1836/1848]: 196–8), and Goethe was even able to appreciate his own *Faust* with fresh eyes by reading the French translation (ibid:330–1). Contemporary Japanese writer and translator Haruki Murakami, best-selling author of *The Wind-Up Bird Chronicle* and *Norwegian Wood*, cites *The Brothers Karamazov* as one of the three books that have meant most to him, alongside F. Scott Fitzgerald's *The Great Gatsby* and Raymond Chandler's *The Long Goodbye*, and states: 'Had it not been for Fitzgerald's novel, I would not be writing the kind of literature I am today (indeed, it is possible that I would not be writing at all)' (Murakami 2013:172). The title of Murakami's non-fiction running memoir, *What I Talk about When I Talk about Running* (2008), is adapted from the title of a short story by Raymond Carver, 'What We Talk about When We Talk about Love' (Murakami 2008:179). So deep is the influence of American literature and culture on Murakami's novels that journalist Sam Anderson, who prepared to write a *New York Times* feature article on Murakami by reading all of his novels, spoke of his shock when arriving in Tokyo to interview the author and finding that Tokyo was not 'a cosmopolitan world capital whose straight-talking citizens were fluent not only in English but also in all the nooks and crannies of Western culture [...] but intensely, inflexibly, unapologetically Japanese' (Anderson 2011). Murakami speaks excellent English and has translated many classic American texts into Japanese, so he is not reliant on translation for his access to Anglophone literature, although he would have been so in his younger years. This is a moot point, however; what is important is that Murakami's evolution as a person and as a writer would be unthinkable without his exposure to non-domestic literature. In this, he is not alone. US exophonic writer Aleksandar Hemon, a Bosnian who found himself in Chicago in 1992 when the Bosnian War broke out and decided to stay in the US, writes of summers spent alone in his family's mountain cabin in Jahorina, 'reading for ten hours straight' (Hemon 2013:68). His reading list included le Carré's Smiley novels, anthologies of contemporary American short stories, Corto Maltese comic books, Tolstoy's *War and Peace*, Mann's *The Magic Mountain* and Kafka's letters (ibid:68–70). Like Murakami, Hemon cites Salinger as an influence; he read *The Catcher in the Rye* in high school and 'often imitated Holden Caulfield's diction (in translation)' (ibid:140). The books Hemon read during the summers of his youth – many of them books-in-translation – permeated his consciousness. *War and Peace*'s Bolkonsky and Natasha showed up in his dreams regularly in the week he spent reading the novel (ibid:69); and on his hikes he 'conducted imaginary conversations with imaginary partners, not unlike the ones between Castorp and Settembrini in Mann's novel' (ibid:70). From the perspective of cognitive literary studies (Jaén and Simon 2012: 20–2), Hemon's reading – much of it done in translation – certainly had mind-altering effects.

A further example of how literature-in-translation becomes part of a writer's personal library, shaping his or her conceptual vocabulary, is provided by an article entitled 'The New Face of India' that appeared in UK newspaper *The Guardian* at the time of Narendra Modi's sweeping success in the Indian election of 2014 (Mishra 2014a). In the article, Indian writer Pankaj Mishra analyses the success of Modi and his party, the Hindu nationalist BJP, within the changing context of contemporary India. Mishra cites two writers who would appear quite far removed from modern India. First, he quotes from Austrian Robert Musil's *The Man Without Qualities*, an unfinished novel set at the end of the Austro-Hungarian Empire that was published in sections between 1930 and 1943. Mishra draws a comparison between the fall of the Austro-Hungarian Empire with its accompanying 'breakdown of values' at the end of the Great War (2014a:2), and the topsy-turvy political situation in India, hinting at a similarity between Musil's fictional murderer Mossbrugger and Modi, who has been accused of orchestrating a massacre against Muslims in his home state of Gujarat in 2002. Second, in his critique of Modi's orchestration of populist gatherings, Mishra references German philosopher Walter Benjamin, using him to argue the point that 'rallies, parades and grand monuments do not secure the masses their rights; they give them no more than the chance to express themselves' (ibid:4). The references to Musil and Benjamin place contemporary political events in India in a different frame. Writing for a Western audience, Mishra is suggesting that India is not as much of a world apart as we might imagine it to be, and reminds us that Europe too has seen eras of 'normalisation of violence and injustice' (ibid:2). As a writer, Mishra has harnessed world literature to 'attribute new value to what once may have been unfamiliar' (Grossman 2010:x) for Western readers, but also to attribute new value to the familiar, to affect a shift in the current domestic perception of India through his rhetorical invocation of Musil and Benjamin. In personal correspondence, Mishra explained that 'I don't believe the modern world, and India in the age of global capitalism and mass media, can be understood without their [*writers like Musil, Nietzsche, Weber, Benn, Simmel, Mann, Broch, Benjamin and Arendt*] help' (Mishra 2014b). Translation thus allows ideas to circulate and move beyond their historical and cultural context, making new understanding – new ways of thinking and seeing – possible.

Just as writers are altered by the foreign texts they read in translation, so too are audiences altered by texts that they would otherwise not encounter. Simultaneously, texts themselves are altered by travelling beyond the borders within which they originally operated and by being put to uses for which they were perhaps not conceived. Within this dynamic of exchange, English holds a particularly powerful position, given its global influence and the fact that it is often used as a bridging language. Non-Anglophone publishers typically use English as the language for the sample translations they send to publishers around the world in order to try to sell the rights to their books, and English translations are sometimes used as bridging texts for indirect translation – also known as relay translation – between less common language pairings. In Croatia, for example, translator Maja Soljan, who does not speak Japanese, has translated several of Haruki Murakami's books via English, as there is only one working Japanese-Croatian translator and he is unable to take on all of the commissions offered to him (Soljan 2014). In the light of the cultural dominance of English, Grossman argues that UK and US publishers 'have an ethical and cultural responsibility to foster literature in translation' (2010:59). PEN does much to encourage publishers to live up to this responsibility by providing financial support for the translation and promotion of literature-in-translation in the form of programmes such as Writers in Translation. One of the books supported by PEN, Iraqi writer Hassan Blasim's short-story collection *The Iraqi Christ* (2013), translated by Jonathan Wright and published by Comma Press, won the 2014 Independent Foreign Fiction Prize, the first work of Arabic literature to do so in the history of the prize. *The Iraqi Christ*, which features surreal and often graphically violent stories is, in the words of the IFF judges, 'a classic work of post-war witness, mourning and revolt' (Booktrust 2014). It has never been published in Arabic. In this example, as in numerous examples of Soviet novels being made available abroad in translation prior to a Russian-language edition (Clark 2011; Mancosu 2013), translation provides censored authors with a voice. The cultural dominance of the English language means that it can serve as a particularly powerful medium for the transmission of such voices.

Beyond rescuing texts from the silence imposed by censorship, translation can also play a role in bringing forgotten or underappreciated texts to the attention of a wider audience, and can sometimes have a boomerang effect on a text's status in the source culture. US translator Peter Filkins discovered Holocaust survivor H.G. Adler's novel *Eine Reise* by chance, in Schoenhoff's Foreign Books in Cambridge, Massachusetts, in 2002. After reading only two pages, Filkins was 'compelled by the haunting power of Adler's voice from beyond the grave' (Bard College at Simon's Rock 2013) and knew that he would have to translate *Eine Reise* into English. Although a small circle of academics had long been familiar with Adler's work, his literary texts were entirely inaccessible to an Anglophone readership and were largely ignored in Germany. As Filkins points out in his introduction to *The Journey*, you will be unlikely to find H.G. Adler in any of the usual reference works on Holocaust literature (Filkins 2008:x), although his non-fiction works on the Holocaust, *Theresienstadt 1941–1945* (1955) and *Der verwaltete Mensch* [Administered Man] (1974), were well-known and well-received during his lifetime; the former title won the Leo Baeck Prize and is a foundational text of Holocaust Studies. Adler, whose first wife and parents-in-law perished in the camps, wrote five novels, but only three were published in his lifetime. Filkins reflects on the reasons for Adler's obscurity, mentioning 'bad luck and the quirks of publishing' and the fact that 'the times were not ready for Adler, nor was he at ease with them' (ibid:xi). Adorno's famous maxim that 'To write poetry after Auschwitz is barbaric' (1967:34) reflected and confirmed the contemporary unease felt at attempts to approach the Shoah through literature. Filkins begins his introduction to *The Journey* with a quote from the English translation of German writer W.G. Sebald's novel *Austerlitz* (2001) (Filkins 2008:ix), in which Jacques Austerlitz expresses his regret that he had not managed to seek out

Adler before the writer's death in 1988 in order to talk to him about Theresienstadt (Sebald 2001:331). This borrowing underlines the role and the task that Filkins has taken upon himself: the role of witness – to Adler, to Adler's experiences in the Shoah and to his literary exploration of the Shoah. This carries with it the urgent responsibility of bringing Adler's work to a wider audience, of making sure his writing is brought from the periphery to the centre, both in its domestic literary polysystem (a polysystem comprises the systems that structure a given national literature and the relations and hierarchies that exist between them (Even-Zohar 2012 [1978])) and in the English-language polysystem. One of the remarkable effects of Filkins' discovery and translation of Adler's novels has been to raise Adler's profile in his language of composition, German, and to promote critical engagement with his work more generally. Several of Adler's non-fiction titles have been reissued in German over the last two years; an Italian translation of *Eine Reise* was published in 2010; Adler's book on Theresienstadt will be published for the first time in English in 2015; academic interest in Adler has blossomed. Through Filkins' efforts, Adler has 'gained value through being translated into a prestigious language and thus anointed, can reenter the culture of origin' (Massardier-Kenney 2010:27). Filkins, meanwhile, is at work on a major biography of Adler, which will be published by Oxford University Press. This is the first English-language Adler biography and consolidates Filkins' role as witness to Adler's life and work. Filkins' promotion of Adler certainly bears out Peter Newmark's comment that successful translation is likely to have much to do with 'the translator's empathy with the writer's thought' (Newmark 1981:54).

The broadly 'humanist' case for translation that I have outlined here has its roots in the late antique/early medieval concept of *translatio studii*: 'the transferal of the classical learning of Athens and Rome to Paris' (Bolduc 2006:4) that brought about a literary 'transcend[ence of] geographical and temporal boundaries' and that was interwoven with the 'increasing importance of the vernacular' in the High Middle Ages (ibid:5). As such it reflects a particular view of the world, one in which enabling the spread of ideas and engaging with the other is a means to greater intercultural understanding and ultimately to improved interpersonal and international relations. This, of course, is an ideological *Weltanschauung* in itself. Translation motivated by humanist principles has an essential faith in communication and hence in translatability; but what if translation denies and eradicates difference rather than opening our eyes to it? Where is the line between engaging with the other and gathering intelligence? Between allowing ideas to travel and evangelising? Has, as Emily Apter suggests, 'the right to the Untranslatable [been] blindsided' (2013:8) through the prioritizing of translation's communicative function? Mona Baker argues that the 'master narrative of the translator as an honest intermediary, with translation repeatedly portrayed as a force for good' is misleading (2005:9) and that translators, far from building bridges, 'participate in very decisive ways in promoting and circulating narratives and discourses of various types. Some promote peace, others fuel conflicts, subjugate entire populations, kill millions' (ibid:12). Even if we presume the best of intentions – and this is not always the case – translators and translating cultures can escape neither the web of ideology nor the individual and collective unconscious. Before turning to look at ideologically motivated translation in more detail, let us briefly consider twentieth-century Bible translation as an example of the fuzzy dividing line between Christian humanist and 'ideological' approaches to translation.

The translation of a sacred text such as the Christian Bible is fraught with challenges. The truth claim of and divine inspiration attributed to sacred texts means that the decontextualization that occurs in translation, when the text's message is separated from its original form, is problematic for believers. It is for this reason that Muslims insist on the authority of the Qur'an in Arabic, which cannot be superseded by a translation. Centuries of hermeneutic tradition and 'devoted attachment' (Nida 2003 [1964]:179) to particular versions of texts on a personal and institutional level only add to the complexity of re-translating the Bible. The 1950s and 1960s saw a 'turning point' in Bible translation, following the discovery of the Dead Sea Scrolls in 1947, new developments in linguistics and anthropology and the convening of the Second Vatican Council in 1965 (Zogbo 2011). During this period US linguist Eugene Nida was asked by the United Bible Societies to investigate why so many translations of the Bible were 'not only difficult to understand, but [. . .] also frequently misunderstood' (Nida 2003 [1964]:ix). Translations intended for evangelical purposes in non-Christian communities appeared not to be having the desired effect of converting the population to Christianity. In two detailed studies, one co-authored with Charles Taber (Nida 2003 [1964]; Nida and Taber 1974), Nida, acknowledging that a Bible translation could have a variety of purposes, concluded that where the translator was 'motivated by a sincere humanitarian purpose, namely, to convey an important message in an intelligible form' (2003 [1964]:152), a translation that followed the principles of dynamic equivalence would be most likely to achieve this aim. Dynamic equivalence in translation means that 'the relationship between receptor and message should be substantially the same as that which existed between the original receptors and the message' (ibid:159). In other words, the text should serve to spread the 'good news' of Christianity as it did in the early days of the Christian Church. Dynamic equivalence can be achieved by making formal adjustments so that the target text uses 'the closest natural equivalent to the source-language message' (ibid:166). In this vision of translation, close engagement with the target culture will equip the translator with the necessary linguistic and cultural knowledge to produce a dynamically equivalent translation. Nida gives numerous examples of this type of knowledge and its implications, such as the fact that Shilluk, which is spoken in what is now South Sudan, uses the phrase 'to spit on the ground in front of' to describe the concept of repentance, referencing the custom of plaintiffs and defendants spitting on the ground in front of each other to indicate closure when a court case has been concluded. In Shilluk, therefore, the metaphor of spitting on the ground would serve as 'the more meaningful idiom' for the Biblical concept of repentance (ibid:158).

Nida's approach has its methodological flaws on a linguistic level: its 'focus on sentence-level-and-below linguistics' (Mojola and Wendland 2003:5), for example, and its assumption that we can access source-text meaning (ibid:7), a claim which renders it essentially irreconcilable with a poststructuralist view of language that sees meaning as fluid, created in the interplay between author, reader, text and the wider culture they inhabit. From an ideological standpoint, too, dynamic equivalence has its critics, summed up by Lawrence Venuti's view that it 'seeks to impose on English-language readers [...] a distinctly Christian understanding of the Bible' (1995:23), i.e. it does not allow any access to the text that would lie outside the framework of the Christian faith, precluding the reading of 'sacred' texts as works of literature or historical sources. But Pym argues that 'when dealing with the translation of sacred texts, there is a level at which ethical discussion simply has to accept the commitment of the faithful' (Pym 2012:110), a statement that suggests the devout have privileged access to these texts and to the translation thereof. Like many translators of secular texts, Nida's commitment to the text and the task at hand is rooted in a belief that the message held by that text is worthwhile and, furthermore, communicable – 'the writers of the Biblical books expected to be understood' (Nida and Taber 1974:7) – and that its movement into other cultures and languages should be facilitated. Nida shares Luther's democratic view of the Bible as a text for the people, a text that must meet people where they stand, in their own language (ibid:31). For Nida, translating in a dynamically equivalent fashion is an act of Christian humanism that provides readers with democratic access to a life-enriching text; for Venuti, and for others, it is ideologically charged, a crude form of cultural colonialism.

## Why do we translate? Ideological agendas

> It is perfectly natural for the human mind to resist the assault on it of untreated strangeness; therefore cultures have always been inclined to impose complete transformations on other cultures, receiving

> these other cultures not as they are but as, for the benefit of the receiver, they ought to be.
>
> Edward W. Said, *Orientalism* (2003 [1978]:67)

Said's seminal work of postcolonial theory, *Orientalism* (2003 [1978]), examines how the West constructed the East from the late eighteenth century and onwards through the colonial era, and how this image of the 'Orient' continues to affect our attitudes towards the Middle East today. Orientalism is an ideology – that is to say, it is a way of looking at the world, or a portion of the world; it is the 'impos[ition of] a pattern – some form of structure or organization – on how we read (and misread) political facts, events, occurrences, actions, on how we see images and hear voices' (Freeden 2003:3). Although the term 'ideology' dates from the French Revolution – Destutt de Tracy published a book entitled *Projet d'éléments d'idéologie* in 1801 – and was initially concerned with the study of ideas (Destutt de Tracy 2012 [1801]), our contemporary understanding of it is heavily influenced by its Marxist inflection, beginning with Marx and Engels' *The German Ideology* (written 1845–6 but not published in its entirety until 1932), which sees ideology as an illusory force that works to conceal the material reality of capitalism, upholding the economic and social status quo for the benefit of the ruling class (Marx and Engels 1970). Understood in this sense, ideology can be made visible, and then either deliberately embraced or consciously resisted. From this stems a more everyday usage of the term, which has come to describe the sum of one's political outlook on society, be it socialist, conservative, liberal or neo-liberal, which in turn informs people's voting behaviour and political decisions. But 'ideology' also has a more abstract, subconscious meaning, as Freeden's definition implies: as an all permeating force of which we are partly or fully unaware and which colours not only our behaviour but our very perception of the world. This interpretation owes much to Louis Althusser, who, in a merging of Marxist and psychoanalytic theory, suggested that our very sense of self takes shape within an ideological framework and that our tastes, values and desires are acquired through our participation in the ideological practices that structure ordinary life: going to school, attending church, going to work, watching television and reading the newspaper, and fulfilling our ordained role within family structures (Althusser 2014).

No matter which definition of ideology we embrace, it is clear that literary translation, as a human activity taking place in the era of late capitalism, is inevitably ideologically situated. Since translators work within the marketplace – although, as we have already noted, not all literary translation is profit-driven – they are a part of an ideological system (capitalism) that governs their mode of production. In fact, from a Marxist point of view, many of the woes of the profession could be attributed to translation's dominant mode of production: a translator's work is almost always owned by somebody else, be it the author, the foreign publisher or the domestic publisher. The translator is inadequately compensated and is often only saved from the fate of alienated labour by those other rewards that Pym has identified (2012:124–5). As a social and economic practice, translation cannot help but serve, to a greater or lesser extent, the ideological ends of the system in which it is situated. Like Orientalism, translation will always convert the foreign from something into something else, to a large extent because the vast majority of translations are commodities, produced for a particular market and sold to generate a profit. But ideology is both a conscious and an unconscious force, and hence can – and, as Venuti has argued, should – be resisted, by individuals and by groups: 'translators must [...] force a revision of the codes – cultural, economic, legal – that marginalize and exploit them' (Venuti 1995:311).

In this section we will be looking at how ideology affects the politics and ethics of the practice of literary translation in the Anglophone world. What does ideology have to do with our motivations for translating? Those translation theorists who argue that we should not always translate (e.g. Pym 2012), that we should not translate for the ignorant reader (e.g. Scott 2012a) or that we all too easily forget the importance of untranslatability (e.g. Apter 2013) do so because they see the decision to translate – rather than not to translate – as ideologically motivated in itself, having to do with humanist belief in translation as a means, and perhaps *the* means, to greater understanding between peoples. Both Scott and Pym argue that translation may in fact undermine this goal (Scott 2012a:17; Pym 2012:167).

Since ideology operates both consciously and unconsciously, a translator may be actively and openly in pursuit of a particular ideological agenda, as is the case with overtly feminist translation practices (see von Flotow 1997 for an overview of such practices); be entirely or partially unaware of the ideological forces operating upon him or her – one might argue that Simone de Beauvoir's first English translator H.M. Parshley falls into this category (Simons 1983; Moi 2002); be aware but powerless or unwilling to resist; or be caught between several camps, functioning as 'a kind of double agent' (Tymoczko and Gentzler 2002a:xix). The evidence for ideological motivation may be partially or completely hidden and must therefore be sought in statements made by translators, but also in analyses of translation products (Berman 2012; Toury 1995). And, depending on one's usage of the term, there are various kinds of ideologies, or at least various levels upon which ideology is operative: at the level of the socio-economic organization of society (capitalism, communism, feudalism); at the level of religion, gender, race or the nation; and at the level of the particular truth claims of systems of knowledge (e.g. psychoanalysis, Marxism, humanism). As we continue to investigate why we translate, how might potential answers to that question be motivated ideologically? And what might the implications of this be for how we translate?

## Ideology in translation: colonialism

Translation can serve dominant ideologies – nations, institutions and ideas that already hold power and influence, or weaker and emergent ideologies – constituencies of various kinds seeking empowerment and a stronger voice, or both at the same time. Much valuable research has been done within Translation Studies on how translation intersects with ideology and power (see, for example, Lefevere 1992; Álvarez and Vidal 1996; Tymoczko and Gentzler 2002b; Calzada Pérez 2003; Tymoczko 2010), with particular attention being paid to the role of translation in colonial and postcolonial contexts (see, for example, Niranjana 1992; Tymoczko 1999; Bassnett and Trivedi 1999; Simon and St-Pierre 2000; Batchelor 2009) and how translation can further imperial interests or promote decolonization. Indeed, these topics have been the dominant field of enquiry in Translation Studies since the early 1990s. One straightforward example of how translation can strengthen the hold of empire can be found in the Maori-language translation of the Treaty of Waitangi (1840), by which Great Britain assumed sovereignty over New Zealand. This translation has been shown to be inadequate on a number of levels (Fenton and Moon 2002). Completed by an Anglican missionary, Henry Williams, the translated treaty simplified the complex English text and omitted important details, resulting in a translation that served the needs of the colonizers. Unsurprisingly, debate over the legitimacy of the treaty continues to the present day. Another example of how translation can serve a dominant ideology is Sir Richard Francis Burton's translation of *Alf Laylah wa-Laylah*, the collection of medieval Arabic stories known to contemporaneous readers of Burton's version as *The Book of the Thousand Nights and a Night*; this first appeared in 1885, when British colonial activity in the Middle East was particularly intense. There is some doubt as to the originality of Burton's translation – he has been accused of plagiarizing from John Payne's earlier translation, published between 1882 and 1884 (Irwin 1994:29) – but the 'obtrusive and often supernumerary footnotes' (ibid:32) that accompany Burton's translation are certainly his own work. In these footnotes, which are 'fascinating, titillating, digressive, conversational and controversial in tone' (Sallis 1999:57), Burton occupies a position of authority over the text and over the Middle East. The footnotes include digressions on the sexual habits of Orientals ('we do not find in The Nights any allusion to that systematic *prolongatio veneris* which is so much cultivated by Moslems under the name Imsák = retention, withholding *i.e.* the semen' (1885:76)), on their customs ('Easterns as a rule sleep with head and body covered by a sheet or in cold weather a blanket. The practice is doubtless hygienic, defending the body from draughts when the pores are open; but Europeans find it hard to adopt; it seems to stop their breathing' (ibid:18–19)) and on their religions ('the strict Moslem is a model Conservative whose exemplar of life dates from the seventh century. This fact may be casuistically explained away; but is not less an obstacle to all progress and it will be one of the principal dangers threatening Al-Islam' (ibid: 167)). Said argues that although Burton's writings on the region, including his translations, are born of first-hand experience – Burton spoke fluent Arabic and even completed the pilgrimage to Mecca – his claim to mastery of the Orient through knowledge 'elevates Burton's consciousness to a position of supremacy over the Orient' and in this he as an individual merges with the imperialist project 'which is itself a system of rules, codes, and concrete epistemological habits' (Said 2003 [1978]:196). The imperialist, Orientalist claim to knowledge is a means of exerting control from without, a denial of sovereignty and a rejection of cultural fluidity and complexity. The *Explanatory Notes on the Manners and Customs of Moslem Men* which accompany Burton's translation confine the Middle East within their expository framework in precisely this fashion. Colonial and neo-imperialist agendas have also been served by translation carried out in the context of missionary activity, which often had secondary effects beyond the immediate goal of evangelization. Israel has looked at the 'civilizing process' of religious conversion in nineteenth-century India (2006:453), which helped the British consolidate their hold on the sub-continent, and Carcelen-Estrada, among others (see, for example, Colby and Dennett 1995), has argued that the activities of SIL and other missionary groups in Latin America during the Cold War were 'an extension of anti-communist controls' that were very much in the interests of the US (2010:68).

### Ideology in translation: systems of thought

Translation can not only uphold dominant systems of power such as colonialism and its constitutive ideology, Orientalism, it can also weaken the force of new ideas trying to gain a foothold and prevent more established ideas from developing. Simone de Beauvoir's seminal work of feminist philosophy *Le deuxième sexe* (1949) and Sigmund Freud's collected writings on psychoanalysis both have controversial Anglophone translation histories which demonstrate how translation can have ideological effects even where it may be difficult to attribute an overtly ideological intention. De Beauvoir's work was translated into English by a US zoologist, H.M. Parshley, an expert on human sexual behaviour and reproduction but who had no previous translation experience. *The Second Sex*, as de Beauvoir's book was titled in

English, was published in the US in 1953 by Knopf. The problems with Parshley's translation have been well documented by feminist theorists (Simons 1983; von Flotow 2000; Moi 2002). Simons was the first to bring English readers' attention to the fact that 10 per cent of the text's original material was missing from the translation, that seventy-eight women's names, and with them a significant body of women's history, had been deleted from the text and that philosophical terms related to existentialism, such as Sartre's *la réalité humaine* (erroneously rendered as 'the real nature of man') had been mangled in translation (Simons 1983:563). The latter category of deformity in particular gave the impression that 'Beauvoir is a sloppy writer, and thinker' (ibid). Nonetheless, Simons comes to the conclusion that all of this damage to de Beauvoir's text was unlikely to have been 'the result of some kind of sexist plot' (ibid). Moi too stresses that 'Parshley should not be seen as the villain of the piece' (2010:5). Parshley was enthusiastic about de Beauvoir's work and felt quite strongly that it should be translated. But if one cannot attribute intent to undermine de Beauvoir's pioneering feminist philosophy to the translator, where can or should one attribute blame? Publisher Knopf's role in editing and promoting *The Second Sex* has been examined by several scholars (Englund 1994; Bogic 2011), who have concluded on the basis of the Parshley–Knopf correspondence that much of the impetus for textual cuts came from the publisher in a drive to simplify the text for the American reader (Bogic 2011:161–2). There was also a failure on Parshley's part to apprehend the text as a work of philosophy: his preface to the translation states that 'Mlle de Beauvoir's book is, after all on woman, not on philosophy' (Parshley 1997 [1953]:8); his 'philosophically deaf ear' (Moi 2002:1014) and ignorance of existentialism were compounded by the publisher's belief that existentialism was 'a dead duck' (Blanche Knopf, cited in Bogic 2011:160). The temporal proximity of Parshley's translation to de Beauvoir's text may have exacerbated this myopia. So while there was certainly no ideological ill intent towards de Beauvoir's text, the failure of the translator to read the book as a philosophical text, the publisher's preoccupation with sales and its inability to find a translator better suited to the task all combined to undermine *The Second Sex* and its effects as a pioneering work of feminist philosophy. The recent re-translation of the text by Constance Borde and Sheila Malovany-Chevallier (2009) has, according to Toril Moi, done nothing to correct this position. Moi describes her experience of reading this new translation as like 'reading underwater': 'it [is] no more reliable, and far less readable than Parshley' (2010:6).

A further example of how translation can affect systems of knowledge, whether emergent or established, is to be found in the translation of the writings of Sigmund Freud. Until the first decade of this century, Freud's works were probably best known to English-language readers through the twenty-four-volume Standard Edition, edited by psychoanalyst

James Strachey, who had been one of Freud's patients, in collaboration with Freud's daughter, Anna Freud, and translated by Strachey and his wife, Alix, a fellow psychoanalyst, with the assistance of Alan Tyson. Copyright on the Standard Edition is held by the Institute of Psychoanalysis, home of the British Psychoanalytical Society; this is the edition of Freud's works that the Institute uses in its training programme. The Standard Edition has been critiqued for its 'formality and would-be accuracy', which has none of the 'charm, flexibility, and force of Freud's Viennese expression' (Mahony 1987:18), and for its imposition of a standardized terminology reliant on dense scientific neologisms that do not reflect Freud's more everyday language (Bettelheim 1984 [1982]). When Penguin commissioned new translations of Freud's work in the early 2000s, interested in 'how one might make a Freud for the new century' (Phillips 2007:36), the Institute of Psychoanalysis sent a solicitor's letter to the managing director of Penguin pointing out that these new translations were not to draw on the Standard Edition (ibid:37). Phillips wittily suggests that, from a psychoanalytic point of view, the Institute cannot have been motivated merely by its stated fear of loss of income from sales of the Standard Edition. Rather, the fears surrounding the re-translation of Freud's writings have to do with transference (in the psychoanalytic sense):

> In producing and promoting and defending the Standard Edition, the institutes of psychoanalysis were not in any way controlling the interpretation of Freud's texts. I think it is possible, to put it in psychoanalytic language, that there is a wish to control – odd as it might sound – the diversity of personal histories that are brought to bear on Freud's texts by having a variety of translators, none of whom may have been analysed [...], and many of whom may have different views about Freud's language. The Standard Edition, whatever else it is, is one man's transference to Freud's words, a transference that Freud himself was acquainted with and had, to some extent, analysed; and it was supervised by a committee of senior analysts. Given what analysts know about the power of transference – the power of transference to translate its objects – there could be real fears about what might be done to Freud's texts in the apparently innocent name of new translation.
> 
> (Phillips 2007:37)

Phillips goes on to argue that an understanding of transference as a means of bringing something new into being rather than as a misreading or distortion opens up the possibility, through re-translation, of engaging anew with Freud's texts, which may in fact be 'of indeterminate use' (ibid:36): as literature, as science or as both. He further argues that a new translation – viewed as an alternative to Strachey's

Standard Edition but not as a replacement – might even allow psychoanalysis to progress as a science (ibid:36). If one subscribes to Phillips' view then the negative ideological effects of the Standard Edition may be to freeze psychoanalysis in a particular moment, to hinder its ongoing development or afterlife and to prescribe the value of Freud's texts for the individual reader and society at large.

## Ideology in translation: textual decision-making

Thus far, we have considered examples of how translation can support dominant systems of government and/or thought, and work to suppress emergent ideas that may have the potential to transform established ideologies. The ideological effects of these translations are more straightforwardly observed than the motivations behind them, which can be nebulous and in need of distillation. But certain theorist-translators are very explicit about their ideological approaches to translation, and these approaches often align with a desire to challenge the (collective) self and to encounter the 'other'. In an essay that has become one of the central texts of contemporary Translation Studies, 'La traduction comme épreuve de l'étranger' (1985), translated into English by Lawrence Venuti as 'Translation and the Trials of the Foreign', French translator and translation theorist Antoine Berman argues that 'the properly *ethical* aim of the translating act [is] receiving the Foreign as Foreign' (Berman 2012:241). What does Berman mean by this? Berman understands translation as a unique opportunity to establish 'a relationship between the Self-Same (*Propre*) and the Foreign' (ibid:240). The target reader should experience the full strangeness of the foreign text, and the target language should be derailed by its collision with the source language. Translation is also an occasion for the foreign work to be tested through its 'uproot[ing] from its own *language-ground*', something that has the potential to reveal its 'most original kernel' (ibid). Berman's description of the encounter of reader and translation, of translating language and translated language, conjures up both a mystical and an unsettling event. The reader should feel disturbed by the translated text, the boundaries of the translating language will be placed under strain and the foreign text will have to prove its worth as it leaves the comfort of its own language behind and strives for 'success' in another. Yet Berman's esoteric and violent account of the translating act also features a detailed, twelve-point, micro-textual description of how translations fail to achieve their properly ethical aim. For Berman, we translate in order that readers and texts might encounter the other, and this necessitates a certain method of translating which has come to be labelled 'foreignization', although the term is not Berman's own and is defined in his essay only by default, through his twelve-point 'negative analytic' (ibid:242), a list of domesticating and deforming tendencies that occur in translation. Pym has criticized Berman's ethics as stemming from an ideological viewpoint similar to Schleiermacher's, one that has a vested interest in keeping the foreign foreign – one that 'assumes a clear border between cultures' (Pym 2012:10) – but I would argue that a more generous interpretation of Berman's use of the word 'foreign' places his argument in a different light. The nature of the self's encounter with the other as sketched by Berman differs from a humanist-ideological belief in the value of intercultural knowledge and exchange, in the sense that Berman's ethics are more textual in nature. His concern is with the pursuit of literary integrity, with allowing literature to function as literature and with permitting the literary work to unfold its poetic effects. The 'foreign' in Berman's essay is as much the stylistic otherness of the individual literary text as the fact of its existence in a foreign language. This would explain his interest in the trial undergone by the foreign text in translation: translation is perhaps the ultimate test of literariness. In this respect, Berman's approach is not entirely 'a consideration of the benefits of the Other for the Self', as Batchelor suggests (2009:236), since the Other – the literary text – also benefits from the trial of translation (Batchelor makes the same point about Lawrence Venuti's approach, but there the criticism may well hold true.) Nor does Berman's approach assume an investment in cultivating distinct cultures: the hybrid language that must result from the posited collision of languages suggests that he was not particularly invested in maintaining borders.

What might Berman's textual ethics – the 'positive counterpart' (Berman 2012:242) to his negative analytic – look like in practice? To arrive at some sort of model, one must work backwards from the negative analytic, which is illustrated with examples drawn from literary prose. The 'shapelessness' and 'lack of control' that is characteristic of the novel in particular means that it is a challenge for the translator to 'avoid an arbitrary homogenization' (ibid:243), but also that the deforming tendencies which result from the (often unconscious) drive to homogenize are less easily observed. Berman cites Dostoevsky as an example of an author whose work has been deformed in French translation. It is certainly the case that in the English-speaking world and in France there has been a movement since the 1990s to produce translations that respect Dostoevsky's polyphonic style (France 2000:595). Although the 'pioneering versions' of British translator Constance Garnett 'allowed [Dostoevsky's] strange new voice to invade English literature' (ibid:596), her work has also been criticized for 'muting Dostoevsky's jarring contrasts, sacrificing his insistent rhythms and repetitions, toning down the Russian colouring, explaining and normalizing in all kinds of ways' (ibid:595). Other post-Garnett translators have also come in for criticism on grounds ranging from 'lack[ing] some of the excitement of the foreign' (ibid:596) to 'produc[ing] texts which lack a distinctive voice' (ibid). Russian-US translation team Richard Pevear and Larissa Volokhonsky, who are often referred to simply as P/V, have been at the forefront of the movement to introduce Anglophone readers to a new kind of Dostoevsky. P/V have acknowledged that they were drawn to re-translate Dostoevsky's novels because they felt that previous translations had not done justice to his polyphonic style (Pevear 1990:xi). Pevear offers the reader a sense of the translators' ethos by stating that 'a smooth translation of Dostoevsky would be what Paul Valéry called a "résumé that annuls resonance and form"' (1994:xxiii). The Garnett (1931) and P/V (1994) translations of the novel Бесы [*Besy*] (1872), which has been variously translated into English as *The Possessed*, *Demons* and *The Devils*, are contrasted in the following short extract. The scene depicted occurs early on and shows Stepan Trofimovich in conversation with the narrator. Trofimovich is in an emotional state, concerned that his forthcoming marriage to Darya Pavlovna is a cover for 'someone else's sins': a sexual indiscretion that may have taken place in Switzerland.

> 'But, *mon cher*, don't crush me completely, don't shout at me; as it is I'm utterly squashed like . . . a black-beetle. And, after all, I thought it was all so honourable. Suppose that something really happened . . . *en Suisse* . . . or was beginning. I was bound to question their hearts beforehand that I . . . *enfin*, that I might not constrain their hearts, and be a stumbling-block in their paths. I acted simply from honourable feeling.'
>
> 'Oh, heavens! What a stupid thing you've done!' I cried involuntarily.
>
> 'Yes, yes,' he assented with positive eagerness. 'You have never said anything more just, *c'était bete, mais que faire? Tout est dit*.‡ I shall marry her just the same even if it be to cover 'another's sins'. So there was no object in writing, was there?'
>
> (Dostoevsky, trans. Garnett 1931:110)

> 'But, *mon cher*, don't crush me finally, don't yell at me; I am quite crushed as it is, like . . . a cockroach, and, finally, I think it is all so noble. Suppose there had indeed been something there . . . *en Suisse* . . . or there was beginning to be. Oughtn't I to question their hearts first, so as . . . *enfin*, so as not to hinder their hearts or stand in their way like a post . . . solely out of nobility?'
>
> 'Oh, God, what a stupid thing to do!' burst from me involuntarily.
>
> 'Stupid, stupid!' he picked up, even greedily. 'You've never said anything more intelligent, *c'était bete, mais que faire, tout est dit*.‡ I am getting married anyway, even if it's to 'someone else's sins,' and so what was the point of writing? Isn't that so?'
>
> (Dostoevsky, trans. Pevear and Volokhonsky 1994:122–3)

‡ 'it was stupid, but what can be done, all has been said.'

Eighty years separate these two translations, which may account for some of the differences in lexical choices. Garnett is a creature of her age, hence the ennobling expression 'heavens!' and the dated use of 'object' to indicate 'sense' or 'purpose'. But there is nothing particularly modern about the Pevear and Volokhonsky version either – the translators work with dictionaries to ensure that their lexical choices do not post-date the text in question (Remnick 2005). In their translation, Trofimovich's diction is more meandering and vague on the one hand ('Suppose there had indeed been something there [...] or there was beginning to be') contrasts sharply with Garnett's more direct 'Suppose that something really happened [...] or was beginning') but is blunter and funnier on the other ('stand in their way like a post' rather than 'be a stumbling-block in their paths'); and whereas in Garnett's clarifying version Trofimovich is marrying for a reason, 'to cover "another's sins"', in the P/V version he is quite literally and more unusually marrying '"someone else's sins"'. Even in this short excerpt, there are notable variations between the two translations in terms of their attitudes to syntax, punctuation and repetition. Garnett creates several new sentences, conforming to conventional English patterns of speech, where P/V allow Trofimovich to ramble on; Garnett opts for lexical variation ('crush' and 'squashed' to P/V's 'crush' and 'crushed'); similarly, Garnett has Trofimovich answer the narrator's accusation of stupidity with 'Yes, yes'; P/V have him echo the phrasing of the narrator's accusation with 'Stupid, stupid!'); Garnett also uses the active voice ('I cried') whereas P/V's passive 'burst from me' is more iconic of the involuntary nature of the narrator's statement. P/V's decision to use the word 'finally' twice, where Garnett uses first 'completely' and then 'after all', makes Trofimovich's intended meaning much more ambiguous and hints at the French adverb 'enfin', which Trofimovich uses elsewhere; this heightens the overall impression of French interference in his Russian. For somebody, like me, who does not read Russian, it is of course impossible to tell how each version relates to Dostoevsky's prose without recourse to expert opinion; but even without this, it is clear that the two sets of translators give us a very different Dostoevsky, and that over the course of a lengthy novel the sum of such subtleties will become very significant indeed. This does not necessarily mean, however, that one translation is better or worse than the other, simply that the translations are creatures of different times, places and translational sensibilities, and that each pursues its own goals.

Berman may seem an unusual choice to include in a discussion of ideological motivations for translation, since his focus is textual rather than overtly political. Yet the idea of encountering the foreign in a certain manner, whether this is through confrontation – perhaps even violent confrontation – or in a more benign, assimilated form that softens 'the assault on [the human mind] of untreated strangeness'

(Said 2003 [1978]:67) is a feature of much ideologically motivated translation. Berman reminds us that every language and culture is ethnocentrically structured, i.e. focused primarily inward, and that ethnocentric deforming forces 'form part of the translator's being, determining the *desire* to translate' (Berman 2012:242). The inclination to transform other cultures 'for the benefit of the receiver' (Said 2003 [1978]:67) will always be present in the act of translation; the extent to which we resist or acquiesce depends very much upon our ideological standpoint.

US translator and theorist Lawrence Venuti has played a substantial role in shaping contemporary Translation Studies with his overt marriage of the textual and the political. His *Translation Studies Reader* has become the textbook of choice for many MA and PhD programmes on both sides of the Atlantic, informing the discipline's canon, but it was his two programmatic monographs, *The Translator's Invisibility* (1995) and *The Scandals of Translation* (1998), that added weight to its postcolonial turn in the 1990s. In *The Translator's Invisibility* Venuti traces the history of translation in the English-speaking world and argues that fluency in translation has a tradition reaching back to seventeenth-century Britain. Domestication, the term Venuti uses to describe the then current dominant mode of translation, assimilates foreign literature to the literary norms of the target language, resulting in smooth, natural texts that read as though they were originally written in English. This serves to strengthen Anglo-American cultural hegemony over the rest of the world because it deprives us of an awareness of what lies beyond our borders. For Venuti, any answers to the questions of why and how we translate must take their impetus from the geo-political situation within which the translator finds him- or herself. In the second half of the twentieth century, there was a 'trade imbalance' (1995:17) that led to a situation of 'unequal cultural exchanges' (ibid:20) in which the Anglo-American market exported far more literature than it imported, thus limiting readers' exposure to difference. Statistics reveal that this situation has not changed much in the new century: Batchelor's analysis of the situation of the sub-Saharan Francophone African novel showed that of 1515 such novels published from the 1920s up to and including 2008, only seventy-two had been translated into English (Batchelor 2009:16). Venuti argues further that the small amount of literature that has been translated into English has tended to be subject to the extreme 'ethnocentric violence' (Venuti 1995:20) of a domesticating approach to translation, which neutralizes the reader's confrontation with the foreign. Translation can thus buttress a neo-imperialist stance towards the rest of the world.

In Venuti's view, English-language translators should work to redress this state of affairs, and he advocates several means by which this might be achieved. First, the translator can shrug off the cloak of invisibility and adopt a foreignizing approach to the translation of literary texts. Venuti's foreignization differs from that of Schleiermacher and Berman's in that 'the foreign text is privileged [...] only insofar as it enables a disruption of target-language cultural codes' (Venuti 1995:42). A foreignizing approach in Venuti's sense draws upon the resources of the target language to foreignize by analogy – he references Philip Lewis here, whose aim as a translator was to 'recreate analogically the abuse that occurs in the original text' (Lewis 1985:43) – rather than by literal fidelity to the source text (Venuti 1995:291). In effect, translators are to create an artificial foreignness in the target text, a foreignness that does not depend on the foreignness of the source text for inspiration. This can be achieved using the resources that English makes available, 'introduc[ing] discursive variations, experimenting with archaism, slang, literary allusion and convention' (ibid:310), creating a stylistic mélange. A further means of raising the profile of translation, according to Venuti, is to highlight the role of the translator using paratextual and extratextual means, cultivating a role for translators as literary experts and public intellectuals (ibid:311). Conversely, the translator can also choose to remain cloaked – adopting 'a canonical discourse (e.g. transparency)' (ibid:310) – in order to 'smuggle' a subversive text into the target culture. The choice of strategy and accompanying method 'should be grounded on a critical assessment of the target-language culture, its hierarchies and exclusions, its relations to cultural others worldwide' (ibid:309).

Venuti believes that contemporary Anglophone translators should translate in order to redress the balance of political and cultural power – to confront English-language readers with difference so that they come to think of themselves as only one culture among many, rather than as an imperial centre. Pym is dismissive of the ideology that informs this view: '[it is] as if, in the pipedreams of New York intellectuals, a change in literary translating would somehow make a whole society aware of what it is doing in the world' (Pym 2012:17). He finds fault with Venuti and, by extension, with Berman, for their investment in translations that are difficult to read since these are, he argues, elitist and hence unlikely to have a wider impact (ibid:35). US scholar Douglas Robinson agrees that Venuti's work displays 'uncomfortable rapprochements with elitism' (1997:99), but he also argues elsewhere, in a critique of Berman's approach and 'timid foreignism' in general (ibid:95), that 'radical and aggressive domestication' (ibid) – Venuti's foreignization under a different name – is 'the most effective way to unsettle the complacent reader' (ibid:96). Venuti himself warns that foreignizing translation should 'stop short of the parodic or the incomprehensible' (1995:311), also arguing that the significance of a particular text may warrant a domesticating approach to its translation. While one is sympathetic to Pym's insistence that the translator cannot operate outside the commercial realm, which is what the translator risks when 'playing with language alone' (Pym 2012:35), the situation of translation in the late capitalist marketplace is shockingly asymmetrical: there are a handful of dominant export literatures rather than an equitable exchange of literatures across linguistic boundaries. Resistance may have to be afforded wherever windows of opportunities exist, however small or elitist. A more fruitful critique of Venuti's position is made by Batchelor, who argues that in Venuti's drive to overcome ethnocentrism, he is ethnocentrically concerned only with 'the benefits of the Other for the Self' (Batchelor 2009:236). His foreignization is not motivated by a textual ethics of respect for literary integrity, and it may even falsely represent the Other in its attempts to disrupt dominant target-language values. Venuti's ethnocentrism may also extend to the erroneous assumption that there is such a thing as a transnational Anglo-American literary culture. To fully appreciate Venuti's position, as well as that of his critics, it is worth considering what a domesticating translation might look like and the relationship between this approach to translation and the literary marketplace.

## Defining domestication

There are a variety of levels on which a text might – theoretically speaking – be domesticated: references to culturally specific elements such as social practices or food items could be removed or replaced; even more radically, a text could be relocated to a domestic setting. 'Difficult' texts might be made more readable by eradicating foregrounded stylistic features, replacing unusual lexical items and turns of phrase with more everyday language and normalizing syntax. Genre fiction could come to resemble its domestic equivalent, even where two national versions do not straightforwardly align. Domestication could also manifest itself as censorship, with elements considered offensive or inappropriate in the receiving culture being removed or rewritten, perhaps leading to substantial abridgement. If one shares Venuti's point of view, a domesticating approach reflects a need or a desire to deny difference, assimilate the other, strengthen one's own hegemonic position and create a false sense of the universality of a particular national position. But translators and publishers who openly aim for domestication would not explain their motivations in these terms. Translations are commodities that can make money: domestication is seen as the prerequisite for readability and hence the route to commercial success. Barry Cunningham, founder and Managing Director of children's publishing house Chicken House, and the editor who pulled J.K. Rowling's Harry Potter from the slush pile, implicitly defines domestication as a form of localization or rebranding:

> Once we've got the translation, we treat it almost like it's an entirely new book. This is an opportunity to make the book work in another language, and so we might go back to the author and look again at

certain points. We're very active on this front, and all the German authors we've worked with have been very pleased with this approach. A good example is Kirsten Boie and *The Princess Plot* – we directed it in a slightly different way and it's been hugely successful in America.

(Cunningham, cited in *New Books in German* 2011:6)

There is evidence of this method in Chicken House's treatment of a number of picture storybooks by Cornelia Funke, each of which features a young female heroine who cleverly subverts expectations of her gender. Although these were received as feminist picture storybooks in the German-speaking world, they were not overtly packaged as such, nor did they form a thematic series. Originally published several years apart as independent titles, *Prinzessin Isabella* (1997) [Princess Isabella], *Der geheimnisvolle Ritter Namenlos* (2001) [The Mysterious Knight Nameless] and *Käpten Knitterbart und seine Bande* (2003) [Captain Crinkly Beard and His Crew] became *Princess Pigsty* (2007, trans. Chantal Wright), *The Princess Knight* (2004, trans. Anthea Bell) and *Pirate Girl* (2005, trans. Chantal Wright) respectively in their English translations. With *Pirate Girl* in particular, the focus of the book was shifted away from the pirate captain, named Firebeard in the English version, to the little girl, Molly, who is captured by Firebeard's crew and eventually liberated by her pirate mother, Barbarous Bertha. This shift of focus was achieved not by rewriting, but by changing the title of the book and the cover illustration: Captain Firebeard and his crew, cutlasses aloft at the helm of their ship, were replaced by Molly, relaxing with a picnic basket in her small boat. *Der geheimnisvolle Ritter Namenlos* was also renamed to make it clear that the story had a female protagonist. The rebranding was successful; these books have been overwhelmingly perceived by parents and hailed by critics as a series of feminist tales for a new generation (see, for example, Webb 2007; McDonald 2012; Alderson 2015). In the German context, feminist narratives in books for children and teens are more common than they are in the UK; ironically, the title changes hide the fact that the source culture may be more progressive than the importing culture.

Writers and translators rarely object to small measures such as these, implemented with the goal of making a book more successful in the marketplace, though some scholars have argued that they may not be as insignificant as they appear (Sonzogni 2011). Domestication, however, can go much further than such rebranding. Barry Cunningham implies that the ideal children's book for an international publisher – his own publisher, Chicken House, is owned by Scholastic and publishes titles from the Chicken House list with partners in Germany and the Netherlands – is one which is easily transferable: 'if I believe a story's appeal is only strong because of its setting, or is so severely limited by its domestic preoccupations, then I won't choose it' (Cunningham, cited in Engberg, 2010). Children's publishers may argue the value of universalism on the grounds of their readers' more limited experience of the world – although one might argue that exposure to difference is all the more important for precisely this reason – but the practice of toning down local colour has certainly not been confined to works translated for a juvenile audience. Venuti criticizes Italian translator William Weaver for eradicating the culturally specific in this fashion, citing the example of the Anglicization of *tagliatelle* and *ricotta* as 'noodles' and 'cream cheese' in Italo Calvino's short-story collection *Cosmicomics* (Venuti 2005:181–2), for which Weaver won the 1969 US National Book Award in the Translation category. In his defence, Weaver argued that 'thirty years ago nobody in the US knew what ricotta was' (ibid:183). Today, prevailing attitudes among readers appear to have shifted, and the provision of local colour, particularly in genre fiction, is generally seen as an exotic enrichment. Novelist Ann Cleeves describes it as voyeurism, in a positive sense. She enthuses that the cultural particulars in translated crime fiction provide 'snapshots of different domestic lives, the food they eat, the pictures on the walls, the way they bring up their children' (Cleeves 2014). It is certainly difficult to imagine a contemporary reader feeling shaken by the fact that Polish prosecutor Teodor Szacki eats 'a piece of fresh chuck steak [. . .] served with prunes, a heap of buckwheat and a pint of cold beer' (Miłoszewski 2012:352) in Antonia Lloyd-Jones' translation of Zygmunt Miłoszewski's noir novel *A Grain of Truth*. Distinguished UK translator Anthea Bell maintains that 'readers should [not] be deprived of the foreign element in a translated text', but that 'the reader should [not] be *made* to confront the otherness of the foreign culture' (Bell 2004:16) and that readable texts attract readers and make money for publishers (ibid), a fact which presumably should also make translators happy. What Bell is advocating here may not necessarily be consonant with domestication in the sense of eradicating the culturally specific, perhaps only implying that the syntax of the target text should not be wildly disruptive and the translation not overly literal. Although Bell aims to be invisible in the texts she produces (Bell 2004, 2006), she has certainly been a very visible proponent of translation off the page and is interviewed regularly in the UK press, particularly in relation to those translations that are received as such in UK culture, the highly successful Asterix series being one example (see, for example, Lathey 2012; Armitstead 2013). Thus Bell's life work has undoubtedly helped bring about a situation in which foreign cultural specificity is (within limits) acceptable to UK readers, and in this respect she is very much a 'foreignizer', despite her distaste, on a stylistic level, for awkward prose and translationese.

If reading tastes have evolved so that local colour – the culturally specific – is no longer as problematic as it may once have been, the debate about domestication naturally shifts to the arena of style. Stylistic domestication implies the imposition of target-language grammatical and stylistic norms on the foreign text in the name of producing a 'readable' or 'accessible' text. An extract from Thomas Mann's novel *Der Zauberberg* (1924) [*The Magic Mountain*] provides an interesting case study. At the very beginning of this novel we are introduced, in a lengthy sentence full of sub-clauses, to Hans Castorp, who is travelling to Switzerland to visit his cousin in a sanatorium. Here is the sentence in the two existing translations of the novel, by Helen Lowe-Porter (1927) and John E. Woods (1995) respectively:

> Hans Castorp – such was the young man's name – sat alone in his little grey-upholstered compartment, with his alligator-skin handbag, a present from his uncle and guardian, Consul Tienappel – let us get the introductions over at once – his travelling-rug, and his winter overcoat swinging on its hook. The window was down, the afternoon grew cool, and he, a tender product of the sheltered life, had turned up the collar of his fashionably cut, silk-lined summer overcoat.
> (Mann, trans. Lowe-Porter 1946:3)

> Hans Castorp – that is the young man's name – found himself alone in a small compartment upholstered in gray; with him he had an alligator valise, a present from his uncle and foster father – Consul Tienappel, since we are naming names here – a rolled-up plaid blanket, and his winter coat, swinging on its hook. The window was open beside him, but the afternoon was turning cooler and cooler, and, being the coddled scion of the family, he turned up the silk-lined collar of his fashionably loose summer overcoat.
> (Mann, trans. Woods 2005:3)

German has complex rules of syntax which can defer verbs to the end of sentences, place extended attributive clauses before nouns and regulate the order in which information appears in a sentence (time elements appear before 'manner' elements, which appear before elements that indicate place). Mann exploits these resources fully, his language 'generat[es] complex hypotactic sentences in which entire series of clause elements are stacked in a process of retardation and anticipation' (Horton 2013:86). In the German source-text version of the above opening, Castorp's 'place', his precise location in the train compartment, is given only after the description of his belongings, out of grammatical necessity, but it also draws attention to the 'amiably garrulous' narrator of the novel (Beddow 2001:140):

> Hans Castorp – dies der Name des jungen Mannes – befand sich allein mit seiner krokodilsledernen Handtasche, einem Geschenk

seines Onkels und Pflegevaters, Konsul Tienappel, um auch diesen Namen hier gleich zu nennen, – seinem Wintermantel, der an einem Haken schaukelte, und seiner Plaidrolle in einem kleinen grau gepolsterten Abteil; er saß bei niedergelassenem Fenster, und da der Nachmittag sich mehr und mehr verkühlte, so hatte er, Familiensöhnchen und Zärtling, den Kragen seines modisch weiten, auf Seide gearbeiteten Sommerüberziehers aufgeschlagen.

(Mann 1972 [1924]:3)

[gloss] Hans Castorp – this the name of-the young man – found himself alone with his crocodile-leather handbag, a present of-his uncle and guardian, Consul Tienappel, in-order also this name here immediately to name, – his winter-coat, which on a hook swung, and his plaid-roll in a small grey upholstered compartment; he sat at-a pulled-down window, and because the afternoon itself more and more cooled-down, so had he, family-little-son and tender-one, the collar of his fashionably wide, in silk worked summer-overcoat up-turned.

Interestingly, both English versions make a number of identical decisions in their rendering of this sentence. Both translations have moved Castorp's location into first place, directly after the verb, and inverted the order in which his possessions are listed, from crocodile-leather handbag, winter coat and plaid roll, to crocodile-leather handbag, plaid roll and winter coat. Both translations begin a new sentence at the point where the German uses a semi-colon, although Woods is more successful in giving this part of Mann's sentence the drawn-out feel that it has in the German by positioning Castorp in relation to the open window as Mann does (contrast 'The window was open beside him' with 'The window was down'), and by using a progressive rather than a simple verb (contrast 'The afternoon was turning cooler and cooler' with 'The afternoon grew cool').

Horton points out that Lowe-Porter's 'conception [of translation] is wholly target-oriented' (2013:57) and that she was open about the 'frequent need for syntactic rearrangement and simplification' (ibid:58). Her translations have certainly been criticized for this, sometimes fiercely (Koch-Emmery 1952/3; Buck 2001). Woods' translation, on the other hand, is more respectful of the 'sequential structure of Mann's original' (Horton 2013:94) – so in the passage above, where Lowe-Porter has created the one-word premodifying adjective 'grey-upholstered', Woods' translation retains the wordiness of Mann's preposition-led extended attribute phrase, even though this must necessarily come after the noun in English. However, Horton concludes that over the course of the novel, both translations display the same fundamental target-orientation (ibid:119) and that Woods in fact 'dissolves approximately the same number of complex structures' as Lowe-Porter (ibid:120). In light of this, we might conclude that the plaid roll has been moved from the end to the middle of the list of Castorp's belongings in both translations because, unlike the handbag and the winter coat, it is not followed by a digressive or descriptive sub-clause qualifying it further. The reader is therefore given somewhat of an informational reprieve before encountering the winter coat swinging on its hook at the end of the enumeration of Castorp's belongings. The splitting of the sentence into two after the description of Castorp's summer coat would also seem to fulfil the function of allowing readers to catch their breath. The translations thus conform to the sensibility of English syntax. Yet the convoluted syntax in Mann's novel is iconic, i.e. performative of the narrative's overall sense of time: Hans Castorp's initial three-week visit to his cousin in a Swiss sanatorium leads to the discovery of his own illness and an incredible subsequent seven-year stay. Mann himself pointed out that at nine-hundred pages *Der Zauberberg* had 'spatially and spiritually' far outgrown what its author had originally planned for it (Mann 1972 [1924]:xiv); the story had run away with him, and its nine-hundred pages certainly run away with the reader. And English is in fact capable of respecting Mann's sequential structure without risking eccentricity – Castorp's location *can* be revealed last, the rug can certainly follow the coat and the sentence can run on instead of being divided into two:

> Hans Castorp – for this was the name of the young man – unaccompanied except for his crocodile-leather handbag, which had been a present from his uncle and guardian, one Consul Tienappel – a further name to add to the one above – his winter-coat, which was swinging on a hook, and his plaid travelling blanket, was seated in a small compartment that was upholstered in grey; the window beside him was pushed down and because the afternoon was growing ever cooler, he, the cosseted baby of the family, had turned up the collar of his fashionably loose, woven silk summer coat.
>
> (my translation)

The resulting sentence is perhaps more difficult and imposes a different, more Germanic reading speed upon the reader.

### *Defining foreignization*

If Mann's *The Magic Mountain* furnishes an example of one of the levels on which domestication might operate, what might foreignization, as conceived of by Venuti, look like in practical terms? In *Revenge* (2013), a collection of dark and surreal interlinked short stories by Yoko Ogawa, translated into English by Stephen Snyder, we know that we are not in a contemporary English-speaking society in the Northern hemisphere because people bow to one another, words are written in characters, the location features loquat and eucalyptus trees, sake is drunk and incense is lit on family altars. Other than these clues, however, there is little about the lexis or syntax that would suggest we are abroad; the language conforms in all ways to the norms of contemporary English. In fact, speakers of UK English will immediately be struck by the American lexis and phraseology (e.g. a family has a 'cookout' (ibid:121); one character says, 'He was supposed to *come see* me last night' (ibid:53, my italics), a grammatical construction which signals to UK readers that the book is not located in their cultural and linguistic space but could perhaps – were it not for the aforementioned cultural details – be a product of North America. Occasionally, however, the familiar and the strange collide, as in the following passage taken from the story 'Lab Coats'

> 'He was full of excuses again. Something about the train getting stuck in snow. He claimed he never even got there, that he sat on the train the whole time and had to come back without seeing them. Can you believe the nerve? He expects me to believe a story like that with the cherry trees already in bloom.'
>
> (ibid:53)

This sounds as though it has been uttered by a native speaker of English, particularly the expression 'Can you believe the nerve?', but the appearance of cherry trees as a self-evident cultural and seasonal marker gives the Anglophone reader pause for thought. Cherry blossom is, of course, an indicator of spring in Europe and North America, too, but other flowers – crocuses, snowdrops, daffodils – are more likely to be the first harbingers of spring in the cultural imagination. In Japan cherry blossoms have great cultural significance: they are a symbol of life and new beginnings. The Japanese practice *hanami*, or gazing at the cherry blossoms, and have picnics among the trees when they come into bloom. With the reference to cherry trees, the speaker of these lines, a hospital secretary who is having an affair with a married doctor, not only invokes a particular cultural space, but on a more metaphorical level she may also be suggesting that the initial bloom of the affair has faded, meaning that she is less likely to believe her lover's excuses. The domesticated speech contrasts sharply with the particularity of the cultural reference; although the speech patterns of Ogawa's characters suggest that the reader is in a US cultural space, the juxtaposition of domestic speech and foreign cultural elements destabilizes this assumption. This discontinuity or heterogeneity might well be an example of the type of foreignization Venuti is advocating. Thus, ironically, domesticating aspects in a translated text can augment its foreignness by creating stark juxtapositions and thematic or stylistic incoherences.

Venuti also defines foreignization in terms of the selection of texts for translation. Certain texts will have a foreignizing effect on the receiving culture irrespective of the translator's approach, simply because they belong to a genre that does not exist in that culture, or because they foreground themes that are unknown there. In this sense, but also in others, Lorena Terando's translation of María Eugenia Vásquez Perdomo's *testimonio*, *Escrito para no morir: Bitácora de una militancia* (1998), Vásquez' account of the eighteen years she spent as a member of the insurgency group Movimiento 19 de Abril (M-19) in Colombia, embodies an ideologically motivated, foreignizing approach to translation which goes beyond activism on the textual level alone. The translator of *My Life as a Colombian Revolutionary: Reflections of a Former Guerrillera* (2005) shows herself ever mindful of 'the context of literary production' (Appiah 2012 [1993]:342), possessing what Spivak refers to as 'a tough sense of the specific terrain of the original' (1993:188), as well as of the political relations that hold between Colombia, the point of origin for the Spanish-language text, and the US, the receiving nation. Terando's pursuit of the project began as she worked on her doctoral thesis entitled 'Toward an Understanding of the Matrix Linking Human Rights and Testimony, Witnessing and Peace' (2001) at SUNY Binghamton. The thesis looked at the *testimonio* in Latin American literature, a genre that has many permutations but that can broadly be defined as an autobiographical text in which the 'I' is emblematic of the collective and that aims 'to bear witness to a silenced or unacknowledged story of trauma, to give voice to the voiceless' (Gates-Madsen 2012:87). Terando focused on the issues surrounding the translation of *testimonios* by two women writers: Vásquez' text, and poems by Consuelo Avila, a former leader of the Communist Party in northern Colombia who died in 1987, collected under the title *Bajo mis pies no florecen amapolas* (1998) [*Beneath My Feet Poppies Do Not Bloom*].

Terando's research and resulting translations were an attempt to challenge dominant narratives on three levels: first, Terando was keen to 'provid[e] a view of Colombia and its civil war that challenges the dominant discourse in the US, that would make it hard to reduce Colombia to coffee and drugs' (Terando 2014a); second, her decision to focus on *testimonios* by women was a feminist one, an acknowledgement of the facts that 'the space of revolution is not compatible with traditional gender roles' (Terando 2001: no pagination (Chapter 1)) and that both Vásquez and Avila had made great personal and gendered sacrifices in the pursuit of their political and revolutionary goals; third, Terando actively supported Vásquez and Avila's project of writing an alternative history (Terando 2014a), one that is narrated from a perspective that stands outside the dominant power structure (in this respect the *testimonio* is related to that other characteristic genre of Latin America, the magical-realist novel). As the translator of a testimonial text, Terando occupies a position not dissimilar to that taken up by H.G. Adler's translator Peter Filkins; and, in fact, Terando explicitly compares the reading and translating of Holocaust literature to the reading and translating of Latin American *testimonios*. All readers of testimonial texts are challenged by the traumatic and painful experiences to which they become witnesses, but the translator carries a double burden, 'negotiat[ing] the hazards of reading with the risks of testifying' (Terando 2001: no pagination (Chapter 1)). In Terando's case, the risks were all too tangible: following her visit to Colombia in 1999 to interview Vásquez and meet Avila's family – a visit which took place two years after Colombian guerrilla groups ELN and FARC had been placed on the US's list of terrorist organizations – she was placed under investigation by the FBI for drug trafficking, kidnapping and extortion; the chair of her dissertation committee and others were interviewed in connection with these allegations (Terando 2014b). Terando was also mindful of the consequences for Vásquez of publishing the translation, and her negotiations with the publisher over the title of the translation were informed by this awareness (Terando 2014b).

*My Life as a Colombian Revolutionary* is an example of a 'thick translation': 'a translation that seeks with its annotations and its accompanying glosses to locate the text in a rich cultural and linguistic context' (Appiah 2012 [1993]:341). The translation is prefaced by an introduction on twentieth-century Colombia, written by Arthur Schmidt, a scholar of Latin American history. The reader's immersion in the cultural context initiated by the introduction is continued by the translation itself: on the occasion of their first appearance, Spanish-language borrowings that describe Colombian food items, articles of dress and features of the national system such as types of school and political groupings are typically italicized and footnoted; and in subsequent presentations of a previously footnoted terminus, the word or phrase remains in Spanish but is no longer italicized. This can mean, particularly in the early stages of the book, that the reader is confronted with a considerable amount of new information in a short space of time. In the chapter 'Turmoil at the Nacional' (Vásquez Perdomo 2005:22–37), for example, in which Vásquez narrates her first year at the Universidad Nacional in Bogotá and her involvement with leftist political groups, one scene takes place in the campus' Central Café, a place frequented by virtually all of the 5,000 students at the Nacional. 'Old-timers' of the leftist cause point out significant political figures and their affiliations to Vásquez and other newcomers, and in rapid sequence the reader encounters political groupings and termini such as *Camilistas*, *mamerto*, *JUPA*, *Cabeza de Turco*, *JUCA* and *ELN*, all of which are explained in the footnotes. What emerges is a sense of Colombia's socio-political complexity, a refusal to simplify this for the US reader and an implicit expectation of engagement therewith. In the same chapter, the footnotes explain words such as *berraco/-a*, 'a very common Colombianism [that] can mean tough, wonderful, courageous, capable, difficult, painful, and other things, depending on the context' (ibid:26) and *pastusa* boots, 'lace-up boots made of raw, untanned leather, almost yellow because undyed, ankle height, rubber soled, hand sewn, good for hiking, and aesthetically military' (ibid:28). These footnotes are more richly textured than ordinary scholarly definitions and give a voice to the translator in her role of cultural interpreter. They confront the US reader with the specificity and otherness of Colombian history and culture. In choosing to retain *berraca* and *pastusa* and by defining them in such detail, rejecting any simple equivalence, the translator is highlighting the signifying power of these terms in context. The fact that the boots, worn by university students, are 'aesthetically military' is clearly consequential. Later in the chapter, when Vásquez abandons her 'bourgeois' miniskirts and eyeliner, which have been criticized by a fellow student, in order to stress her 'revolutionary vocation' (ibid:30), she begins wearing *pastusas*. One might contrast the detail surrounding this type of footwear with a footwear reference in another text, Mikhail Bulgakov's *The Master and Margarita*, in the translation by Diana Burgin and Katherine Tiernan O'Connor, who 'strove for an accurate, readable American English translation' (Burgin and O'Connor 1995:vii). There, on the very first page, the poet Ivan Nikolayevich Ponyryov is described as wearing 'sneakers' (Bulgakov 1995:3), which has none of the contextual richness – the sense of time and place – of *pastusas*.

*My Life as a Colombian Revolutionary* is an example of a text carefully selected by the translator for ideological reasons, in full awareness of its position within the domestic and indeed the continental polysystem – the *testimonio* is a Latin American genre, and the women's revolutionary *testimonio* is a feminist expression thereof – but also with an eye to the contribution the text might make to the image of Colombia in the US. Terando's thick translation approach ensures 'that the setting could not be mistaken for a Midwestern town' (Terando 2014b) and her willingness to accept the unwarranted consequences of her commitment to translating the text – a commitment which allows Vásquez' *testimonio* to reach new readers, with whom 'the path of memory is negotiated' (Vásquez Perdomo 2005:xxxv) – is a powerful example of foreignization, and of ideologically motivated risk-taking, in translation.

The domestication–foreignization binary has had an unfortunate tendency to dominate methodological discussion in Translation Studies. This is a legacy of the long history of binary thinking about translation and, more recently, of the persuasiveness of Venuti's arguments, not to mention the dominance of ideology as a field of enquiry within Translation Studies since the 1990s. As we have seen, however, domestication and foreignization are difficult to define: not only have they been understood in various ways and given different nomenclature over the course of their historical trajectory, but translated texts rarely reveal evidence of a militant adherence to one or the other of the two approaches. What tends to get lost in the political debate over the two poles is style, the manner in which a text makes itself stand out from other literary texts, its relationship to the language in which it is written and how its style relates to its 'content'. The danger with both domestication and foreignization, if we pretend for a moment that there is some clarity and consensus as to what each of these approaches involves, is that both can undermine the stylistic integrity of the foreign text. Domestication does this by ignoring the tension between the source text and source language in the process of making the text conform to the norms of the receiving language. Without this tension, Scott argues, 'the ST might be assumed to exemplify the SL rather than constructing its own linguistic being' (2000:2). Foreignization, hijacking the text for a political cause in a manner that is more focused on the 'self' than on the 'other', is potentially guilty of a similar disinterest in the text's poetics. The increased focus of literary translation studies on translation as reading and writing offers a welcome way out of this binary, and it is with this topic that our exploration of why we translate continues.

## Why do we translate? Translation as a mode of reading and writing

> Creativity on the part of the translator is always linked to the possibilities for creative reading by the reader of the translation.
> Jean Boase-Beier, *A Critical Introduction to Translation Studies* (2011:54)

> The translator, we should know, is a writer too. As a matter of fact he could be called the ideal writer because all he has to do is write; plot, theme, characters, and all the other essentials have already been provided, so he can just sit down and write his ass off.
> Gregory Rabassa, *If This Be Treason* (2005:8)

> Übersetzung ist eine Form.
> Walter Benjamin, 'Die Aufgabe des Übersetzers' (1991 [1923]:9)

Thus far the responses to the question of why we translate have focused on the effects of the act of translation: both humanists and ideologically motivated translators want to change the world in some way (or to prevent it from changing). It is, however, also possible to consider the question from the perspective of the cognitive and creative gains of the translation process for the translator. Translation offers a particularly intense reading experience and can afford the reader a more nuanced understanding of a text. One might conclude from this that translators are in a position to become privileged explicators of their source texts – super-readers – who bring a sensitivity to literary criticism informed by the peculiar nature of their mode of textual engagement. Translation is also a form of creation; the process results in a new literary text, which implies that translation is a form of creative writing. This section will examine in detail these answers to the question of why we translate.

### Translation as a mode of and a response to reading

All translation involves reading. Any position that claims that one of the motivations for translation resides in the pleasure and benefits of reading, and of an implicitly translational mode of reading, requires a theoretical framework that explains what it means to read a literary text and what is different or special about the specific form of readerly engagement with a text that occurs in the process of translation. Literary texts differ from non-literary texts in a number of respects (Boase-Beier 2011:35–46): they employ stylistic features such as metaphor more frequently than non-literary texts; they do not straightforwardly reflect the 'real world' (in fact, they very often create fictional worlds); they 'embody a state of mind' (ibid:46) to a greater extent than other types of text; and because of this they require a greater investment from their readers. Cognitive scientists Dan Sperber and Deirdre Wilson's theory of relevance posits that utterances are 'relevant' when there is a pay-off between the effort we invest in processing them and the degree of cognitive benefit obtained (Sperber and Wilson 1995:261). Drawing on this theory and on Ernst-August Gutt's work on relevance (2000 [1991]), Jean Boase-Beier, a pioneer in the field of cognitive stylistic approaches to translation (Boase-Beier 2002a, 2002b, 2003, 2004a, 2004b, 2006, 2011), argues that it is the 'open-endedness' (2011:43) of literary texts that makes reading them such a rewarding activity. This open-endedness is created by the presence of weak implicatures, i.e. weakly implied meanings that the reader assumes were intended by the author, however distant, nebulous or constructed that author may be, and that the reader invests effort in processing (Boase-Beier 2006:31–49). Literature's poetic effects, which in this model are the cognitive rewards specific to reading, can include a range of emotional, physical and intellectual responses (Boase-Beier 2011:38). One of these responses, and here Boase-Beier cites Attridge, and traces a trajectory back to Walter Benjamin (ibid:108), may in fact be translation itself. Viewed in this light, reading has to be understood as a creative act, a search for meaning(s) in the textual clues available to us. Translation, Boase-Beier argues, springs from the same motivations that lead us to read; indeed, translation is a response to reading: we read/translate because reading/translating is a pleasurable activity that cognitively and creatively engages us and has poetic effects. At the same time, translation is a special kind of reading in so far as it 'bod[ies] forth its object' (Steiner 1998 [1975]:316). So in translation, the reading of a text provokes a direct response in the form of a further written (or performed or voiced) text. Translation differs from other types of reading (Boase-Beier 2006:24) in the close attention paid by the reader to style, in the necessity of creatively negotiating certain external and internal constraints, which can include the nature of the translation commission, the linguistic constraints imposed by the forms of the source and target languages and differences in cultural norms (Darwisch 2008: 210–11; Boase-Beier and Holman 1999) and in the translator's 'hear[ing] in the text echoes of the translation it is about to become' (Boase-Beier 2010:32).

To illustrate the kind of reading that listens in to the text for 'echoes' of its translation and to demonstrate why the intensity of this type of reading may itself furnish the primary motivation for translating, I would like to present a translator's reading of a poem. I have chosen Canadian poet J. Mark Smith's 'Germans', taken from the collection *Notes for a Rescue Narrative* (2007).

**Germans**

> I studied the looms, puzzled by that technology.
> Warm day bees' murmur filtered through the open building.
> In one cool high-ceilinged room with hide chairs
> and a rough old wooden table, Nina said
> you would have been the padre who sat in the backroom
> with *Nachmittagskaffee* and worked on Latin a few hours,
> then got up in late light
> to watch the weavers, to admire their skill,
> not take it up.
>
> We snoozed after lunch, I could hear her snoring
> and then the nearing crunching of a hiker's boots on the trail.
> Down from one little peak the marine layer came around,
> and we sensed the day's passing only by the poppies
> closing up
> their fire-orange discs.
> The word 'wrack' is cognate with what? she said.
>
> The Bengali-Californian motel clerk in Lompoc,
> before we even spoke: Germans?

It was the Mission of the *Purísima Concepción*.
Swallows were in the adobe eaves.
We had seen heads drop, upside down, from mud cells,
before they fell through our watching.

The poem's title, a reference to the motel clerk's assumption that the tourist couple – Nina and the unnamed male speaker – are Germans, suggests an ironic embrace of this misidentification and the being-out-of-placeness implied by it. The couple, whom we assume are North American, are not local; they are linguistically and otherwise 'other', even in a place that can accommodate such complex identities as 'Bengali-Californian'. They are intellectuals: for them an afternoon coffee is *Nachmittagskaffee* [afternoon coffee]; they are fascinated by words ('The word "wrack" is cognate with what?'); and although the speaker is admiring of those who work with their hands, he likes to passively 'study' and 'watch' – he does 'not take it up', as Nina superciliously observes, in a short, to-the-point line. The poem is an account of a relationship in decay. The couple know each other too well; the speaker listens to his partner snoring – there is no post-lunch coitus here – and the consonance of 'snoozed' and 'snoring' with the echoing 'n' in the line that follows stresses the over-acquaintance. The poem's soundscape is dominated by a somnolent 'l', from the 'looms' in the first line to the 'fell' of the last. The ominous sense of an approaching end, of which the couple are ignorant, perhaps even deliberately so, is indicated by the development of the marine layer, a characteristic weather feature in California, and by the danger-coloured poppies closing for the night. The couple watches the swallows – monogamous birds, nesting in the eaves – and the swallows watch them, but the couple is removed, uninvolved, mere observers, and the speaker ominously remarks, with an unusual nominalization, that the swallows 'fell through our watching'.

Thus far this may appear to be little more than a variation of close reading as performed by any reader or critic who encounters a poem and seeks to 'understand' it by searching for a narrative, relating stylistic features to the poem's 'content'. Reading-for-translation, however, takes this initial engagement with the text further. If I were to translate this poem into German, would it make sense to maintain the title, for instance? 'German' in this context has particular connotations: the man and woman look out of place because they are educated, middle-class. In a German translation, the couple would 'speak' German and there would be nothing in the poem to indicate their out-of-placeness in their own culture: in particular, the word *Nachmittagskaffee* would no longer be foregrounded as a foreign term, but would disappear into the rest of the poem. Even if German readers did not assume that the speaker and Nina were German, would they understand what it is about the couple that leads the motel clerk to draw his conclusion? In other words, would German readers be able to adopt the necessary external perspective on their own culture in order to grasp how they are perceived abroad and the implication that the couple are un-American in some way? A change of nationality may well be in order to maintain this implication. The translator would want to select a wealthy Western European country that affords its citizens a good education and that sends tourists to the US in significant numbers. The Dutch and the Scandinavians fulfil the former requirement but are from smaller nation states. The French may not send as many tourists to the US as the Germans, but the cultural significance of their nation, and the radical difference of its culture from US culture, is certainly recognized. Perhaps, then, in German, one might title the poem 'Franzosen' [French] and convert *Nachmittagskaffee* into *casse-croûte* [snack] – or if one wanted to multiply the implications of Nina's statement that her partner would be just like the padre who eschews manual labour, then the more infantile *goûter* [a mid-morning or mid-afternoon snack for children] could work well. Translations into other languages would not face the same problem with the title, of course, but the translation would still benefit from the translator's awareness of the title's resonance.

The translator will note other features of the poem as well. The padre's naïve admiration of those who work with their hands finds phonetic expression in the alliteration of 'late' and 'light', 'watch' and 'weavers'. The sharp 'p' consonant in 'passing' and 'poppies' emphasizes the relationship's approaching end. The lack of equivalence between languages means that the translator is unlikely to be able to directly mimic these linguistic features in the target text, but their presence alerts him or her to nodes of meaning in the text and hence to a particular state of mind. In considering what is possible in translation, the significance of the repetition of the 'p' sound will need to be weighed against the symbolism of the poppies with their 'fire-orange' colour indicating the danger of the imploding relationship that the couple chooses to ignore, and the wildflower's association – in the Western world, at least – with conflict and death, but also with an opiate-induced somnolence. The translator can only make these decisions if he or she is paying close attention to the style of the text. Finally, the success of the poem's final, metaphorical line – 'before they fell through our watching' – will rely on the translator making the connection to the 'watch' of the first stanza and the male speaker's stance of aloof observation, but also a recognition of the metaphorical blend of the swallows' physical fall with the idea of something eluding the observers. The translator's stylistically aware, creative engagement with the text should result in a target text that gives its reader equal though not identical 'possibilities for creative reading' (Boase-Beier 2011:54).

## Documentary translation

If translation is a response to literature, a response to the act of reading, and a mode of reading in itself, the text that results from this reading will have readers of its own. Boase-Beier develops Christiane Nord's (1997) theory of translation's 'documentary' and 'instrumental' functions – the potential orientation of a translation towards documenting a source in metatextual fashion vs. its fulfilling a function of its own in the target context – to argue that literary translation is both documentary *and* instrumental (Boase-Beier 2011:62). A translation documents its source, giving the target-language reader an indication of the nature of the (potentially) inaccessible foreign-language text, but it is also instrumental in the sense that it 'manifests the characteristics and effects on the reader so central to the way literature works' (ibid). Not all translators accept this duality. Some, as we will see, argue against the need for a translation to document its source and embrace translation as a form of creative writing. Others refuse any instrumentality and embrace the purely documentary instead, viewing translation as a method of illuminating the source text, with no obligation to produce a target text that functions as literature in its own right. Vladimir Nabokov's translation of Pushkin's *Eugene Onegin* (1964a, 1964b, 1964c, 1964d) is such a text, a text that translation practitioners love to hate. Edith Grossman, for example, dismisses its approach as 'something one might find down a rabbit hole or on the other side of a looking glass' (2010:70). Yet this pedantic text, the *non plus ultra* of literal translation – four volumes in total, featuring an introduction, the translation, the commentary, appendices and the Russian source text – is, in its very refusal to translate in an 'acceptable' fashion, a grudging affirmation of the illuminating, literary critical force of translation and an implicit throwing down of the gauntlet to translators everywhere: to be better, to strive to outdo literal-ness. The premise of Nabokov's refusal to translate Pushkin's verse novel in any fashion other than 'Metaphrase, or turning [his] Authour word by word, and Line by Line, from one Language into another' (Dryden 2012 [1680]:38) is that the contemporaneously existing translations 'unfortunately available to college students' (2012 [1955]:120) were all 'grotesque travesties of their model' (ibid), containing errors, exhibiting 'dreadful verse' (ibid) and revealing an unacceptable ignorance of Russian culture. Nabokov's mention of college students suggests that his primary concerns were didactic and scholarly, and indeed his *Onegin* is widely acknowledged to be a tremendous contribution to Pushkin scholarship. But Coates (1999) argues that from a bio-psychological perspective, Nabokov's advocacy of literal translation was a late development borne of his transition from writing in Russian to writing in English – that it was in fact a response to loss and a form of resistance to assimilation by US culture. His translation, which was intended to be read as a commentary-companion to the Russian text, was an attempt to 'unfold[. . .] the rich specificity of his native culture [and] to gain it the respect and admiration he felt it deserved' (ibid:95). As such it is another example of what Appiah would come to label 'thick translation' (2012 [1993]:341). But in the process of making its readers aware of the text's difference, its essential Russian-ness, Nabokov's *Onegin* ironically also claimed the text for the world literary canon by 'revealing the transcultural, European roots of Russian literature' (Coates 1999:106), attributing sources to Pushkin that 'suggested a mind formed by French and German translations' (ibid:105).

Nabokov's translation is entirely 'documentary'. Rather than retextualizing poetic effects, it seeks to spell out the mechanics of those effects in 'copious footnotes, footnotes reaching up like skyscrapers to the top of this or that page so as to leave only the gleam of one textual line between commentary and eternity' (Nabokov 2012 [1955]:125). So, for example, Nabokov explains his particularly opaque rendering of one line in Chapter Eight, Verse Nine, 'Because, by liking room, wit cramps?' (1964a:295) in the following manner:

> 8/ *Chto ùm, lyubyá prostór, tesnít*: The meaning is: intelligence, needing elbowroom, squeezes fools out. *Prostor* has several meanings, all depending on the idea of spaciousness, such as 'scope,' 'range,' 'open expanse,' etc. The word for 'space' itself is *prostranstvo*.
>
> (1964c:161)

He also comments on the infelicities inflicted on *Onegin* by previous translators and critics. One of his notes on Chapter Two, Verse Two, explains that the Russian word *zámok*, which he translated as 'castle', is a common Russian translation of the French word *château*. He goes on to mock Chizhevski, a Harvard professor whose *Onegin* commentary had been published in 1953, for explaining Pushkin's use of the word as 'perhaps under the influence of the Baltic provinces near by' (Nabokov 1964b:221). Nabokov retorts with the words 'what influence? near what?', dismissing this as 'a typical example of the comic naïvetés in [Chizhevski's] running, or rather stumbling, commentary to *EO*' (ibid).

Nabokov's translation of *Onegin* rests on an assumption that translation implies an intensification of close reading and functions as a particularly fastidious form of literary criticism. That translation and commentary – a particularly translational form of literary criticism – should go hand-in-hand is by no means a new development. Berman argues that the traditional link between the two was lost when literary criticism emerged as an autonomous entity (2008:18) and has only of late been rediscovered: 'Any commentary on a *foreign* work entails translation. *Is* translation, one might even say. Conversely, all translation entails an element of commentary' (ibid, my translation).

Translation as a literary critical tool does not have to take the austere form of 'Metaphrase' accompanied by skyscraping footnotes, however. Gaddis Rose argues for, and models, the reading of a translation or translations alongside the original text. She proposes that we use the documentary potential of translations to enrich our reading encounter with a particular text. This stems from a belief that translations 'articulate [a text's] range of compressed implications' (1997:6) and can therefore enhance our reading experience. Like Nabokov, Gaddis Rose is thinking in terms of the classroom and of the student who is able to read the foreign language, but her strategies have implications for reading outside the classroom and for the reading of translations by the 'ignorant' reader – the reader with no knowledge of the source language – as we will see in the next chapter. She argues that translation opens up a space around the source text, what she calls 'a circumference of interpretation' (ibid:55), that highlights gaps, tensions and concordances between source and target(s), thus provoking the reader's investment and collaboration.

We can investigate the method of reading proposed by Gaddis Rose by focusing on a key verb in Walter Benjamin's essay 'Die Aufgabe des Übersetzers' ['The Task of the Translator'] (1991 [1923]). The opening paragraph of Benjamin's essay is concerned with the relationship between the receiver of the work of the art and the work of art itself. Benjamin rejects the notion that works of art are preoccupied with their audience, thus questioning the notion of the work of art as a communicative act and positioning himself against contemporaneous views of language as a communicative tool (Berman 2008:47). The final line of the first paragraph of the essay states, 'Denn kein Gedicht gilt dem Leser, kein Bild dem Beschauer, keine Symphonie der Hörerschaft' (Benjamin 1991 [1923]:9) [gloss: For no poem is-valid for-the reader, no picture for-the viewer, no symphony for-the audience]. *Gilt* is the third-person singular, present-tense form of the verb *gelten*, and the verb on which our discussion will centre here. Antoine Berman, in *L'âge de la traduction* (2008), his commentary on Benjamin's essay, notes that French translator Maurice de Gandillac, for whatever reason, perhaps because Benjamin's phrase 'seems so paradoxical at first' (2008:47), omitted this sentence from the first French translation.

Benjamin's second paragraph opens by pondering whether translations are primarily produced for readers who do not understand the source language, and the sentence repeats the verb *gelten*: 'Gilt eine Übersetzung den Lesern, die das Original nicht verstehen?' (Benjamin 1991 [1923]:9) [gloss: Is-valid a translation to-the readers, who the original not understand?], which was translated into French by Gandillac as 'Une traduction est-elle faite pour les lecteurs qui ne comprennent pas l'original ?' (Benjamin 2000a:244) [gloss: A translation is-it made for the readers who not understand the-original?]. But, as Berman points out, Benjamin did not say 'est-elle faite' [gloss: is-it made]: he uses the verb *gelten*, which is much like the French *valoir*, as he did in the preceding sentence and as he will do again later in his essay. Berman points out that *gelten* is 'one of those foundational terms that make up the lexical fabric of the text beneath its conceptual fabric' (2008:50) and that the fault of Gandillac's translation 'does not rest with the meaning' – a point with which one might in fact take issue – 'but with its failure to respect the linguistic weft of the text' (ibid:51). The need to be attentive to the patterns of prose (and the frequent failure of translation to do so) is a familiar concept in Berman's work. We find it expressed in the negative analytic, the twelve-point list of translational practices that deform texts, as formulated in the essay translated into English by Lawrence Venuti as 'Translation and the Trials of the Foreign' (2012). What might give a prospective English translator pause for thought here is not the idea of respecting the linguistic weft of the source text, i.e. the networks and patterns that shape the way in which the text signifies, but the fact that the verb *gelten*, which finds a convenient French-language counterpart in *valoir*, finds no simple translation in English. The German verb *gelten* can be transitive or intransitive and has a variety of meanings. Possible English renderings, depending on the context, are 'to be valid', 'to count', 'to be worth', 'to apply' or 'to be considered as': e.g. *eine Fahrkarte gilt* (a ticket is valid), *seine Stimme gilt* (his vote counts), *das Geld gilt nicht viel* (the money isn't worth much or doesn't carry much weight), *ein Gesetz gilt* (a law applies or is applicable) and *er gilt als Fachmann* (he's considered an expert). The verb is often used with the impersonal subject *es* [it] in a similar fashion to the French *il vaut* or *ça vaut*. The meaning that applies in this Benjaminian context is the sense of *gelten* as an intransitive verb meaning 'to be addressed to or destined for', with an overtone of one of its other meanings, 'applies to'; but although the verb *gelten* has a grammatical subject in Benjamin's text (*Gedicht* [poem], *Bild* [picture], *Symphonie* [symphony], and then *Übersetzung* [translation]), it has no subject in the sense of an agent and that is precisely the point. Benjamin is unpicking our desire to conceive of the work of art as a message. Through his choice of verb, Benjamin begins his dismantling of the notion of message by removing the transmitter, the agent, at the same time as he dismisses the importance of the receiver.

As stated earlier, there is no equivalent of *gelten* or of *valoir* in English, which raises the question of what Benjamin's English-language translators did with the verb *gelten*. Here are the four English-language versions of the two lines I have been discussing:

No poem is intended for the reader, no picture for the beholder, no symphony for the listener.

Is a translation meant for readers who do not understand the original?
(Benjamin, trans. Zohn 2000b:15)

> For no poem is intended for its reader, no painting for its viewer, no symphony for its listener.
>
> Is a translation intended for readers who do not understand the language of the original?
>
> (Benjamin, trans. Hynd and Valk 2000c:298)

> For no poem is aimed at the reader, no picture at the viewer, no symphony at the people who are going to hear it.
>
> Is a translation aimed at those readers who do not understand the original?
>
> (Benjamin, trans. Underwood 2009:29)

> No poem is meant for the reader, no picture for the beholder, no symphony for the audience.
>
> Is a translation meant for readers who do not understand the original?
>
> (Benjamin, trans. Rendall 2012:75)

All four sets of translators have opted for the passive voice; all four have used a verb, either 'mean' or 'intend' or 'aim', that implies an agent, a person who means or intends or aims, a message transmitter, and which presupposes the existence of a message. *Gelten* operates more in the realm of applicability or validity, and its other potential meanings crowd in on the way it is used in Benjamin's text. If one reads the German source text alongside the four English translations, and perhaps also with the French translation and with Antoine Berman's commentary which offers re-translations of certain passages from the essay, then *gelten* emerges as a key node in the text, a verb with crucial signifying power. But its significance only becomes clear when we consider its translation into English and observe the difficulty of finding an appropriate equivalent. It is all too easy to criticize existing translations, and that is not the intention behind this approach: rather, the lack of concordance between source and target illuminates the source text, calls attention to 'the ways in which it *makes* its meanings' (Scott 2000:247) and shows the challenges this presents for the translator. It also allows any future translator to 'translate in a re-translational mode' (Berman 2008:20), benefiting from the translational paths already travelled by Zohn, Hynd and Valk, Rendall and Underwood.

Much as Gaddis Rose proposes, translation has of late been rediscovered as a literary critical tool. Texts such as Michelle Woods' *Kafka Translated* (2014), David Horton's *Thomas Mann in English* (2013) and an edited volume entitled *Translated Poe* (Esplin and Vale de Gato 2014), show that there is an increasing awareness and interest in how translation shapes the literary critical reception of foreign texts.

Increasingly, the question of why we translate is answered in terms of translation's potential to reconfigure reading for the individual, for a wider reading public and within the academy.

## Instrumental translation

If reading is creative, as has been argued above, translation too – given that it is a specialized form of reading – must be creative. Boase-Beier argues that the act of reading translated texts is more creatively engaging than the act of reading non-translated texts because of the complex literariness of the translated text (2011:57). A translation is a creative blend of source and target that 'multiplies the voices of the text, by adding the translator's voice' (Boase-Beier 2011:57) and that negotiates the constraints imposed by the lack of equivalence between languages and the need for a translation to document its source. Translation is, in a sense, iconic of the literary; it foregrounds textual possibility, literary capacity, refracted through the person of the translator. This is how it contributes to the 'afterlife' (Benjamin 2012:76) of the literary text, through a continuous re-engagement with its possibilities across time and space.

Given the literary potential of translated texts, it is perhaps little wonder that there are theoreticians who wish to highlight literary translation's 'instrumental' function and are primarily interested in translation as a literary activity in its own right. Perhaps the most intriguing of these is Clive Scott, whose translations and theoretical writings seek to explore the potential of translation as a genre of writing that can enrich and challenge existing forms of literary production, including literary critical writing.

In *Translating Baudelaire*, Scott suggests that new settings should be found for translations: 'translations as part of a diary of reading, translation as an inbuilt supplement to literary criticism, translation as the destination of a creative meditation' (2000:2). Scott shares with Gaddis Rose, Nabokov and Benjamin a belief that translation should not be carried out for, or not exclusively employed by monoglot readers, 'those ignorant of the source language' (Scott 2012a:15). Scott translates for the reader who has linguistic access to the source text, warning that to do otherwise has dangerous implications on a number of levels (Scott 2012a:16–17): for the translator, who then assumes too much authority over the text; for the translated text, whose quality and mission cannot be truly assessed or appreciated under these circumstances; for the practice of translation, which will remain 'second-order' (ibid:16) as long as it strives to fulfil this documentary function; for the reading of translations, which will continue to be inadequately theorized; and finally – and this is where Scott overlaps with Pym (2012) – for the promotion of language-learning. But where Pym advocates, in certain circumstances, non-translation as a response to lazy monoglottism (Pym

2012:133–63), Scott emphasizes 'the multilingualism already in *langage*' (2012a:65), seeking to undermine the compartmentalization of languages *through* translation, rather than through the refusal thereof. Scott is drawing attention to the complexity of the language faculty itself (*langage*): any *langue* (the language used by a particular speech community, which may or may not equate with the language of the nation state) shows traces of other *langues* in its synchronic borrowings and through its historical development; any *langue* encompasses dialects, sociolects, even 'textual languages' (2012a:64), hence the language faculty itself is multilingual. We cannot *not* translate, Scott argues, since 'translation [is] an existential need and condition of reading' (2012b:3). There is an echo of Benjamin here, as there is in all approaches to translation which emphasize the practice as a form of reading. The shift away from translating for the monoglot reader allows Scott to deconstruct Roman Jakobson's distinction between interlingual, intralingual and intersemiotic translation (2012 [1959]:127), since if one frames translation in this fashion then the traditional rationale for interlingual translation – its documentary function – falls away and can then be drawn 'out of its preoccupation with the narrowly linguistic, with issues of fidelity and equivalence, and out of its suspicion of allied practices such as imitation, pastiche, and adaptation' (Scott 2012b:13).

In his most recent writings, Scott explores how translation and literary criticism differ in their respective responses to literature. Literary criticism excludes autobiographical input 'on the grounds that it does not transcend the anecdotal and the impressionistic' (ibid:2). But it is precisely this facet of the translator's encounter with the source text in which Scott has become interested: translation is a site through which to explore the phenomenology of reading and its expression in writing (but also through other media such as photography and performance). Translation Studies has long acknowledged the subjectivity of the translator and his or her presence in the target text, but Scott seeks to chart 'the kinaesthetics of reading: the dynamic of our organism as it is set in motion by the act of reading' (ibid:12). The physical body of the translator and the real-world environment in which his or her reading takes place – or in which a reading experience is remembered, for Scott emphasizes that reading also has an 'after-the fact-ness' that makes it a 'phenomenon of memory' (ibid:62) – is what helps the source text survive, in the Benjaminian sense of *überleben*. The text is reborn – undergoes a 're-styling' (Scott 2012a:34) – through a particular person in a particular time and place. That time and place are much more specific than the UK in the second decade of the twenty-first century. As I read, I have 'moments of turning away' (Scott 2012b:59), so, for example, the fact that I am translating a particular text while sitting in the Shakespeare Institute in Stratford-upon-Avon on a rainy but warmish October day, when the heating inside is overly eager, making it hard

## Why do we translate?

for me to concentrate, while outside the slow-moving gardener spreads out an old embroidered green tablecloth to catch the hedge clippings, and an orange tabby who must belong to one of the neighbouring houses meows to be allowed to enter the world of books (I should wash my hands before I stroke my own cats when I return home, just in case she has fleas or ringworm), this fact will form part of my reading experience, and 'what is autobiographical in reading becomes compositional' (ibid:67) and hence will influence the text that I create. The aim is not to 'modernize' or 'relocate' the source text in the sense of making it relevant to the here and now, but rather to 'tirelessly interrogate[e] [its] textual complacency' (ibid:82), to investigate what it 'makes possible in the way of a new text' (ibid:128). What results from this understanding of translation, Scott argues, is a piece of experimental writing (2012b:4). Experimental because its autobiographical input makes 'its parameters [. . .] difficult, if not impossible, to establish' and because it places the source text 'at the cutting edge of its own progress through time' (ibid). To this one might add that the text type Scott is advocating is experimental in the sense that – as a genre – it does not yet exist to any significant extent in the post-postmodern world, or if it does then we are reluctant to label it 'translation'.

Leaving aside Scott's own translations, which are framed by his theoretical and methodological discussions (Scott 2000, 2006, 2012a, 2012b), are there any contemporary translations that might embody or hint at this type of experimental writing? My own translation of Yoko Tawada's 'Portrait of a Tongue' (2013) is certainly characterized by this approach, although I argue in my introduction to that text that the translational experiment was prompted in large part by the nature of the source text (Wright 2013:26,33); it was not experimental for experiment's sake, although it does emphasize the translator's subjectivity. In a different manner, both Simon Armitage's translation of *Sir Gawain and the Green Knight* from the Middle English (2007) and Seamus Heaney's translation of *Beowulf* from the Old English (1999) identify and build connections between the source and target historical variants of their Englishes, as Scott advocates. Armitage, a Yorkshire man, 'recognizes plenty of the poem's dialect [and] detects an echo of his own speech rhythms' (Armitage 2007:vii); Heaney writes of an illuminating loophole in *Beowulf* – the recognition that the Irish word 'thole' had its roots in the Old English word 'þolian', meaning 'to suffer' – which allowed him a glimpse of a longed-for 'unpartitioned linguistic country [. . .] and entry into further language' (Heaney 1999:xxv). Heaney gives a glimpse of the 'autobiographical input' into his *Beowulf* when he writes of emulating the men in his family he liked to describe as 'big-voiced scullions' (ibid:xxvi) within the poems' cadences, and by using local Ulster words where they seemed 'either poetically or historically right' (ibid:xxix). Armitage, in imitating *Gawain*'s alliterative form

('The fellow in green was in fine fettle./ The hair of his head was as green as his horse', Armitage 2007:13), was also conscious of the poem as performance, of its embodiment in the here and now: 'If the technique is effective, as well as understanding what we are being told we take a step closer to actually experiencing it' (ibid:viii). But both Armitage's and Heaney's translations are still essentially documentary. Ciaran Carson's translation of Dante's *Inferno* (2002) may be less so, in part because of his lack of access to Dante's vernacular and reliance on the translations of others, and because the 'autobiographical input' of his translation is more tangible. Carson's introduction to his translation draws explicit parallels between Dante's Florence and his own Belfast. As Carson walked his city hunting for rhymes he would often head for the old Belfast Waterworks: 'Situated on a rise above the embankment is the Westland housing estate, a Loyalist enclave which, by a squint of the imagination, you can see as an Italian hill-town' (2002:xi). Just as Belfast natives are able to place one another, so too do 'the souls in Dante's Hell reveal themselves by a phrase, by body language' (ibid:xii). When one encounters such lines as 'four majestic shadows loomed towards us/ like one inscrutable, impassive unit' (ibid:26) and 'what holds the future for the citizens/ of my divided city? Is there just one man/ in it? Or are they all sectarians?' (ibid:40), one does not have to 'squint' too much to blend the British army with Dante's universe or to assume that the questions are pertinent to both Dante's Florence and Carson's Belfast.

All three of these translation projects – Carson's, Heaney's and Armitage's – which gesture towards the reading environment that gave birth to them, are by well-established writers and all three are of poetry. Yet the experimental writing that Scott calls for is not supposed to be reserved for established writers of 'original' texts, or indeed for poets. Scott's call to action, to experimentation, is aimed at literary translators. Many translators already unproblematically self-describe as writers and indeed it is not without significance that the British Translators Association is a subsidiary group of the Society of Authors. At the same time, the majority of translators operate with an understanding that translation *is* a derivative activity – the existence of another text being the premise for a translation's existence – and that its documentary function cannot be denied. Pym fiercely argues that translators are not authors since they do not have authorship in a pronominal sense – rather, they occupy 'the alien "I"' (2012:63) and are not 'committed to what the words say' (ibid:66) as authors are. Andrew Chesterman would contest this, however, arguing for an 'emancipatory translation' in which translators own their words and take responsibility for them (2000:87–9). If literary translation is understood as a form of writing, and particularly if it is understood as experimental writing, then there may well be a desire on the part of the translator-writer to be identified as an author/co-creator/writer, even if Pym warns of the unwieldiness of a situation where we note 'explicit discursive positioning for each utterance rendered from another language' (Pym 2012:64). With few exceptions, in any case, the current dominant translation form looks nothing like Scott's experimental writing, or at least not yet. Rather, literary translations occupy a peculiar space where two intellectual models of textual authority are operational: an older model dating back to nineteenth-century literary criticism, where textual authority lies with the author, and a newer, poststructuralist model in which textual authority and the creation of meaning has been relocated to multiple sites and agents. Translators hover between these two positions, remaining faithful to the source text in the sense of fulfilling a documentary function on the one hand, while acknowledging the translator as a subject, and thus claiming more status and visibility for themselves on the other.

This unresolved intellectual tension finds expression in a rhetorically charged debate that raged in the *Times Literary Supplement* in late 2014. In a review ('Faun's Way') of Jean Findlay's biography of C.K. Scott Moncrieff, A.N. Wilson made several provoking claims about Moncrieff, the British translator of Proust, which were countered by Proust expert Christopher Prenderghast within the 'Letters to the Editor' pages and elicited responses from other readers for several weeks after the review's publication. Wilson opens his review uncontroversially by arguing that Moncrieff's domestication of Proust, beginning with his borrowing of the title *Remembrance of Things Past* from a Shakespeare sonnet, had succeeded so thoroughly that 'Proust's masterpiece seem[s] like a work of English, rather than of French' (Wilson 2014:5). Wilson acknowledges the dual authorship of *Remembrance* – the prose Moncrieff's, the characters Proust's – and the debt owed by the English reader both to the translator and to *Remembrance* more generally, which Wilson lauds as a life-enhancing text. Less conventionally, however, Wilson goes on to argue that *À la recherche du temps perdu* may have found, in Moncrieff, its 'chosen translator' (Benjamin 2012:76):

> It is hard not to feel that – just as Luther was the first translator truly to bring out the essence of St Paul – Scott Moncrieff is more Proustian than Proust himself. And you can see why proficient linguists such as Joseph Conrad considered Scott Moncrieff actually to be Proust's superior. [. . .] Might it not be true that Proust, coughing his life away as he failed to finish the masterpiece, actually needed someone else to rewrite it, and make it perfect [. . .]?
>
> (Wilson 2014:5)

Wilson's claim, that the English *Remembrance* was a better text than *Recherche*, but more particularly that Moncrieff may well have been a better writer than Proust, met with a robust rebuttal from

Prenderghast, who dismissed Wilson's assertions as 'genuinely eccentric', 'prima facie unintelligible' and 'counterfactual' (Prenderghast 2014:6). Prenderghast's quarrel is not with the quality of Moncrieff's translation, which he considers 'majestic, if in certain respects flawed' (ibid) – rather, he balks at the idea that Moncrieff could somehow be 'more Proustian than Proust'. This may be an unfortunate formulation and there are certainly contradictions in Wilson's argument. How, for example, can *Remembrance* be both an example of literary domestication (remembering that domestication can mean different things to different people) and 'more Proustian than Proust'? Surely, leaving the matter of the English title aside, *Remembrance* must have been perceived as radically 'other' when it was first published, its Proustian-ness residing precisely in its non-alignment with Anglophone literary norms. And while one could conceivably be more of a Marxist than Marx, it is difficult to imagine what being more Proustian than Proust might practically entail. Leaving aside Wilson's rhetoric, however, Prenderghast's ire appears to have been aroused by the suggestion that Moncrieff's translation might be a more successful, more fulfilling work of art than Proust's novel. This was also Joseph Conrad's claim – dismissed by Prenderghast as 'surely tongue-in-cheek' (2014:6) – namely that Moncrieff's translation 'has revealed something to me and there is no revelation in the other [Proust's novel]' (Conrad, cited in Wilson 2014:5). The position shared by Wilson and Conrad is entirely subjective, of course, but the implication of their position is that translations can be viewed as independent works of art with the capacity to be more successful than the works of art that inspired them – with the necessary caveat that artistic success is a difficult thing to define and to measure. I find this, the idea that a translation might be a better piece of writing than its source text, an entirely unproblematic view, but it clearly strikes at the heart of our culture's anxieties over originality, authorship and the status of the translated text, anxieties from which even professional readers and scholars are not immune. Perhaps, though, the conundrum embodied by translation cannot and should not be resolved; perhaps the practice and those texts that go by the name 'translation' are a necessary reminder of the dubious nature of ownership when the building blocks of what we seek to own are made of language.

## Coda: Babel

And all the earth was one language, one set of words. And it happened as they journeyed from the east that they found a valley in the land of Shinar and settled there. And they said to each other, 'Come, let us bake bricks and burn them hard.' And the brick served them as stone, and bitumen served them as mortar. And they said, 'Come, let us build us a city and a tower with its top in the heavens, that we may make us a name, lest we be scattered over all the earth.' And the LORD

came down to see the city and the tower that the human creatures had built. And the LORD said, 'As one people with one language for all, if this is what they have begun to do, now nothing they plot to do will elude them. Come, let us go down and baffle their language there so that they will not understand each other's language.' And the LORD scattered them from there over all the earth and they left off building the city. Therefore it is called Babel, for there the LORD made the language of all the earth babble. And from there the LORD scattered them all over the earth.
Genesis 11:1–9, trans. Robert Alter (2004:58–9)

This chapter has considered the varied motivations that lead us to translate and the varying values and practices that translations can embody: humanism, ideology, reading and writing. In the Western tradition of thinking about translation, the Biblical story of Babel is seen as translation's metaphorical genesis, the *Ur*-response to the question of why we translate, the *raison d'être* of the practice. Traditionally, Babel has been seen as divine punishment, mankind's comeuppance for its boldness in reaching for the heavens (see, for example, Arnold 2009:118–21), but Scott points towards an alternative reading of Babel as 'God's pushing humanity back on its proper course – the development of fruitful alterity' (Scott 2012a:8; Ost 2009:23–66; Hiebert 2007) in order to argue an affirmative vision of translation as one of the conditions of our 'cultural maturity' (Coogan 2007:25–6) and a motor for the dynamic expansion of language (Scott 2012a:8–11). This is George Steiner's view also, albeit from 'the "Darwinian" view of the psychic indispensability of the prodigality of diverse languages among mankind' (1998 [1975]:xv). Seen in this way, translation is a practice without an end, but not in a futile, Sisyphean sense: that is, not a practice marked by an irreducible unfinishedness or incompleteness (Derrida 1985:165), but a questing, spiritual, fundamentally human endeavour through which we innovatively embrace our 'creaturely condition' (Alter 2004:58), exploring language and, through language, the divine within and without.

## Conclusions

This first chapter has been concerned with the multiple and intersecting motivations for translation. The next chapter will enquire into how translations are – or should be – read and received. The two issues are closely related. If translators wish to change how their work is read, they must first have an understanding of why they translate, both on a global level and in terms of individual texts. Among other considerations, this will always involve an engagement with the consequences of the translating act for the author, source text and culture, for the translating culture and for the translator. Thus Peter Filkins' decision to translate H.G. Adler's work was accompanied by a sense of responsibility towards an author whose work had been so prescient it failed to find the contemporary audience it deserved. The reception of Adler's work in German has been enhanced by the effects of its translation into English, and Filkins has now embraced the role of biographer and Adler expert. Lorena Terando was mindful of the consequences of translation for the lives of the female Colombian activists whose writing she introduced to a US audience, and was very clear about her motivations for wishing to undertake its translation. Her decision had serious personal and professional repercussions, reminding us, in Maureen Freely's words, that although 'our work might begin on the page [...] it rarely lets us stay there' (Freely 2013:126). Freely's statement is borne of her own experience, as Orhan Pamuk's translator, of becoming implicated in the controversy surrounding his novels (Freely 2013). Translators who are engaged with 'the cultural conditions of the translating' (Venuti 2013:247) in this manner will inevitably bring this engagement to bear on how they translate. Filkins' attentive treatment of Adler's modernist style and Terando's detailed footnotes on Colombian political and cultural artefacts bear witness to this. It is, of course, a fact that most literary translators translate a large number of texts that are not of their own choosing. Some of these texts will be a matter of indifference to the translator, and in some cases perhaps even repugnant. Anthony Pym suggests that the fundamental ethical question to be answered by the translator is 'Should I translate?', while acknowledging that not all translators are in a position to be able to answer this question without constraint – financial, political, intellectual or professional (2012:103). He argues that the question is part of an ethical discourse that 'hypothetically envisions the day when all translators will have the power and the honesty to ask themselves, before they undertake a job, if they should really translate' (ibid:104). Formulating an answer to this question, however hypothetical an exercise, helps the translator take a step back and develop a meta-awareness of the implications of the activity in which he or she is engaged; a more conscious approach to translation on the part of the practitioner cannot help but create better conditions for the reading of translations.

### Exercises

1. How do domesticating and/or foreignizing approaches to translation manifest themselves in this excerpt from Jaroslav Hašek's novel *The Good Soldier Švejk*, in the 1973 translation by Cecil Parrott. (The same passage is omitted from Paul Selver's 1930 translation, which abridges the Czech novel.)

'Once we had one of those Hungarian bastards by the throat in Pausdorf, where we sappers went for a drink. I wanted to sock him across the coconut with a belt in the dark – you see we had smashed the hanging lamp with a bottle as soon as it started – but all of a sudden he began to shout:

"Tonda! Why, it's only me, Purkrábek, from the sixteenth Landwehr!"

A mistake was avoided by a hair's breadth. But instead we gave it fair and proper to those Hungarian clowns at Neusiedler See which we went to look at three weeks ago. In a village nearby there was stationed a machine-gun detachment of a Honvéd regiment, and we all happened to go to a pub where they were dancing their Csardas like mad and shooting their mouths off as they shouted: "*Uram, uram, biró, uram*", or "*Láňok, láňok, láňok a faluba*".* We sat opposite them; only we put our belts in front of us on the table and said to ourselves: "You bastards, we'll give it to you hot for your *láňok*", and a chap named Mejstřík who had a paw as big as the White Mountain immediately volunteered to dance and take away a girl from one of these lousy bastards in the middle of the dance. The girls were bloody neat pieces, you know, with plump calves and fleshy arses, and marvellous thighs and eyes. From the way those Hungarian bastards squeezed them you could see that those girls had breasts as full and firm as rubber balls, that they got a great kick out of it and knew their onions.'

* Hungarian songs: 'Mr, Mr, Mr Justice' and 'Girls, girls, girls from the village'.
(Hašek 1973:359–61; footnote is part of the translation).

2. Choose a poem and annotate it in preparation for translation. As you do so, consider the following issues:

What is your immediate 'reading' of the poem? (Who is speaking? What is the poem 'about'?)
Does the text foreground (= call attention to, highlight) particular stylistic features? If so, what might be the function of those features?
How does your own context influence your reading? How might this context find its way into the translation?
Which contextual knowledge might help you understand the poem better? If you were able to question the poet, what might you ask him/her?

## Further reading: learning more about why we translate

In the Bibliography below see Berman 2012; Benjamin 2012; Boase-Beier 2006, 2011; Nabokov 2012 [1955]; Nida 2003 [1964]; Nord 1997; Pym 2012; Schleiermacher 2012; Scott 2012a, 2012b; Tyulenev 2014; Venuti 1995, 1998.

## Bibliography

Adorno, T., 1967 [1951]. Cultural Criticism and Society. In: T. Adorno. *Prisms*. Translated from German by S. and S. Weber. London: Neville Spearman. pp. 19–34.

Alderson, S., 2015. Top 10 Feminist Icons in Children's and Teen Books. *The Guardian*, 7 March. Available at: www.theguardian.com/childrens-books-site/2015/mar/07/top-10-feminist-icons-childrens-teen-books-international-womens-day [accessed 9 March 2015].

Alter, R., trans. 2004. *The Five Books of Moses: A Translation with Commentary*. New York: W.W. Norton.

Althusser, L., 2014 [1995]. *On the Reproduction of Capitalism: Ideology and Ideological State Apparatuses*. Translated from French by G.M. Goshgagarian. London: Verso.

Álvarez, R. and Vidal, M.C., eds. 1996. *Translation, Power, Subversion*. Clevedon: Multilingual Matters.

Anderson, S., 2011. The Fierce Imagination of Haruki Murakami. *The New York Times*. Available at: www.nytimes.com/2011/10/23/magazine/the-fierce-imagination-of-haruki-murakami.html?pagewanted=all&_r=0 [accessed 6 November 2014].

Appiah, K.A., 2012 [1993]. Thick Translation. In: L. Venuti, ed. *The Translation Studies Reader*. 3rd ed. New York: Routledge. pp. 331–43.

Apter, E., 2013. *Against World Literature: On the Politics of Untranslatability*. London: Verso.

Armitage, S., trans. 2007. *Sir Gawain and the Green Knight*. London: Faber and Faber.

Armitstead, C., 2013. Anthea Bell: It's All about Finding the Tone of Voice in the Original. You Have to Be Quite Free. *The Guardian*, 16 November. Available at: www.theguardian.com/books/2013/nov/16/anthea-bell-asterix-translator-interview [accessed 9 March 2015].

Arnold, B.T., 2009. *Genesis*. Cambridge: Cambridge University Press.

Avila, C., 1988. *Bajo mis pies no florecen amapolas*. Bogotá: Editorial Colombia Nueva.

Baker, M., 2005. Narratives in and of Translation. *SKASE Journal of Translation and Interpretation*, 1(1), pp. 4–13.

Bard College at Simon's Rock, 2013. *Simon's Rock Magazine*. Available at: http://simons-rock.edu/_documents/sr-2013-spring-magazine.pdf [accessed 22 October 2015].

Bassnett, S. and Trivedi, H., eds. 1999. *Post-Colonial Translation*. London: Routledge.

Batchelor, K., 2009. *Decolonizing Translation*. Manchester: St. Jerome.

Beddow, M., 2001. The Magic Mountain. In: R. Robertson, ed. *The Cambridge Companion to Thomas Mann*. Cambridge: Cambridge University Press. pp. 137–50.

Bell, A., 2004. Translation as Illusion. *EnterText*. Available at: www.brunel.ac.uk/__data/assets/pdf_file/0005/110696/Anthea-Bell-pdf,-Translation-as-Illusion.pdf [accessed 9 March 2015].

Bell, A., 2006. Translation: Walking the Tightrope of Illusion. In: S. Bassnett and P. Bush, eds. *The Translator as Writer*. London: Continuum. pp. 58–67.

Benjamin, W., 1991 [1923]. Die Aufgabe des Übersetzers. In: Benjamin, W. *Gesammelte Schriften Band IV. 1*. Frankfurt am Main: Suhrkamp. pp. 9–21.
Benjamin, W., 2000a [1923]. La tâche du traducteur. In: W. Benjamin. *Oeuvres I*. Translated from German by M. de Gandillac, R. Rochlitz and P. Rusch. Paris: Gallimard. pp. 244–62.
Benjamin, W., 2000b [1968] [1923]. The Task of the Translator. Translated from German by H. Zohn. In: L. Venuti, ed. *The Translation Studies Reader*. New York: Routledge. pp. 15–23.
Benjamin, W., 2000c [1968] [1923]. The Task of the Translator. Translated from German by J. Hynd and E.M. Valk. In: D. Weissbort and A. Eysteinsson, eds. *Translation – Theory and Practice*. Oxford: Oxford University Press. pp. 298–307.
Benjamin, W., 2009 [1923]. The Task of the Translator. Translated from German by J.A. Underwood. In: W. Benjamin. *One-Way Street and Other Writings*. London: Penguin. pp. 29–45.
Benjamin, W., 2012 [1923]. The Translator's Task. Translated from German by S. Rendall. In: L. Venuti, ed. *The Translation Studies Reader*. 3rd ed. New York: Routledge. pp. 75–83.
Berman, A., 1985. La traduction comme épreuve de l'étranger. *Texte*, 4, pp. 67–81.
Berman, A., 2008. *L'âge de la traduction*. Saint-Denis: Presses Universitaires de Vincennes.
Berman, A., 2012 [2000] [1985]. Translation and the Trials of the Foreign. Translated from French by L. Venuti. In: L. Venuti, ed. *The Translation Studies Reader*. 3rd ed. New York: Routledge. pp. 240–53.
Bettelheim, B., 1984 [1982]. *Freud and Man's Soul*. New York: Vintage.
Blasim, H., 2013. *The Iraqi Christ*. Translated from Arabic by J. Wright. Manchester: Comma Press.
Boase-Beier, J., 2002a. Translating Style. In: S. Csábi and J. Zerkotiwz, eds. *Textual Secrets: The Message of the Medium. Proceedings of the 21st PALA Conference*. Budapest: Eötvös Loránd University Press. pp. 317–25.
Boase-Beier, J., 2002b. Style and Choice: Recreating Patterns in Translation. *Studies in Cross-Cultural Communication*, 1, pp. 1–28.
Boase-Beier, J., 2003. Mind Style Translated. *Style*, 37(3), pp. 253–65.
Boase-Beier, J., 2004a. Knowing and Not Knowing: Style, Intention and the Translation of a Holocaust Poem. *Language and Literature*, 13(1), pp. 25–35.
Boase-Beier, J., 2004b. Saying What Someone Else Meant: Style, Relevance and Translation. *International Journal of Applied Linguistics*, 14(2), pp. 267–87.
Boase-Beier, J., 2006. *Stylistic Approaches to Translation*. Manchester: St. Jerome.
Boase-Beier, J., 2010. Who Needs Theory? In: A. Fawcett, K.L. Guadarrama García and R. Hyde Parker, eds. *Translation: Theory and Practice in Dialogue*. London: Continuum. pp. 25–38.
Boase-Beier, J., 2011. *A Critical Introduction to Translation Studies*. London: Continuum.
Boase-Beier, J. and Holman, M., 1999. Introduction: Writing, Rewriting and Translation. In: J. Boase-Beier and M. Holman, eds. *The Practices of Literary Translation*. Manchester: St. Jerome. pp. 1–17.

Bogic, A., 2011. Why Philosophy Went Missing: Understanding the English Version of Simone de Beauvoir's *Le Deuxième Sexe*. In: L. von Flotow, ed. *Translating Women*. Ottawa: University of Ottawa Press. pp. 151–66.

Bolduc, M., 2006. *The Medieval Poetics of Contraries*. Gainsville, Florida: The University Press of Florida.

Booktrust, 2014. Independent Foreign Fiction Prize Winner Announced. Available at: www.booktrust.org.uk/d/news-and-blogs/news/291/ [accessed 9 February 2015].

Buck, T., 2001. Mann in English. In: R. Robertson, ed. *The Cambridge Companion to Thomas Mann*. Cambridge: Cambridge University Press. pp. 235–48.

Bulgakov, M., 1995 [1966]. *The Master and Margarita*. Translated from Russian by D. Burgin and K. Tiernan O'Connor. London: Picador.

Burgin, D. and Tiernan O'Connor, K., 1995. Translators' Note. In: M. Bulgakov, *The Master and Margarita*. Translated from Russian by D. Burgin and K. Tiernan O'Connor. London: Picador. p. vii.

Burton, R.F., 1885–8. *A Plain and Literal Translation of the Arabian Nights Entertainments, Now Entitled The Book of the Thousand Nights and a Night with Introduction Explanatory Notes on the Manners and Customs of Moslem Men and a Terminal Essay upon the History of The Nights*. Vol V. London: The Burton Club.

Calzada Pérez, M., ed. 2003. *Apropos of Ideology: Translation Studies on Ideology – Ideologies in Translation Studies*. Manchester: St. Jerome.

Carcelen-Estrada, A., 2010. Covert and Overt Ideologies in the Translation of the Bible into Huao Terero. In: M. Tymoczko, ed. *Translation, Resistance, Activism*. Amherst/Boston: University of Massachusetts Press. pp. 65–88.

Carson, C., trans. 2002. *The Inferno of Dante Alighieri*. London: Granta.

Chesterman, A., 2000. Teaching Strategies for Emancipatory Translation. In: C. Schäffner and B. Adab, eds. *Developing Translation Competence*. Amsterdam/Philadelphia: John Benjamins. pp. 77–89.

Clark, K., 2011. Russian Epic Novels of the Soviet Period. In: E. Dobrenko and M. Balina, eds. *Cambridge Companion to Twentieth-Century Russian Literature*. Cambridge: Cambridge University Press. pp. 135–51.

Cleeves, A., 2014. The Top 10 Crime Novels in Translation. *The Guardian*, 22 January. Available at: www.theguardian.com/books/2014/jan/22/top-10-crime-novels-translation-ann-cleeves-scandinavia-montalbano [accessed 9 March 2015].

Coates, J., 1999. Changing Horses: Nabokov and Translation. In: J.Boase-Beier and M. Holman, eds. *The Practices of Literary Translation*. Manchester: St. Jerome. pp. 91–108.

Cohen, S. and Legault, P., eds. 2012. *The Sonnets: Translating and Rewriting Shakespeare*. Brooklyn, NY: Telephone Books.

Colby, G. and Dennett, C., 1995. *Thy Will Be Done: The Conquest of the Amazon*. New York: HarperCollins.

Coogan, M.D., ed. 2007. *The New Oxford Annotated Bible*. 3rd ed. Oxford: Oxford University Press.

Damrosch, D., 2003. *What is World Literature?* Princeton and Oxford: Princeton University Press.

Damrosch, D., ed. 2009. *Teaching World Literature*. New York: Modern Language Association.

Darwisch, A., 2008. *Optimality in Translation*. Patterson Lakes, Victoria: Writescope Pty Ltd.
De Beauvoir, S., 1949. *Le deuxième sexe*, Vols I and II. Paris: Gallimard.
De Beauvoir, S., 1997 [1953] [1949]. *The Second Sex*. Translated from French by H.M. Parshley. London: Vintage.
De Beauvoir, S., 2009 [1949]. *The Second Sex*. Translated from French by C. Borde and S. Malovany-Chevallier. London: Jonathan Cape.
Derrida, J., 1985. Des Tours de Babel. In: J.F. Graham, ed. *Difference in Translation*. Ithaca: Cornell University Press. pp. 165–248.
Destutt de Tracy, A., 2012 [1801]. *Éléments d'idéologie: Idéologie proprement dite*. Paris: J. Vrin.
Dostoevsky. F. 1931 [1872]. *The Possessed*. Translated from Russian by C. Garnett. London: J.M. Dent.
Dostoevsky, F., 1994 [1872]. *Demons*. Translated from Russian by R. Pevear and L. Volokhonsky. London: Vintage.
Dryden, J., 2012 [1680]. From the Preface to *Ovid's Epistles*. In: L. Venuti, ed. *The Translation Studies Reader*. 3rd ed. New York: Routledge. pp. 38–42.
Eckermann, J, P., 1982 [1836/1848]. *Gespräche mit Goethe in den letzten Jahren seines Lebens*. Berlin/Weimar: Aufbau.
Engberg, G., 2010. Bookmakers: Barry Cunningham. *Booklist Online*. Available at: http://booklistonline.com/ProductInfo.aspx?pid=4510409&AspxAutoDetectCookieSupport=1 [accessed 9 March 2015].
Englund, S.A., 1994. A Dignified Success: Knopf's Translation and Promotion of *The Second Sex*. *Publishing Research Quarterly*, 10(2), pp. 5–18.
Esplin, E and Vale de Gato, M., eds. 2014. *Translated Poe*. Bethlehem, PA: Lehigh University Press.
Even-Zohar, I., 2012 [1978]. The Position of Translated Literature within the Literary Polysystem. In: L. Venuti, ed. *The Translation Studies Reader*. 3rd ed. New York: Routledge. pp. 162–7.
Fenton, S. and Moon, P., 2002. The Translation of the Treaty of Waitangi: A Case of Disempowerment. In: M. Tymoczko and E. Gentzler eds. *Translation and Power*. Amherst/Boston: University of Massachusetts Press. pp. 25–44.
Filkins, P., 2008 [1962]. Introduction. In: H.G. Adler. *The Journey*. Translated from German by P. Filkins. New York: Random House. pp. ix–xxi.
Forshaw, B., 2012. *Death in a Cold Climate*. Basingstoke: Palgrave Macmillan.
France, P., 2000. Dostoevsky. In: P. France, ed. *The Oxford Guide to Literature in English Translation*. Oxford: Oxford University Press. pp. 594–8.
Franzen, J., 2013. *The Kraus Project*. Toronto: HarperCollins.
Freeden, M., 2003. *Ideology: A Very Short Introduction*. Oxford: Oxford University Press.
Freely, M., 2013. Misreading Orhan Pamuk. In: E. Allen and S. Bernofsky, eds. *In Translation: Translators on Their Work and What It Means*. New York: Columbia University Press. pp. 117–26.
Frost, C., 2014a. 'Hinterland' Star Richard Harrington Reveals How He Brought More Compassion to 'Welsh Wallander'. *The Huffington Post*. Available at: www.huffingtonpost.co.uk/2014/05/12/hinterland-richard-harrington-interview-wallander-_n_5309832.html [accessed 6 December 2014].

Frost, C., 2014b. 'Hinterland' Co-Creator Ed Thomas Explains Why He Wanted Wales to Have Its Own Detective. *The Huffington Post*. Available at: www.huffingtonpost.co.uk/2014/05/27/hinterland-richard-harrington-welsh-crime-drama_n_5398091.html. [accessed 6 December 2014].
Funke, C., 1997. *Prinzessin Isabella*. Hamburg: Oetinger.
Funke, C., 2001. *Der geheimnisvolle Ritter Namenlos*. Hamburg: Oetinger.
Funke, C., 2003. *Käpten Knitterbart und seine Bande*. Hamburg: Oetinger.
Funke, C., 2004. *The Princess Knight*. Translated from German by A. Bell. Frome: Chicken House.
Funke, C., 2005. *Pirate Girl*. Translated from German by C. Wright. Frome: Chicken House.
Funke, C., 2007. *Princess Pigsty*. Translated from German by C. Wright. Frome: Chicken House.
Gaddis Rose, M., 1997. *Translation and Literary Criticism*. Manchester: St. Jerome.
Gates-Madsen, N.J., 2012. Bearing False Witness? The Politics of Identity in Elsa Osorio's *My Name is Light (A veinte años, Luz)*. In: L. Detwiler and J. Breckenridge, eds. *Pushing the Boundaries of Latin American Testimony*. New York: Palgrave Macmillan. pp. 87–106.
Gilbert, G., 2014. Welcome Piece of Welsh Noir is Set to Make a Killing. *The Independent*. Available at: www.independent.co.uk/arts-entertainment/tv/reviews/hinterland-bbc4-tv-review-welcome-piece-of-welsh-noir-is-set-to-make-a-killing-9298912.html [accessed 6 December 2014].
Grossman, E., 2010. *Why Translation Matters*. Yale: Yale University Press.
Gutt, E-A., 2000 [1991]. *Translation and Relevance*. Manchester: St. Jerome.
Hašek, J., 1973 [1921–3]. *The Good Soldier Švejk*. Translated from Czech by C. Parrott. London: Penguin.
Heaney, S., trans. 1999. *Beowulf*. London: Faber and Faber.
Hemon, A., 2013. *The Book of My Lives*. London: Picador.
Hermans, T., 1996. The Translator's Voice in Translated Narrative. *Target*, 8(1), pp. 23–48.
Hermans, T., 2014. Positioning Translators: Voices, Views and Values in Translation. *Language and Literature*, 23(3), pp. 285–301.
Hiebert, T., 2007. The Tower of Babel and the Origin of the World's Cultures. *Journal of Biblical Literature*, 126(1), pp. 29–58.
Horton, D., 2013. *Thomas Mann in English*. London: Bloomsbury.
Irwin, R. 1994. *The Arabian Nights: A Companion*. London/New York: Tauris Parke.
Israel, H., 2006. Translating the Bible in Nineteenth-Century India: Protestant Missionary Translation and the Standard Tamil Version. In: T. Hermans, ed. *Translating Others*. Manchester: St. Jerome. pp. 441–59.
Jaén, I. and Simon, J. J., 2012. An Overview of Recent Developments in Cognitive Literary Studies. In: I. Jaén and J.J. Simon, eds. *Cognitive Literary Studies*. Austin, TX: University of Texas Press. pp. 13–32.
Jakobson, R., 2012 [1959]. On Linguistic Aspects of Translation. In: L. Venuti, ed. *The Translation Studies Reader*. 3rd ed. New York: Routledge. pp. 126–31.
Koch-Emmery, E., 1952/3. Thomas Mann in English Translation. *German Life and Letters*, 6, pp. 275–84.

Lathey, G., 2012. Anthea Bell, Literary Translator Par Excellence. *Books for Keeps*. Available at: http://booksforkeeps.co.uk/issue/194/childrens-books/articles/anthea-bell-literary-translator-par-excellence [accessed 9 March 2015].

Lefevere, A., 1992. *Translation, Rewriting and the Manipulation of Literary Fame*. London: Routledge.

Lewis, P., 1985. The Measure of Translation Effects. In: J.F. Graham, ed. *Difference in Translation*. Ithaca: Cornell University Press. pp. 31–62.

Mahony, P.J., 1987. *Freud as a Writer*. New Haven/London: Yale University Press.

Mancosu, P., 2013. *Inside the Zhivago Storm*. Milan: Feltrinelli.

Mann, T., 1946 [1927] [1924]. *The Magic Mountain*. Translated from German by H. Lowe-Porter. London: Secker & Warburg.

Mann, T., 1972 [1924]. *Der Zauberberg*. Berlin: S. Fischer.

Mann, T., 2005 [1995] [1924]. *The Magic Mountain*. Translated from German by J.E. Woods. New York: Knopf.

Marx, K. and Engels, F., 1970 [1932]. *The German Ideology*. Translated from German by W. Lough, C. Dutt and C.P. Magill. London: Lawrence & Wishart.

Massardier-Kenney, F., 2010. Translation Theory and Its Usefulness. In: C. Maier and F. Massardier-Kenney, eds. *Literature in Translation*. Kent, OH: Kent State University Press. pp. 22–30.

McDonald, A., 2012. Picture Books About Strong Girls. *No Time for Flash Cards*. Available at: www.notimeforflashcards.com/2012/09/picture-books-about-strong-girls.html [accessed 9 March 2015].

McGowan, G., 2012. Introduction to the Syllabus for EN302 Revolutionary Egypt, *EN302 Advanced Composition: Revolutionary Egypt*. United States Military Academy West Point, unpublished.

Miłoszewski, Z., 2012 [2011]. *A Grain of Truth*. Translated from Polish by A. Lloyd-Jones. London: Bitter Lemon Press.

Mishra, P., 2014a. The New Face of India. *The Guardian: Review*, 17 May. pp. 2–4.

Mishra, P., 2014b. *The New Face of India – References to Musil and Benjamin*. Personal communication, 12 June 2014.

Moi, T., 2002. While We Wait: The English Translation of 'The Second Sex'. *Signs*, 27(4), pp. 1005–35.

Moi, T., 2010. The Adulteress Wife. *London Review of Books*, 32(3), pp. 3–6.

Mojola, A.O. and Wendland, E. 2003. Scripture Translation in the Era of Translation Studies. In: Wilt, T., ed. *Bible Translation: Frames of Reference*. Manchester, St. Jerome. pp. 1–25.

Murakami, H., 2008 [2007]. *What I Talk about When I Talk about Running*. Translated from Japanese by P. Gabriel. London: Vintage.

Murakami, H., 2013 [2009]. As Translator, As Novelist: The Translator's Afterword. Translated from Japanese by T. Goossen. In: E. Allen and S. Bernofsky, eds. *In Translation*. New York: Columbia University Press. pp. 169–82.

Nabokov, V., trans. 1964a. Aleksandr Pushkin's *Eugene Onegin*. Volume 1. New York: Pantheon.

Nabokov, V., trans. 1964b. Aleksandr Pushkin's *Eugene Onegin*. Volume 2. New York: Pantheon.

Nabokov, V., trans. 1964c. Aleksandr Pushkin's *Eugene Onegin*. Volume 3. New York: Pantheon.
Nabokov, V., trans. 1964d. Aleksandr Pushkin's *Eugene Onegin*. Volume 4. New York: Pantheon.
Nabokov, V., 2012 [1955]. Problems of Translation. *Onegin* in English. In: L. Venuti, ed. *The Translation Studies Reader*. 3rd ed. New York: Routledge. pp. 113–25.
*New Books in German*, 2011. Fairy Tale, Fantasy and Folklore. *New Books in German*, 29, pp. 6–7.
Newmark, P., 1981. *Approaches to Translation*. Oxford: Pergamon.
Nida, E. 2003 [1964]. *Toward a Science of Translating*. Leiden/Boston: Brill.
Nida, E. and Taber, C. 1974. *The Theory and Practice of Translation*. Leiden: Brill.
Niranjana, T., 1992. *Siting Translation: History, Post-Structuralism and the Colonial Context*. Berkeley: University of California Press.
Nord, C., 1997. *Translating as a Purposeful Activity*. Manchester: St. Jerome.
Ogawa, Y., 2013 [1998]. *Revenge*. Translated from Japanese by S. Snyder. London: Harvill Secker.
Ost, F., 2009. *Traduire: Défense et illustration du multilinguisme*. Paris: Fayard.
Parshley, H.M., 1997 [1953]. Translator's Preface. In: de Beauvoir, S. 1997. *The Second Sex*. London: Vintage. pp. 7–12.
PEN America, 2015. *PEN/Heim Translation Fund Grants*. Available at: www.pen.org/content/penheim-translation-fund-grants-2000-4000 [accessed 5 February 2015].
Pevear. R., 1990. Introduction. In: Dostoevsky, F. [1880]. *The Brothers Karamazov*. Translated from Russian by R. Pevear and L. Volokhonsky. London: Vintage. pp. xi–xviii.
Pevear. R., 1994. Foreword. In: Dostoevsky, F., *Demons*. [1872]. Translated from Russian by R. Pevear and L. Volokhonsky. London: Vintage.
Pfizer, J., 2006. *The Idea of World Literature*. Baton Rouge: Louisiana State University Press. pp. vii–xxiii.
Phillips, A., 2007. After Strachey. *London Review of Books*, 29(19), pp. 36–8.
Prenderghast, C., 2014. C.K. Scott Moncrieff (Letters to the Editor). *Times Literary Supplement*, 7 November, p. 6.
Pym, A., 2012. *On Translator Ethics*. Translated from French by H. Walker. Amsterdam/Philadelphia: John Benjamins.
Rabassa, G., 2005. *If This Be Treason: Translation and Its Discontents*. New York: New Directions.
Remnick, D., 2005. The Translation Wars. *The New Yorker*, 7 November. Available at: www.newyorker.com/magazine/2005/11/07/the-translation-wars [accessed 2 March 2015].
Robinson, D., 1997. *What Is Translation?* Kent, OH: Kent State University Press.
Said, E., 2003 [1978]. *Orientalism*. London: Penguin.
Sallis, E., 1999. *Sheherezade Through the Looking Glass*. Richmond, Surrey: Curzon.
Schiavi, G., 1996. There Is Always a Teller in a Tale. *Target*, 8(1), pp. 1–21.

Schleiermacher, F., 2012 [2000] [1813]. On the Different Methods of Translating. Translated from German by S. Bernofsky. In: L. Venuti, ed. *The Translation Studies Reader*. 3rd ed. New York: Routledge. pp. 43–63.
Scott, C., 2000. *Translating Baudelaire*. Exeter: Exeter University Press.
Scott, C., 2006. *Translating Rimbaud's Illuminations*. Exeter: Exeter University Press.
Scott, C., 2012a. *Translating the Perception of Text*. London: Legenda.
Scott, C., 2012b. *Literary Translation and the Rediscovery of Reading*. Cambridge: Cambridge University Press.
Sebald. W.G., 2001. *Austerlitz*. Translated from German by A. Bell. London: Penguin.
Simon, S. and St-Pierre, P. 2000. *Changing the Terms. Translating in the Post-Colonial Era*. Ottawa: University of Ottawa Press.
Simons, M., 1983. The Silencing of Simone de Beauvoir: Guess What's Missing from 'The Second Sex'. *Women's Studies International Forum*, 6(5), pp. 559–64
Smith, J.M., 2007. Germans. In: J.M. Smith. *Notes for a Rescue Narrative*. Lantzville, British Columbia: Oolichan. p. 42.
Sofronieva, T., 2012. *A Hand Full of Water*. Translated from German by C. Wright. Buffalo, NY: White Pine Press.
Soljan, M., 2014. *Translating Haruki Murakami into Croatian*. Personal communication, 12 June 2014.
Sonzogni, M., 2011. *Re-Covered Rose: A Case Study in Book Cover Design as Intersemiotic Translation*. Amsterdam/Philadelphia: John Benjamins.
Sperber, D. and Wilson, D., 1995. *Relevance: Communication and Cognition*. 2nd ed. Oxford: Blackwell.
Spivak, G.C., 1993. The Politics of Translation. In: G.C. Spivak. *Outside in the Teaching Machine*. New York: Routledge. pp. 179–200.
Steiner, G., 1998 [1975]. *After Babel*. 3rd ed. Oxford: Oxford University Press.
Steinhöfel, A., 2010. *The Pasta Detectives*. Translated from German by C. Wright. Frome: Chicken House.
Strachey, J., ed. 1953–74. *The Standard Edition of the Complete Psychological Works of Sigmund Freud*. Translated from German by J. Strachey, A. Strachey and A. Tyson. Vols I–XXIV. London: Hogarth Press/Institute of Psychoanalysis.
Terando, L., 2001. Toward an Understanding of the Matrix Linking Human Rights and Testimony, Witnessing and Peace. PhD. State University of New York at Binghamton.
Terando, L., 2014a. *Translating* Escrito para no morir *into English, Part One*. Personal communication, 16 July 2014.
Terando, L., 2014b. *Translating* Escrito para no morir *into English, Part Two*. Personal communication, 5 September 2014.
Toury, G., 1995. *Descriptive Translation Studies and Beyond*. Amsterdam/Philadelphia: John Benjamins.
Tymoczko, M., 1999. *Translation in a Postcolonial Context: Early Irish Literature in English Translation*. Manchester: St. Jerome.
Tymoczko, M., 2010. *Translation, Resistance, Activism*. Amherst/Boston: University of Massachusetts Press.

Tymoczko, M. and Gentzler, E., 2002a. Introduction. In: E. Gentzler and M. Tymoczko, eds. *Translation and Power*. Amherst/Boston: University of Massachusetts Press. pp. xi–xxviii.

Tymoczko, M. and Gentzler, E., eds. 2002b. *Translation and Power*. Amherst/Boston: University of Massachusetts Press.

Tyulenev, S., 2014. *Translation and Society: An Introduction*. New York: Routledge.

United States Military Academy West Point, 2015. *Courses Required for Literature Majors EP351 – World Literature*. Available at: www.usma.edu/dep/sitepages/courses/ep351.aspx [accessed 9 February 2015].

Vásquez Perdomo, M.E., 2000 [1998]. *Escrito para no morir: Bitácora de une militancia*. Colombia: Ministerio de Cultura.

Vásquez Perdomo, M.E., 2005 [1998]. *My Life as a Colombian Revolutionary*. Translated from Spanish by L. Terando. Philadelphia: Temple University Press.

Venuti, L., 1995. *The Translator's Invisibility*. New York: Routledge.

Venuti, L., 1998. *The Scandals of Translation*. New York: Routledge.

Venuti, L., 2005. Local Contingencies: Translation and National Identities. In: S. Bermann and M. Wood, eds. *Nation, language, and the ethics of translation*. Princeton: Princeton University Press. pp. 177–202.

Venuti, L., 2013. Towards a Translation Culture. In: L. Venuti. *Translation Changes Everything*. New York: Routledge. pp. 231–48.

von Flotow, L., 1997. *Translation and Gender*. Manchester: St. Jerome.

von Flotow, L., 2000. Translation Effects: How Beauvoir Talks about Sex in English. In: M. Hawthorne, ed. *Contingent Love. Simone de Beauvoir and Sexuality*. Richmond, VA: Virginia University Press. pp. 13–33.

Warwick Research Collective, 2015. *Combined and Uneven Development: Towards a New Theory of World-Literature*. Liverpool: Liverpool University Press.

Webb, S., 2007. Review: Princess Pigsty. *Inis – The Children's Books Ireland Magazine*. Available at: www.inismagazine.ie/reviews/book/princess-pigsty [accessed 9 March 2015].

Wilson, A.N., 2014. Faun's Way. *Times Literary Supplement*, 31 October. p. 5.

Woods, M., 2014. *Kafka Translated*. New York: Bloomsbury.

Wright, C., 2013. *Yoko Tawada's 'Portrait of a Tongue': An Experimental Translation*. Ottawa: University of Ottawa Press.

Zogbo, L. 2011. Bible, Jewish and Christian. In: M. Baker and G. Saldanha, eds. *Routledge Encyclopedia of Translation Studies*. Abingdon: Routledge. pp. 21–7.

# 2 How do we read translations?

> Reading-in-translation is a fundamental mode of relating-to-translation. We cannot even think of experiencing translation if we do not read in translation. The latter should be a prerequisite for any translation pedagogy. Reading translations is not simply a matter of comparing them to their originals. It is an act *sui generis*.
>
> Antoine Berman, *L'âge de la traduction*, trans. Chantal Wright (2008:31)

Professional associations of literary translators in the Anglophone world, among them the UK's Translators Association (TA) and the American Literary Translators Association (ALTA), have long fought for two basic related translational rights: for the translator to have his or her name mentioned in any journalistic or scholarly review of the work he or she has translated, and for the publisher of a translation to feature the translator's name prominently on or near the cover of the book. The latter is now mostly codified in the translation contract long before the manuscript is delivered, yet it is still rare for the translator's name to feature on the front cover of the book alongside the author's, the inside cover being the more usual position. Exceptions to this rule include translations by prominent writers with name recognition, particularly in cases where very little or nothing is known about the original author, which creates a space for another writer to step in, as is the case with Seamus Heaney's intralingual translation of *Beowulf* (1999), but also in cases of interlingual re-translations of canonical texts where the translators have garnered a substantial reputation over the course of the re-translation project, e.g. Richard Pevear and Larissa Volohonsky's re-translations of nineteenth-century Russian classics. It is still not unusual to pick up a cheap reprint of a canonical text such as a translation of Grimm's fairytales and to find no information whatsoever about the translator, or for Amazon to fail to distinguish between different translations in their 'look inside' feature. Where book reviews are concerned, the policy on including or omitting the translator's name varies from publication to publication and from reviewer to reviewer. Professional associations such as the TA typically respond to omissions with a letter or an e-mail politely reminding the reviewer of his or her discourtesy and underlining the translator's contribution. Social media now affords translators another means of drawing attention to this issue. Translator Helen Wang, who is one of a group of translators to tweet under the handle @TranslatedWorld, introduced the hashtag #namethetranslator in December 2013 with the aim of increasing awareness and to try to make it standard practice to acknowledge the translator (Wang 2014). Nonetheless, the omissions continue and with them the frustration of the profession and the sense that its work is not appreciated because it is not apprehended in the first place. This sense of frustration can be compounded by the failure of translation reviews to engage with the nature of the process and the product, exemplified by what translator Esther Allen identifies as the single adverb approach to translation, whereby the translator has translated 'capably', 'deftly', or, at the more negative end of the spectrum, 'poorly' or 'execrably' (Allen 2014:26), and by the almost inevitable appearance of the old translation chestnut that suspects something of having been 'lost in translation'. (Ronald Christ, one of Gregory Rabassa's former students, reports having heard Rabassa say that the only thing that gets lost in translation is the money (Christ 2010:85).) Late capitalism can be blamed for some of this: literature is a commodity like any other on the market; only a discerning consumer will have a sense of the actors and processes involved in the production of a translation. A recent survey by the UK's Authors' Licensing and Collecting Society (ALCS) revealed that in 2013 the median income of the professional author – that is, an author who dedicates the majority of his or her time to writing – was just £11,000, well below the minimum income standard of £16,850 (ALCS 2014:5). Given that translation is considered second-order literary work, the implications of the author's dismal situation for the (dependent) translator's livelihood and status are bleak. One begins to wonder whether books too should carry Fairtrade certification to indicate that those involved in their creation have been adequately paid and treated.

For the reasons outlined by Venuti in *The Translator's Invisibility* (1995) and *The Scandals of Translation* (1998), reasons that were explored in the previous chapter, contemporary mainstream Anglophone publishers have tended to champion a school of translation that harks back to an approach identified by the poet John Dryden as 'Imitation', where a translator 'writes[s], as he supposes, that Authour would have done, had he liv'd in our Age, and in our Country' (2012 [1680]:40). This domesticating approach to translation makes translation, and the translator, invisible, undermining any attempt to build what Venuti calls 'a translation culture' (2002:247). Domestication is motivated, on the part of the publisher, by a sense that translation works against a book's marketability.

There is a growing conviction among certain Translation Studies scholars that translators are, in part, responsible for their own undervaluing. Lawrence Venuti, himself a literary translator whose oeuvre extends from Tarchetti to contemporary Italian noir, argues quite vehemently that 'if translators want to change the cultural marginality of translation, they need to change the ways that they themselves think about and represent their work' (2002:248). He makes the case that there will be no change to the cultural status quo as long as practising translators continue to eschew theory and write about their work in 'belletristic' fashion (ibid:247), concentrating on 'comparing the translation to the source text instead of taking into account the cultural conditions of the translating' (ibid:247). In other words, translators need to reflect on why and how they translate (and the relationship between the two), both generally but also in relation to specific texts, and to develop a sense of how this relates to the translation practices of earlier epochs so that current thinking and practice are placed in context (ibid). Venuti notes the absence of any significant inquiry into 'translated textuality' (Venuti 2013b:6) – what kind of texts translations are, with the attendant implications for how we read them. In a similar vein, Scott critiques the failure of literary translation studies to formulate an 'adequate reader response theory' (2012a:17), arguing that even if we produce a translation with the 'ignorant' reader in mind, we still do not know 'what constitutes a proper use of the reader's intelligence and imagination' (ibid).

This second chapter is concerned with how translations are – or should be – read, by book reviewers, by students and scholars and by 'everyday' readers; for critique, for study and for pleasure. The following questions will be at the forefront of the discussion:

- Is a literary translation a special kind of text? Does (or should) reading a literary translation feel different from reading a non-translated literary work?
- How do we (or should we) discuss and review literary translations?
- How do we read a translation for scholarly purposes?
- How do we assess the 'success' of a literary translation?

## Are literary translations special? Are they – should they be – read differently?

Boase-Beier, whose work we encountered in the previous chapter, argues that a literary translation *is* a special kind of text (Boase-Beier 2011:59–72). A translated literary text is neither fully documentary nor instrumental and in fact 'achieves its instrumentality by virtue of being documentary' (2006:28). This dual function or role can be accounted for by understanding translation as a 'blend' (Boase-Beier 2011:67).

A blend is a 'creative cognitive structure' (ibid) in which two or more mental spaces are combined, resulting in a dynamic new entity that shares some of the elements of its input spaces but also has its own unique properties or emergent structure (Boase-Beier 2011:67–72; Fauconnier and Turner 2002; Stockwell 2002:96–8). The input spaces for a translation are, on the one hand, the foreign source text, which is a mental space with a real-world counterpart, and, on the other, an imagined non-translated text written in the reader's language (English, in our context), which the reader equates with the foreign source text. The blend which arises from the meeting of these two mental spaces is the translation. As a blend, a translation is a distinct type of text that demands a special kind of reading. It enjoys dual authorship (each translation has at least one author and at least one translator); it started life in one or more specific source cultures, and now finds itself in a new receiving culture or cultures; finally, in the process of rewriting the source text's style using the resources of the target language, the translator has facilitated a linguistic encounter which leaves traces in the language of the translation. These traces are not only traces of the source language as harnessed in the source text but, as Theo Hermans argues, the 'visible traces and direct interventions' (2014:287) of the translator, whose attitude towards the text he or she has translated is inevitably inscribed therein and can be detected, Hermans further argues, by the speculative reader (ibid:296–9). For all of these reasons, and because translation operates under constraints (beginning with the basic fact of the non-equivalence of languages) which have to be creatively negotiated (Boase-Beier and Holman 1999), Boase-Beier asserts that 'the creativity involved in writing and reading a literary text is enhanced when it is translated' (2011:57).

Other voices in Translation Studies agree that translations are distinct types of text, even if they disagree on the precise nature of the relationship between source and target. As we saw in the first chapter, Scott rejects literary translation's documentary function – its obligation to give the 'ignorant' reader an account of the inaccessible source text – but he nonetheless asserts the fundamental connectedness of source and target and the need to read the target with an awareness of its source in order to appreciate the nature of the translator's readerly and writerly engagement with that text. Where Boase-Beier sees the reader's voice blended with the author's in an emergent structure, Scott's 'translation as experimental writing' sees the translator's 'readerly autobiography becom[ing] part of the writerly biography of the other' (2012a:180). Here the reader-translator is inscribed in the text in a much more forceful and visible manner.

A variety of theoretical positions – each with their own attendant terminology – all highlight the intrinsic hybridity of the translated text. From the perspective of postcolonial theory, for example, a translation is an appropriation, a text that we make our own to a greater or lesser degree so as to avoid the full alienation of engagement with the foreign: the source text's 'otherness is [. . .] differed-deferred into an other self who resembles us, however minimally' (Spivak 1993:181). This is the ethnocentric violence of which Venuti speaks (1995:20). By contrast, Chesterman, who sees Translation Studies as a branch of memetics (the study of memes – units of culture that reproduce themselves), argues that translation is a process in which 'mutation or modification is normal, not exceptional' (2009:84). The mutation that occurs as the source text is 'copied' results in a new kind of text, one that both resembles its source and introduces variation. There clearly is a general consensus that a translation is a special kind of text: a blended or hybrid entity that is connected in a unique way to a preceding text; a text that has multiple voices and that has undergone a process of mutation or transformation. It is therefore to be expected that the experience of reading a translation will differ from that of reading a non-translated text.

Theoretical engagement with the question of whether and to what extent the reader should be aware that he or she is reading a translation has been a constant companion to the practice of translation and was most succinctly expressed for the modern era by Schleiermacher when he asked whether the translator should leave the reader or the author 'in peace' (Schleiermacher 2012:49) – in other words, whether the translator should make the reader or the author move further in the literary encounter. As we have already seen, various theorists have answered Schleiermacher's question in different ways. Venuti's foreignizing approach to translation, for instance, is rooted in the conviction that reading a translation *should* be a different type of reading experience, one that calls attention to the foreign origins of the text in our hands by highlighting the presence of the translational voice through disruptive textual strategies. Only thus can the Anglo-American world move beyond its current cultural imperialism. Less radically, David Damrosch, writing from a World Literature perspective, suggests that we read world literary texts (which can be written in our own language or be translated) in terms of 'likeness, of unlikeness, and of a shifting like-but-unlike relation to our own world' (Damrosch 2003:159), seeking out a middle ground between experiencing alienation and practicing assimilation.

Either way, if we accept the above arguments that translations *are*, in fact, special kinds of text, we can be confident in arguing that if we read them with an awareness of their translated nature – whether this is the minimal awareness brought about by the presence of the translator's name on the cover or the maximal awareness created by an interventionist or experimental translation strategy – then the benefits for us as readers will be considerable. Many readers purposefully seek out translations, for many of the reasons that motivate the act of translation in the first place and that were explored in the first chapter: humanism, ideology and because translation is a very particular mode of reading and writing. Waisman argues that our 'need – or desire – for alterity [...] factor[s] in as a significant player in our need for translation' (2010:73). If we interpret 'alterity' here in the broadest possible sense, as 'otherness', 'difference', 'contrast', 'challenge', 'novelty', then we can see that translation has much to offer and we can assume that engaged readers will be prepared to invest the necessary effort to derive maximum benefit from the text. Part of this effort, Venuti suggests, should be a willingness to conceive of translation as 'an act of interpretation' (2002:244) that is tied to that particular cultural moment. In other words, the reader should be aware that a translation represents a particular reading of a source text and ask why a source text should have been translated into the target culture at that particular moment. Engaging with the translator's motivations and methodology – facilitated by the translator's critical awareness of these and willingness to highlight his or her rationale and approach both in paratexts, i.e. in a translator's preface or afterword, and extratextually, e.g. at literary events or in the media – will aid the reader of the translation in reading and assessing the text.

In recent years, several translation theorists and practitioners have formulated guidelines to aid readers in their approach to translated texts. The nature and detail of the guidelines varies according to the audience. Readers of translations may be book reviewers, whose task is to deliver some sort of judgement or recommendation that may or may not lead the reader of the review to purchase the title in question. Readers of translations may also be university students on a World Literature or Comparative Literature course who are learning to write literary criticism and must find a way to approach a foreign text that features a dual authorial voice and to negotiate its relationship to more familiar, domestic literature. Finally, there is the general reader, who may or may not be aware that the book he or she is reading is a translation and who may or may not have deliberately sought out a translated text.

The clichés of the translation book review were recently addressed by translator Esther Allen in 'Lost in the Book Review' (2014). Allen offers reviewers several pieces of advice: 'that they envision the translator as having played an active and creative role in the book under review'; 'that they feel free to judge the piece of writing that is before them on its own internal merits rather than becoming ensnared in the briarpatch of accuracy' (2014:31); that they are cognizant of the fact 'that realism [by which Allen means the ability of the translator to recreate features of the original such as voice and momentum so that these are convincing in translation] requires skill'; and, finally, that the translator should be thought of 'not only as actor [...] but as set and costume designer, as well' (ibid:32), by which she means that the translator is not a ventriloquist but also sets the scene through lexis, voice and cultural detail. For the university student, David Damrosch's advice on how to approach translated literature, particularly his *How to Read World Literature* (2009), is invaluable; and for the instructor of a literature-in-translation class, Carol Maier and Françoise Massardier-Kenney's edited collection *Reading in Translation: Issues and Practice* (2010) offers advice ranging from how to select an appropriate translation for a university course to case studies of reading national literatures in translation. Lawrence Venuti's 'How to Read a Translation' (2004), which is aimed at the general reader, features a five-pronged set of guidelines, which are reproduced below:

1. Don't read just for meaning, but for language too; appreciate the formal features of the translation;
2. Don't expect translations to be written only in the current standard dialect; be open to linguistic variations;
3. Don't overlook connotations and cultural references; read them as another, pertinent layer of significance;
4. Don't skip an introductory essay written by a translator; read it first, as a statement of the interpretation that guides the translation and contributes to what is unique about it;
5. Don't take one translation as representative of an entire foreign literature; compare it to translations of other works from the same language.

(Venuti 2004:109–15)

Venuti warns the reader not to expect smooth prose and to be aware of the translator's presence, both in the language of the text and in paratexts, but he also takes up issues that preoccupy World Literature – the inevitable decontextualization that occurs when we remove a text from its source language and culture, for example, and the challenging presence of alterity – and suggests ways of dealing with these.

The first step in approaching a translation, then, is to realize that it is a translation; but how do we then assess it? Engaging with a translation's paratexts will, hopefully, give the reader an insight into the translator's motivations and goals, but, as is the case with any work of literature, there are necessary limits to the explanatory powers of the people involved in its creation, and a translation should certainly not be judged solely on the basis of whether it achieves its stated aims, since the motivations for its creation may not be entirely apparent to itself and may also be concealed from others. The purpose of our reading will also inevitably shape our assessment of a translated text: reviewers judge, students and scholars critique and seek textual evidence to support a particular interpretation and the general reader may read with any number of purposes in mind. Polyglot readers might choose to read their translation in tandem with the source text. Engaged readers might ask why the text in their hands entered the target culture at a particular moment, particularly if there is a significant gap between the dates of source- and target-text publication, or, if the text is a re-translation or a revised translation, what the reasons for the re-translation or the revised translation might be. Regardless of whether a translation is read alongside – or even with a memory of – a source text or perhaps an earlier translation, and regardless of whether the translation has embraced a documentary function or firmly rejects it, in most cases it does seem important that a translation function instrumentally – that is to say, as a literary text in its own right. The degree of its dependence, independence or co-dependence on a source text may vary, but its own literariness will be paramount in any assessment of its success as a literary text – bearing in mind that the term 'literary' can be applied in a wide variety of ways to a wide variety of texts, ranging from works of genre literature to avant-garde experiments and non-fiction texts.

The sections that follow will offer readings of several translations, positing different contexts for each reading. They will begin by examining several reviews of translated books, considering the elements that might constitute good and bad reviewing practice. I will then offer my own review of a re-translation of Austrian writer Ingeborg Bachmann's poetry, entitled *Enigma* (2011), considering what this new translation by Mike Lyons and Patrick Drysdale has to offer a much translated poet. The chapter will then proceed to consider what needs to be taken into consideration when reading literary translations for scholarly purposes, taking three translations of Freud's *Bruchstück einer Hysterie-Analyse* (2007 [1905]), popularly known as the Dora case, as its focus. Finally, it will look at the question of how we assess the 'success' of literary translations, exploring this issue through a comparative analysis of Ralph Mannheim and Breon Mitchell's respective translations of Günter Grass' *The Tin Drum* (1959).

## How do we, or should we, review translations?

> 'You've never called me by my name! You don't know me!'
> Milan Kundera, *Ignorance*. Trans. Linda Asher (2002:187)

On 12 December 2004, BBC Radio 4's *A Good Read*, presented by Sue MacGregor and featuring guests Clare Balding and Andrew Collins, reviewed Milan Kundera's novel *Ignorance* (2002), translated from the French by Linda Asher. Asher's translation had been awarded the 2003 Scott Moncrieff Prize, an annual prize given for an English translation of a French work of literary merit and general interest. Kundera's novel, which is described by Balding, who selected it for review, as a 'book more about theory than it is about character' (BBC Radio 4, 2004), follows the return of two Czech émigrés to Prague following the fall of the Iron Curtain. The *Good Read* review, which is overwhelmingly positive, superficially notes the theme of translation implicit to the novel – the translation of the self across temporal, linguistic and geographical boundaries, and political systems – and links this to *Ignorance*'s status as a translated novel. Balding finds that the removal of meaning that occurs when one translates one's self, as the characters in the novel have done, is echoed in the novel's translated-ness; this 'add[s] another layer' to the reading experience. Despite Balding's perception of this link, however, MacGregor fails to perceive non-standard language use in the translation as a positive feature – one that might highlight the theme of displacement – and conceives of both self-translation and textual translation almost exclusively in terms of loss. The review discusses the episode in which Irena, one of the two émigrés, returns to Prague after many years spent in Paris and takes a case of Bordeaux with her to share with her old Czech friends (Kundera 2002:35–8). Her friends ignore this exotic import and insist on drinking the local beer. The episode is read as an example of dislocation and loss; the reviewers ignore the transformational possibilities that relocating the self can offer despite Irena's clear insistence in the narrative on being accepted for who she is – a changed person marked by the experience of emigration – or not at all, and despite the ambiguous ending of the episode, when one of Irena's friends decides that they will open one of the bottles of red wine after all.

The translation comes in for heavy criticism by MacGregor for its supposed 'infelicities': Kundera, she remarks, was 'not terribly well served' by his unnamed translator who, for instance, uses the formulations 'the Paris airport' and 'the Prague airport' rather than referring to those airports by their specific names. (MacGregor herself erroneously refers to the Prague Spring as the Czech Spring, aptly demonstrating that the *mot juste* sometimes eludes us all.) There is a suggestion that the translator's Americanness may be to blame for this non-standard nomenclature. Conversely, the translator receives no credit when the novel's phrasing is judged a success. Towards the end of the review discussion turns towards a 'beautifully described coupling' that typifies Kundera's skillful handling of middle-aged love affairs. One sentence in particular is singled out by Collins as 'brilliant': 'slightly solemn and thus embarrassing, as [. . .] the lovers confront a future they are suddenly required to take on' (Kundera 2002:190). In this context the reviewers' discussion of a sexual episode featuring a different couple, in which Irena ends up in bed with a man she knows from the past who fails to recognize her, becomes loaded with irony. 'You don't know my name, you don't know who I am', Irena tells her lover, as though she were voicing the translator's lament over her lack of visibility. To add a further layer of irony, the words Balding cites here are not actually a quotation but a paraphrase, an approximation of what Asher actually wrote.

The *Good Read* review of Asher's translation thus typifies a range of bad practices in translation reviewing. No attempt is made to distinguish between the author's language and the translator's language, or even to acknowledge the complex interweaving of the two. Asher is blamed when things go wrong (the airports) but not praised when things go right (the 'beautifully described' sex scene). The novel has not been sufficiently domesticated for the reviewer's taste: the Americanness of the language jars, reminding UK readers that this text is not of their culture. Certain expressions are foregrounded by virtue of their divergence from common usage ('the Paris airport'), but no consideration is given to whether there might be a reason for this beyond incompetence. Perhaps it was the author's choice? MacGregor remarks that she was 'brought short by the translation [. . .] now translations of foreign novels are so good that one expects them to be excellent'. Although 'good' is not explicitly defined, the discussion as a whole suggests that for MacGregor, a good translation is smooth and fluent and does not draw attention to itself – precisely what Irena does by taking wine to the beery city of Prague. The review does not investigate its own assumptions, nor sufficiently interrogate the interaction between the novel's thematic focus and its textual qualities.

Let us turn to another example of a review, one that is far more sensitive to the presence of the translator within the translated text. The *Times Literary Supplement* review (Bird 2014) of Oliver Ready's re-translation (2014) of *Crime and Punishment* by Dostoevsky comes from the pen of an academic expert who is able to read Dostoevsky in the original and is thus well-positioned to assess the relationship between source and target. Robert Bird, the author of a monograph on Dostoevsky's life and work, poses the question of what is different about Ready's generation of translators, and why *Crime and Punishment* is being re-translated now, after the famous P/V versions of the 1990s. He does this, in an agile rhetorical manoeuvre, by making a connection between the radicalism of youth in 1860s Russia, as depicted in the novel itself, and the radicalism of a new generation of translators (ibid:4–5). Ready's generation, Bird argues, can benefit from the advantages of scholarship unavailable to previous generations of translators, 'the numerous studies of the historical realities behind the novel, from its urban geography to its constant references to current events' (ibid:5). The younger generation of translators are also linguistically better attuned, having 'spent much more time in Russia than their forebears' – perhaps because of the changed geo-political situation since the fall of the Iron Curtain. Bird has a strong sense of how the translator's style ('clipped but precise') interacts with Dostoevsky's style ('the tension between reticence and verbosity that characterizes [his] prose') and of where Ready differs from P/V ('errs even more on the side of fidelity, preserving Russian words such as *papirosa* and *burnous*, which are hardly familiar to readers with no Russian and require explanatory footnotes') (ibid). The review assesses the effects of the translator's stylistic choices, noting that these choices go 'a long way towards a fuller representation of [Dostoevsky's] characters' eccentric physiognomies', but that at times Ready's fidelity 'afflicts the syntax of the translation' (ibid). Bird is critical of Ready's phrasing for occasionally sounding too contemporary ('Can one say: "Both your items . . . were found at *hers*"?' – one can, if one is of Ready's generation) but also for sounding too British ('Mummy'; 'poppycock') (ibid). Both of these features appear to Bird to be unwelcome reminders that the text is being filtered through the here and now of a particular translatorly subjectivity, and the latter also 'raises the unwelcome spectre' of Dostoevsky's first and much criticized English-language translator, the Edwardian Constance Garnett (ibid). Interestingly, the Britishisms that Bird singles out for critique are resolutely uncontemporary, suggesting that Ready may have adopted a foreignizing mixture of registers in the style advocated by Venuti (Venuti 1995:311). There are echoes in Bird's critique of the Atlantic divide felt by the reviewers of Kundera's American *Ignorance*. Unlike MacGregor and her guest reviewers, however, Bird catches himself before he progresses too far down the road of what Allen has labelled 'nitpicking' (Allen 2014:27) by acknowledging that 'it would be a mistake [. . .] to judge any translation as a set of equivalences between two sign systems', even arguing that 'the novel is very much about the ability of signs to entrap people in structures of necessity' (Bird 2014:5), thus making the implicit case that the new translation of *Crime and Punishment* contributes to the afterlife of the text, allowing it to make its meanings in a new context. Bird concludes that Ready's new translation does indeed succeed in 'implicating new readers in Dostoevsky's old novel' (ibid). His review asks the question that we should always ask of any re-translation: why now? We should ask this not because a re-translation must justify itself by pointing to the shortcomings of previous translations – a re-translation may be motivated by the simple fact that a translator feels an affinity for a particular text – but because to do so is to pay attention to the 'cultural conditions of the translating' (Venuti 2002:247).

A third example of a translation review, and one which offers a fresh approach to its task, is 'Sniffle', Sheng Yun's review of Mai Jia's *Decoded: A Novel* for the *London Review of Books* (2007). Yun, like Bird, is a scholar proficient in both the source and target languages of the translated work under discussion. Yun's lengthy review is unimpressed by the source text and places responsibility for its 'bad writing' (2014:41) squarely on the author's rather than the translator's shoulders: 'The translator, Olivia Milburn, has done her best, but there isn't a lot to work with' (ibid:40). (The *LRB* subsequently corrected the print version's omission of the novel's second translator, Christopher Payne, on its website, although Payne is not credited in the UK edition of *Decoded*.) In the absence of any literary qualities worthy of discussion, the reviewer makes the productive choice to present a thorough contextualization of the translation. The review thus considers a number of topics: Mai Jia's status in China and the effects of the translation of *Decoded* thereupon; the novel's critical reception in the English-speaking world and how this relates to our understanding of Chinese literature; and, finally, throwing in a potted history of Chinese literature, how Chinese literature has been affected by its cultural encounters with the Western and South American other.

Yun begins by deconstructing the proclamation made by *The Economist* in relation to *Decoded*: 'Finally, a great Chinese novel' (*The Economist* 2014:88). He makes the point that Mai Jia is essentially a Chinese Dan Brown rather than a serious man of letters, and that if his novel is heralded in the West, it is because it conforms to a genre familiar to us: the airport novel. In fact, as Yun points out, the novel form as such is a late nineteenth-century import to China: 'The educated Chinese elite has never really valued fiction. The Chinese word for novel, *xiao shuo*, means "small talk": poetry and the essay are the carriers of Chinese intellectual heritage' (Yun 2014:41). Mai Jia's fiction is a hybrid, influenced by the translated fiction that flooded China in the 1980s during a time of what polysystem theorists would call a turning point in the literary polysystem (Even-Zohar 2012 [1978]:164). This turning point arose because of the copyright vacuum that resulted from China's belated subscription to the World Copyright Convention (Yun 2014:40). García Márquez topped the list of foreign bestsellers, and Yun observes that it took Nobel-prizewinner Mo Yan 'twenty years to shake off the García Márquez effect' (ibid:41). Tellingly, *The Economist*'s review explicitly compares *Decoded* to the magical realism of García Márquez, with its other points of reference drawn from the Anglophone world (the Australian writer Peter Carey and the English writer Tom McCarthy) (*The Economist* 2014:88). But here the reference to Márquez is simply to hail Mai Jia's novel as something familiar (and hence good); no attempt is made to contextualize the perceived link between one literary tradition and the other. This decontextualization of the novel, quite a typical feature of translation reviews, affects our appreciation of the Chinese literary landscape of which 'only a small fragment [...] has been read overseas' (*The Economist* 2014:88). Further on in the same paragraph, *The Economist*'s unnamed reviewer places responsibility for the poor reception of Chinese literature abroad with the literature itself, stating that 'almost none of the thousands of translated [Chinese] works has held its own as a novel that book-lovers with no special interest in China will relish' (ibid). Not only is this an uncritical conflation of quality (or at least of readerly appeal) with accessibility and familiarity, but the casual reference to the supposed 'thousands' of Chinese books that have been translated also demonstrates an incredible ignorance of the material facts of translation publishing.

Yun's contextualization, by contrast, reveals much about the literary relations that hold between national literatures: in the case of Mai Jia, who was particularly influenced by Borges during the boom in translated fiction, and indeed in the case of other contemporary Chinese fiction writers, the West is to a certain extent receiving a refraction of its – and South America's – exports. But the Anglophone West is largely oblivious to how it has shaped what it is now receiving from China, just as it is oblivious to or willingly ignorant of the politics of the original text and of the translation. Mai Jia is 'an establishment figure', 'a Red writer' (Yun 2014:40) who, like other members of official Chinese writing associations, receives a salary from the Chinese government. Yun tells us that Mai felt compelled to play down what was in fact a 'marginally favourable' review by translator Perry Link in the *New York Times* because of Link's 'dubious' political credentials: Link has been banned from entering mainland China because of his translation of *The Tiananmen Papers* (2001) (ibid). Mai therefore stressed the negative aspects of Link's review in a statement on Weibo, the Chinese version of Twitter, suggesting that Link had objected to the absence of any dissident sentiment in *Decoded*. This reviewing spat is but one example of how the decision to translate reverberates back into the target culture. Yun points out, too, that the novel's domestic reputation, and through it Jia's literary status, was much boosted by the fact that a publisher as reputable as Penguin had decided to publish *Decoded* in translation.

Yun's review suggests a number of strategies for best practice in translation reviewing. It does not immediately come to the conclusion that the text's aesthetic failures are the translator's doing and will in fact not even accept the excuse that Jia writes under conditions of government censorship ('The Soviet Union was a fully censored environment, but there were good poets, novelists and composers', 2014:41). Its informed contextualization of the reception and impact of *Decoded* in both source and target cultures fully acknowledges that the text partakes in a complex dynamic of exchange and that the effects of the translation are more than simply textual. The review also contains something quite rare in translation reviewing: in its discussion of a passage that deviates from the literal sense of the original Chinese, it seeks an explanation other than the translator's incompetence:

> the narrator finds Rong's notebook and returns it to his wife, then asks her if she ever really loved the geeky savior of the nation. 'I love him as I love my country,' she says. (Mai Jia is a staunch patriot.)

'Do you regret marrying him?' he asks. The narrator sees 'that this question took her by surprise; she opened her eyes wide, stared at me and replied excitedly: "Regret? When you love your country, how can you regret it? No! Forever the answer will be no –!" Her eyes immediately filled with tears and she began to sniffle as if she was about to cry.' In the original that last sentence actually reads: 'I saw her eyes suddenly fill with tears, and felt a twitch in my nose. I wanted to cry.' Translators must do as they see fit, even if it means a bit of role-swapping. But Milburn's got the tone right: we find the same uninflected faith in nation and party in Mai Jia's other novels [...] and even if she botched the translation, it's an authentic touch to have the hero's dreary wife affirming the author's dreary values.

(Yun 2014:40)

Yun does suggest that Milburn has probably made a mistake here, but rather than berating her incompetence the review assesses the aesthetic and cognitive effects of the mistake, thus treating the translation as an independent work of literature. Yun implies that attributing the 'sniffle' to Rong's wife rather than to the narrator reveals or foregrounds an important aspect of the novel: by emphasizing her cloyingly sentimental patriotism but leaving the narrator's (and perhaps the reader's) eyes dry, the mistranslation is perfectly in keeping with *Decoded*'s 'Red' tone. The translator's attitude towards the text may well have found an outlet (conscious or unconscious) for expression here, an opportunity to indicate her non-alignment with the narrator's and the writer's 'reported speech' (Hermans 2014). Yun's point here is in line with recent developments in translation theory; both Scott and Venuti have argued for a more nuanced approach to 'errors' in translation in precisely this vein, suggesting that the reader's default assumption should not be that the translator is incompetent, nor that mistakes are without literary value. The reader should be 'mindful of the possible 'deeper' sources of mistranslation' (Scott 2012a:29), which may have to do with the translator's unconscious attitude towards the text and which can be investigated by reading translations psychoanalytically (Berman 2012; Venuti 2013a). We will return to this point in the discussion of errors in the translation of Freud's 'Dora'.

---

*Enigma*. Selected Poems by Ingeborg Bachmann. Translated by Mike Lyons and Patrick Drysdale. 2011. Ariadne Press, 132 pp.

The final poem in *Enigma*, Mike Lyons and Patrick Drysdale's translations of selected poems by the Austrian writer Ingeborg Bachmann, caught my eye immediately. Mike Leigh's *Mr Turner* had recently been in cinemas, a film in which Leigh sensitively, humorously and – by almost universal critical consensus – magisterially explores Turner's person and considers the pursuit of artistic endeavour. In Lyons and Drysdale's translation of 'William Turner: Backlight', the final two lines read 'To himself he gave little thought/ and allowed himself no perspective'. In choosing this poem as one of the bookends of *Enigma*, a collection which numbers eighty poems in total, the translators appear to be gesturing towards Ingeborg Bachmann's depression and tragic end at the age of forty-seven: the poet, who had developed a substance abuse problem, fell asleep in bed in her Rome apartment with a lit cigarette and died three weeks later from her injuries. But their choice also affirms Bachmann as a great artist, since 'what matters is the fall of light' and this was Bachmann's métier. The page, poetry's canvas, was to be stretched 'across a land with meagre sun' as the painter-poet 'brushed in the tracks reaching for the sky'. Capturing light in a painting, capturing lived experience in a poem lies at the heart of the artistic endeavour, and is sometimes pursued to the detriment or in wilful ignorance of one's physical and emotional wellbeing. 'William Turner: Backlight' is also a response to *Enigma*'s opening poem, 'Estrangement', an early text in which the physical senses – sight, hearing – fail to serve the poetic voice with the necessary materials for her craft: 'Before my eyes the forest flees,/ before my ear the birds close their mouths'. By the final line of the poem the voice laments that 'I can no longer see a path in any path'. When the reader reaches 'William Turner: Backlight', the artistic crisis, if not the personal one, has been resolved, but the network of signification in which these two poems partake has been loosened by the decision to translate a key noun using two different words. In German, the final line of 'Estrangement' reads 'Ich kann in keinem Weg mehr einen Weg sehen' [literally, I can no longer see a path in any path]. In 'William Turner: Backlight', the artist 'streifte/ die Wege nah an den Himmel' [brushed [in] the paths close to the sky]. In German, this latter line suggests the artist's physical traversal of the landscape – the walking that Leigh captures so well in his film – but also the sublime nature of Turner's brushstrokes with their evocation of the heavens. In 'Estrangement', Lyons and Drysdale have rendered *Weg* with 'path', but in 'William Turner: Backlight', they have translated the plural of that noun [*Wege*] with 'tracks', and so the sense of redemption via the artistic path – the brushstroke, the poetic line – is weakened. This is not intended to be a 'lost-in-translation' lament of the most unhelpful variety, but a measuring of the translated poems against a statement made by another of Bachmann's translators, Peter Filkins, in the introduction to his own translations of Bachmann's collected poems, entitled *Darkness Spoken*: 'the reader may often be inclined to wonder about the *where* and the *when* of any poem, but never the *who*, for the continuity of Bachmann's voice is the central source of her poetic authority' (2006a:xxvi). Paying attention to signifying networks not only intratextually but intertextually – from poem to poem – must be one of the hardest of the translator's tasks, and particularly hard in English, where our literary unconscious tells us to avoid repetition and where the lexical richness of the English language tempts us towards variation. The reward when it succeeds, however, is an integrity of poetic voice and the strengthening of signifying networks.

It behoves us to judge the translated poems' success in their own terms – as English poetry – rather than by constant comparison to the German original. Nonetheless it is difficult for somebody who reads German and is familiar with Bachmann's poetry to entirely forget her poetic voice and her physical one, too, preserved for us in various recordings and now accessible on websites such as lyrikline.org, where Bachmann can be heard reciting her own work. Both of Bachmann's voices, the poetic and the actual one, are sonorous and serious, even when they are playful. There is at best a sense of melancholy, at worst a sense of menace – whether it be the Nazi past rearing its head or the spectre of personal unhappiness and depression – 'time on loan, repayment due,/ appears on the skyline' ('Time on Loan'). This poem contains a welter of images, of hounds snapping at one's heels, fish guts gone cold, one's lover being buried alive in sand, but the poem also announces that there is no time to dwell on these harbingers of doom, for 'harder days are coming'. Here, as in the poem 'Every Day', bravery is called for: 'Lace up your boot', the addressee of 'Time on Loan' is told. The German language has a word for this kind of bravery, *Zivilcourage*, the courage of the civilian to stand up and be counted in difficult circumstances. In 'Every Day', medals are awarded 'for deserting the flag/ for valour when facing the friend,/ for betraying despicable secrets,/ and for disobeying/ every order'. Bachmann may have been reflecting on the failure of her own society to take a stand in the face of National Socialism, but her poem belongs to no time and place, and speaks equally to the modern world's Edward Snowden or Chelsea Manning, both of whom have paid a price for their *Zivilcourage*. The light and the dark, the beauty and the beast go hand-in-hand in Bachmann's texts, and Lyons and Drysdale capture some of these juxtapositions beautifully, as in 'From the corpse-warmed portico of heaven steps the sun' in 'Message', and 'Wherever we turn in the deluge of roses,/ the night is floodlit by thorns' in 'In the Deluge of Roses'. One of Bachmann's most famous poems, 'Explain to Me, Love', in which the poetic voice is tempted to set aside her own doubts and thoughts by the ease and joy with which the natural world goes about courtship and romance, is rhythmic and full of beautiful imagery in Lyons and Drysdale's translation. The uncovered head of the figure evoked in the first stanza 'has tantalized the clouds' and his or her face is 'struck blind by cornflowers'; similarly 'the dove turns up his feathered collar ruff,/ the air, too full of cooing, stretches out'. The lightness of this poem with its images taken from the natural world contrasts with the mourning of 'A Kind of Loss', one of the poems written after Bachmann's relationship with Swiss writer Max Frisch had ended, which references the everyday objects and routines of an intimate relationship: 'The keys, the teacups, the bread-basket, sheets and a bed./ A trousseau of words, of gestures, brought with me,/ employed, consumed'.

'Bohemia Lies on Sea', which Bachmann 'reckoned to be her finest poem', as Hans Höller tells us in the afterword to the Lyons/Drysdale translation, is less successful. The German title, 'Böhmen liegt am Meer' [literally, Bohemia lies on the sea], contains a definite article, *dem*, which has been merged with the preposition *an*. The translators have taken the decision to omit this article. Even if one were not familiar with the German title, the wording of the English title, which finds a refrain in the body of the poem, would strike a discordant note. It is of course possible to say that one is 'on land' or 'on sea' in specific collocations, and the UK has numerous seaside towns with this nomenclature – think of Clacton-on-Sea or Southend-on-Sea – therefore one must assume that this was a deliberate choice on the part of the translators. The real Bohemia is landlocked, of course, but the metaphorical Bohemia and the Bohemia of Shakespeare's *The Winter's Tale* can lie by the sea since these are spaces of utopia and fiction, and this is a poem about hope, in part the hope offered by a world without borders. But in the lines 'If Bohemia's still on sea, then I believe the seas again./ And if I still believe in sea, then I hope for land', the omission of the definite article and indeed the choice of preposition upset the rhythm. Peter Filkins' 'If Bohemia still lies by the sea, I'll believe in the sea again. And believing in the sea, thus I can hope for land' seems preferable here. There are a few other awkward choices that affect the flow of this poem: 'I find Bohemia there again' would have been better expressed in the future tense, to match the future tenses of the first three lines ('If houses hereabouts are green, I'll step inside a house./ If bridges here are sound, I'll tread on solid ground./ If love's labor's lost for ever, I'll gladly lose it here), which contribute to the utopian atmosphere of the poem. The colloquial and contemporary register of 'if only a bit' in the line 'I'm bordered still by a word and by another land,/ I'm bordered, if only a bit, by all things more and more,' is jarring.

Bachmann certainly emerges as a fine and enduring poet from this new translation, minor quibbles aside. What is a shame is that Lyons and Drysdale have not been afforded an introduction or afterword of their own in *Enigma*, so the rationale for their re-translation of a selection of Bachmann's poems must be gleaned from the paratexts surrounding their work. The back cover – which presumably represents the editor's vision – tells us that *Enigma* is a translation for the general reader and the non-German-speaking student of literature, not for the academic or the reader who can access the source language. The translators have attempted to stay close to both meaning and form and have used rhyme where there is rhyme in the original. The collection aims to promote Bachmann's reputation as a 'world poet'. In the preface, written by Bachmann's brother, Heinz Bachmann, we learn that Mike Lyons and Patrick Drysdale are theatre translators and that theirs are the first UK versions since Michael Hamburger's 1967 translations for *Modern Poetry in Translation*. Why is it that a UK readership requires a UK Bachmann (Filkins''American' poems precede the collection by only five years)? How its Britishness furthers its ambition to promote Bachmann's status as a 'world poet' and what it is about this translation that ties it to

> a particular national space remains unclear. I noted only some small differences in vocabulary that might reflect the differing cultural sensibilities of the two nations: for example, in the poem 'Harlem', where Filkins has translated Bachmann's 'schwarze Stadt' [black city] as 'ghetto', the UK translators opt for 'black-skinned city'. One hopes that the emphasis on the poems' Britishness is more of a marketing ploy than the outcome of a conviction that Bachmann's texts required a domestically acceptable form. In fact, the back-cover blurb may in this respect do the translation a disservice. What Lyons and Drysdale encounter is a voice of such poetic power that it calls out for frequent re-translation as a mode of discovering it anew. What the translators achieve is the creation of a poetic voice that resounds (almost) consistently through their collection, as it does in the poem that gives the collection its title, 'Enigma'. Here once again our time is up, 'Nothing more will come', but this inevitability is met with a lightness of touch: 'You really shouldn't cry,/ the music says. Otherwise/ no one/ says/ a word'.

## How do we read a translation for scholarly purposes?

When we read a text for scholarly purposes rather than to make a value judgement like a literary critic or for pleasure like the general reader, then we are either looking for information, or for evidence that supports a particular argument or bolsters a theory. As we have seen, however, 'translated textuality' is a complicated beast, and constructing an argument using evidence from a translated text is less straightforward than constructing an argument using evidence from a text that was originally composed in the language in which it is being read. To begin with, the words on the page are not the author's words; they are the translator's words, and this immediately makes statements such as 'Simone de Beauvoir argues' or 'Bruno Schulz's striking use of metaphor' problematic, for how can we be sure that de Beauvoir really argued this in French or that Schulz's metaphors are actually present in the same way in the original Polish text? Furthermore, if it has been brought to our attention, as is the case with de Beauvoir's *Le deuxième sexe*, that scholars have serious misgivings about existing translations, that these translations at worst distort and perhaps even censor the source text and at best fail to do justice to it, then how can any statement about a text that derives from its English translations have validity? How do we reconcile our dependence on the translated text, our need to use it for scholarly purposes, with its contingent and slippery nature?

It certainly does no harm to begin from the premise that translation in a Babelian world is all we have. Translation gives us access to texts that would otherwise remain inaccessible – and here we arrive back at the humanist case for the translational endeavour. It is inevitable that foreign texts are refracted (Henitiuk 2012) or mutate (Chesterman 2009) on their journey into the target culture and that a text's reception in that culture will therefore be shaped by its translations and may differ quite substantially from its reception in the source culture and other cultures into which it might be translated. In cases where only one translation of a text exists, its power to influence our readings will be all the greater. Even though translated texts may be flawed, they can nonetheless be formative. The English-speaking world's reception of Dostoevsky is unthinkable without Constance Garnett's translations, which 'allowed this strange new voice to invade English literature' (France 2000:596), even if Garnett has been much criticized (May 1994:37–42) and 'superceded' by other translators in recent years. Psychoanalyst Adam Phillips, who edited the New Penguin Freud and was eager to see what new translations might do for Freud's texts, professes his admiration for Strachey's Standard Edition of Freud's works (Phillips 2007:36), a translation that critics have attacked on a number of counts, not least for its creation of a medical-scientific jargon that does not match Freud's preference for terminology drawn from the everyday (Bettelheim 1984; Mahony 1987:171).

If a translation is seriously flawed, it is likely – particularly in the contemporary critical environment, which is much more sensitive to the dynamics of translation – that scholarly readers with knowledge of the source text will bring our attention to it, as Toril Moi has done in the case of the most recent translation of *Le deuxième sexe* (Moi 2010) and as competent book reviews should also do. Such metatexts will be invaluable in drawing the monolingual reader's attention to possible areas of difficulty. If there are minor but glaring errors in a translation, the observant reader should generally be able to spot these because they will appear out of place, even nonsensical, and disrupt the flow of the English text. Errors may also become apparent as readers compare different translations, where these are available, although consensus across a number of translations does not necessarily prove any outlier wrong, as mistakes may be repeated across several translations. And for all the anxiety engendered by reading 'only' in translation, it is important to remember that if a text is translatable in the Benjaminian sense – if its literary qualities are such that it calls out for its own translation – then it is likely to transcend any infelicities in a particular translation, and if it is translated sensitively, it may even become a 'better' (a more interesting, more literary) text in translation.

When reading in translation for scholarly purposes, the reader can be equipped for the unique demands and benefits of translated textuality through an awareness of certain facts: that the text in the reader's hands has come from another place, culture and language and has been made accessible through the agency of the translator; that the translator is embedded in the translated text and that it therefore has multiple authors; and that there is no simple equivalence between languages – and, finally, that for these reasons the translation process will inevitably bring with it transformations, refractions, errors, distortions, implicit or explicit commentary, insights, gain and loss. The presence of such elements – and we will only truly be able to identify these if we are sufficiently familiar with the source text to know that they belong to the translation alone – reflects the instability and multiplicity of the literary text, so that in fact translation highlights something very basic about the nature of literature. It will be important to demonstrate this awareness of the nature of the translated text when using material from it to construct an argument, particularly at the micro-linguistic level. If an argument hinges on one word, consultation with a different translation may reveal that this word is no longer present, that it has been compensated for elsewhere in the text with a different word, phrase or structure or that its signifying power is now altogether absent. Similarly, a crucial sentence may have moved from the active into the passive or merged with another sentence. A character's attitude might be more concrete or more ambiguous in a particular translator's voice and could also be affected by the differences in cultural norms between source and target cultures (e.g. a speech act may be considered direct to the point of rudeness in one culture and perfectly civil in another). Textual evidence from a translation needs to be used with greater sensitivity, and where multiple translations are available it will always be beneficial to draw upon them. This is not to say that one cannot construct an argument on the basis of a translated text. Critical nodes in the translation, which will become particularly apparent from a comparative analysis of different translations of the same text, will be suggestive of critical nodes in the source text itself and are likely to be central to its meaning-creation. Such nodes may also lead the reader to 'speculate about how translators position themselves [...] and what purpose the positioning serves' (Hermans 2014:297).

### Translations of Freud's 'Dora' on the couch

Freud's early psychoanalytic case study of a female hysteric, which is entitled *Bruchstück einer Hysterie-Analyse* (2007 [1905]) [literally, Fragment of a Hysteria-Analysis] but is more commonly known as 'Dora' after the pseudonym Freud gave his patient Ida Bauer, will serve as an illustration of the issues surrounding reading in translation for scholarly purposes. I choose this text because Freud remains a routine reference point for literary critical work, irrespective of whether the literary critic in question can access his work in German or not, and because the literariness of Freud's texts – their tendency to signify in the complex and unstable ways characteristic of literary works – is both undeniable and threatening to those invested in fixing their meaning. Freud's work, we should remember, is read by multiple constituencies for multiple purposes – as literature, as theory, as science and to train psychoanalysts of various schools. There is, in other words, much at stake in its interpretation. The Strachey Standard Edition of 1953 has been joined by two new translations of 'Dora' since copyright expired on Freud's work: a 2006 translation by Shaun Whiteside, which is part of the New Penguin Freud series, and a 2013 translation by Anthea Bell, published as an Oxford World Classic. Dora, a young woman from a bourgeois Jewish family who begins analysis for various hysterical symptoms that include breathlessness and losing her voice, eventually breaks off her analysis before its completion. Her treatment at Freud's hands has been described as 'one of the great psychotherapeutic disasters' (Mahony 1996:148).

We will begin our case study by considering the issue of errors in translation, looking at why they call attention to themselves, what motivates them and at their effects on the text and the reading experience. In the course of her psychoanalytic treatment, Dora relates to Freud two key incidents involving the predatory sexual overtures of Herr K., an older married man. Herr K. is a family friend who also happens to be the husband of the woman with whom Dora's father is conducting a long-term affair. In one of the two incidents related by Dora, which occurs – in Freud's account – when Dora is only fourteen, Herr K. lures Dora to his shop, grabs her and kisses her. Both Herr K. and Dora keep the incident a secret and Dora does not speak of it until one of her therapeutic sessions with Freud (Freud 2007 [1905]:30). In Whiteside's translation, there is an error – easily identifiable to a reader of German – in the paragraph in which Dora relates this incident to Freud. Freud tells his reader that neither Herr K. nor Dora 'ever mentioned this little scene, and Dora claims to have kept it a secret even *at confession at the spa*' (Freud, trans. Whiteside 2006:21, emphasis my own). The 'scene' described does indeed take place in a spa town – this is the town identified by the letter B. to which the Bauer family moved on the grounds of Dora's father's poor health – but Dora's confession about the scene with Herr K. does not take place there. If the reader consults the other two translations of the Dora case, it will become clear that there is a lack of agreement on the location/occasion of the confession. Bell, for instance, writes that neither party 'ever mentioned this little scene, and [Dora] said she had kept the secret to herself until she confessed it in the course of treatment' (Freud, trans. Bell 2013:23). The Standard Edition tells us that they '[n]ever mentioned the little scene; and according to her account Dora kept it a secret till her confession during the treatment' (Freud, trans. Strachey 2001:28). All three translations agree a confession took place, but Whiteside's translation with its rendering of 'in the course of treatment' as 'at the spa' may lead readers who lack the contextual knowledge that Dora is Jewish to believe that Dora has participated in a Catholic sacrament.

Why might the translator have confused the spa town with the course of treatment that Dora is undergoing? The German word that Freud uses for the town of B. and for Dora's treatment is in fact the same: *Kur*. The town of B. is a *Kurort* (literally, a cure-place). Even today, Germans, Austrians and Swiss go on *Kur* in spa towns, a holiday that involves taking the waters, enjoying the fresh air and following a diet. But the term *Kur* has also been used since the sixteenth century to describe medical care in general, eventually coming to be understood in its current sense of 'treatment'. The psychoanalytic therapeutic method that was still in its infancy during Dora's treatment was christened with the English phrase 'talking cure' by Bertha Pappenheim, a patient of Freud's mentor and colleague Josef Breuer, who is better known under the pseudonym Anna O. (Freud and Breuer 2004:34). It is the German cognate *Kur* that is used at the very beginning of the paragraph in which the 'scene' with Herr K. is related. It describes the treatment that Dora is undergoing with Freud. In Whiteside's translation this line is rendered as 'After the first difficulties of the cure had been overcome' (Freud, trans. Whiteside 2006:20), whereas in the Standard Edition and in Bell's version the term 'treatment' is used instead (Freud, trans. Strachey 2001:27; Freud, trans. Bell 2013:22). Whiteside too prefers the word 'treatment' to render *Kur* in other instances (Freud, trans. Whiteside 2006:17: 'even then I suggested psychological treatment').

Whiteside's 'error' is more than it seems. It may in fact be a motivated error, albeit an unconscious one, one of the many choices made by the translator in the course of bringing the work from German into English. As we have already noted, Venuti has argued that in the work of experienced translators, errors need not be seen simply as instances of carelessness, but may point to a deeper psychological mechanism at work that has to do with the translator's feelings towards the text, feelings that may in fact illuminate the text further since they spring from an intense engagement with its every word. Venuti further argues that this textual relationship can be psychoanalysed (Venuti 2013a). In the case of Freud's 'Dora' – one of the founding texts of psychoanalysis: a therapeutic technique that employs free association as part of its toolkit – it is perhaps not far-fetched to suggest that the translator's lexical choices reveal something about his own and Freud's associative processes. In the example discussed above, Whiteside must have associated the German noun for 'confession', *Beichte*, with the term used for the Catholic sacrament – in German as in English there is an overlap between the secular and religious senses of the terms. But the translator's misreading highlights the fact that Freud's lexical choice is an interesting one to describe a therapeutic technique that is still being refined and which, in Dora's case, is far from perfect. In other words, there is a curious aftertaste of the religious to Freud's scientific method which the mistranslation unwittingly highlights. The translator's error also draws our attention to the fact that Freud appears to be associating the spa town (*Kurort*) in which much of Dora's narrative takes place with the therapeutic sessions (*Kur*) taking place between him and Dora. This may be part of the counter-transference – the phenomenon whereby the analyst transfers feelings onto the analysand, just as the analysand transfers feelings onto the analyst – that characterized Freud's therapeutic relationship with Dora but which was not properly theorized or acknowledged at the time of her treatment (Mahony 1996). The translator's misreading thus draws our attention to an interesting and revealing linguistic 'complex' within Freud's text, one that might become apparent to readers who are prompted by the logical incoherence of Whiteside's phrase to consult the text's other translations or the source text itself.

A further example of a motivated error on the part of the translator occurs in Whiteside's rendering of one of Freud's iterations of Dora's symptoms ('Husten und Stimmlosigkeit', Freud 2007 [1905]:29), described in the various translations as 'the cough and the loss of voice' (Freud, trans. Strachey 2001:27), 'the coughing and mood swings' (Freud, trans. Whiteside 2006:20), and 'the cough, the loss of voice' (Freud, trans. Bell 2013:22). The Whiteside translation jars with the other two here, suggesting either an error in one or all of the translations or a hermeneutic difference of opinion. Consultation with the German text reveals that over the course of the case study, the symptoms attributed to Dora by Freud and her father include both *Verstimmung* (Freud 2007 [1905]:26, 28) and *Stimmlosigkeit*. *Verstimmung* is indicative of some degree of mood shift but it is also used to describe the out-of-tuneness of a musical instrument. *Stimmlosigkeit* refers to loss of voice, a symptom that Freud also describes using the technical term *Aphonie* (aphonia) (Freud 2007 [1905]:26). On this particular occasion, Dora has lost her voice, but Whiteside's error is far from random and is motivated by the morphological relationship between the two German words, which both contain *Stimm*, found in *Stimme* (voice) and *stimmen* (to agree or to tune). The translator's 'error' once again draws attention to Freud's networks of signification and to the fact that Dora's symptoms centre on a lost or off-kilter 'voice'. This is surely of importance for a narrative in which Dora's voice reaches us only through Freud the narrator, and is perhaps indicative of Freud's subconscious awareness of this fact. For the reader of Freud in translation, it may be difficult to assess which, if any, of the translations contains an error, or if the discordant translations highlight an ambiguity in the source text itself. The close relationship between the two symptoms of coughing and voice loss might lead the reader to believe that this is the correct translation. Then again, since Dora's symptoms are always both physical *and* emotional, this may be an erroneous assumption, and once again it would be dangerous to presume that the majority rendering is in the right, as translation errors can be perpetuated from translation to translation, sometimes over centuries. What this example highlights is the need to be attentive to variations across translations and cautious when constructing an argument on the basis of close reading in translation.

The reader's understanding of the critical events and symptomology of Dora's case is dependent upon the translators' interpretation of Freud's narrative and therefore of his voice. For present-day translators of 'Dora', the well-known criticisms of the Standard Edition and the wave of psychoanalytic and feminist psychoanalytic literary criticism that peaked in the 1990s, with its particular critique of Dora's treatment at Freud's hands (see, for example, Bernheimer and Kahane 1990; Mahony 1996), will inevitably influence their attitudes towards both Dora and Freud and hence will find expression in their texts. The decisions involved in rendering Dora's hysterical symptoms and the medical conditions of other 'characters' in the Dora story are a good example of this. The Standard Edition's preference for medical terminology has been noted already. Thus, in Strachey's translation, Dora suffers from 'chronic dyspnoea with occasional accesses' (Freud, trans. Strachey 2001:21), a description which is likely to have the non-medically trained reaching for the dictionary, whereas in Whiteside's translation Dora is suffering from 'a chronic respiratory illness with occasional violent aggravations' (Freud, trans. Whiteside 2006:16). Bell's phrasing is much more mindful of the lay person and in fact reflects Freud's own terminus, the prosaic *Atemnot* [literally breath-need] (Freud 2007 [1905]:23): 'permanent and sometimes very marked breathlessness' (Freud, trans. Bell 2013:16). There is a general tendency in the two most recent translations to avoid overly medical terminology in the mode of the Standard Edition and to clarify in those instances where such terminology is used – note Bell's 'aphonia or voice-loss' (ibid:19). In one particular instance – Freud's discussion of Dora's father's syphilis, contracted before his marriage to Dora's mother – this serves to make the situation much clearer for the modern reader. Thus the Standard Edition's 'and since the patient admitted having had a specific infection before his marriage, I prescribed an energetic course of anti-luetic treatment' (Freud, trans. Strachey 2001:19), which has a Monty Python-esque 'say no more' quality for the modern reader, becomes in Bell's version a much more straightforward 'and after he had admitted to a specific infection before his marriage, I prescribed a course of vigorous anti-syphilitic treatment' (Freud, trans. Bell 2013:15). Dora's main symptoms following her family's move to Vienna (Freud 2007

[1905]:25) are variously described as 'low spirits and an alteration in her character' (Freud, trans. Strachey 2001:23), 'mood swings and character changes' (Freud, trans. Whiteside 2006:17) and 'low spirits and a change in her character' (Freud, trans. Bell 2013:18). 'Low spirits' and 'mood swings' are the translators' renderings of *Verstimmung*. On a later occasion, this descriptively ambiguous term of Freud's is translated as 'depression' (Freud, trans. Strachey 2001:24)), 'mood swings' (Freud, trans. Whiteside 2006:18) and 'bad temper' (Freud, trans. Bell 2013:19). There is tremendous variation here, suggesting a range of behaviour and a spectrum of severity from irritation and grumpiness to melancholia and a psychiatric disorder. The diagnosis of hysteria is one that would no longer be made today, of course, and to a certain extent the lexical variation in the translations reflects the fact that a particular individual's *Verstimmung* – their out-of-tuneness – is very much in the eye of the beholder (Freud's, in this case), but it also draws our attention to the complexity of mental illness and the potential for shifting, and gendered, diagnosis over time.

Freud's attitude towards Dora is given different nuances in the various translations. The *taedium vitae* from which she is described as suffering (Freud 2007 [1905]:26) is either insincere ('not entirely genuine' (Freud, trans. Strachey 2001:24), 'probably not meant seriously' (Freud, trans. Bell 2013:19)) – thus placing Dora at fault – or 'probably not to be taken seriously' (Freud, trans. Whiteside 2006:18), which implies that Dora could indeed be tired of life but that Freud chooses to believe that her sentiments are not genuine. Dora's father, as quoted by Freud (Freud 2007 [1905]:28), describes her as suffering from 'suicidal ideas' (Freud, trans. Strachey 2001:26), 'ideas of suicide' (Freud, trans. Bell 2013:21) or 'notions of suicide' (Freud, trans. Whiteside 2006:19). 'Notions', much more so than 'ideas', suggests that Dora's expressions of suicidal thoughts are treated dismissively by the men in her life, thus constructing a particular picture of these men for the reader. Dora is described as busying herself 'with attending lectures for women and with carrying on more or less serious studies' (Freud, trans. Strachey 2001:23), but in Whiteside and Bell's translations the qualifying 'more or less', which belittles either her efforts at education or the quality of the education on offer, has vanished. In Whiteside's translation, furthermore, the audience for the lectures that Dora attends has lost its gendered aspect (Freud, trans. Whiteside 2006:17).

The precise nature of a further incident with Herr K., which occurred after the shop incident but was the first of the two incidents to be related to Freud, and which occurred while Dora and Herr K. were taking a walk after a boat trip (Freud 2007 [1905]:27), is interpreted very differently by the three translators. In the Standard Edition, Herr K. 'makes her a proposal' (Freud, trans. Strachey 2001:25), which is quite ambiguous, implying a range of behaviours from a marriage proposal to a sexual overture. In Whiteside's version, Herr K. makes a much more old-fashioned 'declaration of love' (Freud, trans. Whiteside 2006:19). In Bell's translation – which, it should be noted, is the only translation of 'Dora' by a woman thus far – Herr K. 'makes advances to her' (Freud, trans. Bell 2013:20), a much more aggressive act. Freud's infamous hypothesis that Dora had felt Herr K.'s erection during the shop incident (Freud 2007 [1905]:31) and that she must necessarily be hysterical because she had failed to feel sexual excitement during this encounter (ibid:30) is given different inflections in the various translations:

> This perception was revolting to her; it was dismissed from her memory.
> (Freud, trans. Strachey 2001:30)

> This – to her – repellent perception was excised from memory.
> (Freud, trans. Whiteside 2006:22)

> This perception, which disgusted her, was removed from her memory.
> (Freud, trans. Bell 2013:24)

In Whiteside's translation, the use of dashes to emphasize that another woman – or a man – might not have found this sensation repellent reinforces Freud's extraordinary point of view, which essentially condones Herr K.'s sexual aggression towards a teenage girl.

Freud cannot help but reveal himself through his narration of 'Dora' and his interaction with the reader, of whom he demonstrates an 'abiding awareness' (Mahony 1987:55). The reader is essential to Freud's endeavours since, as Mahony has argued, his texts manifest the quality of *pensée pensante* or 'processiveness, ongoing, progressive, evolving, or unfolding movement' (ibid:120–1) and this thinking out loud requires witnesses, interlocutors, addressees. Bettelheim argues that Freud addresses the reader directly because he saw this inclusive appeal as a way of combating 'the universal wish to remain unaware of one's own unconscious' (1984 [1982]:7). In the Standard Edition, however, the presence of the reader has been much reduced. Where the reader is directly invoked in Freud's narrative through the use of the pronoun *wir* [we] in German, this is often eradicated. For example, the Stracheys translate 'It will be remembered' (Freud, trans. Strachey 2001:49) where Bell opts for 'Let us remind ourselves' (Freud, trans. Bell 2013:71) and Whiteside 'Let us recall that' (Freud, trans. Whiteside 2006:71). In the postscript to his case study of Dora, Freud muses on the necessity of sacrificing a general account of the therapeutic process in order to produce a clear narrative for the case study (Freud 2007 [1905]:110). Not to have made this sacrifice, he argues, would mean, in the words of the Standard Edition, that 'the result would have been almost unreadable' (Freud, trans. Strachey 2001:112), but for whom? In Whiteside's version, as in Bell's, the focus of Freud's concern is clear: 'it would certainly have made a disagreeable experience for the reader' (Freud, trans. Whiteside 2006:100) and 'it would probably not have been a pleasant experience for the reader' (Freud, trans. Bell 2013:96). The reader's sense of Freud's voice, of his behaviour and his attitude towards Dora and the extent to which he involves the reader in this early case study can vary tremendously according to the translation one reads. Freud's conclusion that Dora must be in love with Herr K. is put to her, in the Standard Edition, in words which suggest no doubt as to this fact on Freud's part and make Dora seem petulant in her refusal of Freud's fait accompli ('When I informed her of this conclusion she did not assent to it', Freud, trans. Strachey 2001:37), but in the other translations Freud's words are much more speculative and allow Dora space for dissent ('When I put this conclusion into words, she rejected it', Freud, trans. Bell 2013:31; or 'When I voiced this deduction, Dora disagreed', Freud, trans. Whiteside 2006:28). Freud's words in German, 'Als ich diese Folgerung aussprach, fand ich keine Zustimmung bei ihr' (Freud 2007 [1905]:39) (literally, as I uttered this conclusion, I found no agreement in her), put the emphasis on the analyst, who fishes in vain for a particular response to an idea that may only have come into being at the moment of being spoken aloud.

There are other such examples that affect our understanding of how Freud conducted and conceived of this new *Kur*. When reflecting upon his analysis of the first of Dora's two dreams, Freud remarks upon his failure to enquire into a statement made within the dream by Dora's father (Freud 2007 [1905]:91), concluding that if he had done so it would probably have revealed the structure of the dream to be more complicated but also rendered it 'easier to penetrate' (Freud, trans. Strachey 2001:92). The presence of such a sexually charged word to describe the process of dream interpretation is highly suggestive and pushes the reader towards a particular view of the process; yet if we consult the other two translations, the word 'penetrate' has vanished, replaced with 'more transparent' (Freud, trans. Bell 2013:79) and 'easier to recognize' (Freud, trans. Whiteside 2006:78). Bell's translation is equivalent to the German term used by Freud ('durchsichtiger'), but Strachey's lexical infelicity may indeed tap into the undertone of Freud's text as a whole. Similarly, in the postscript to his case study, Freud reiterates his belief that sexuality is crucial to an understanding of the psychoneuroses (Freud 2007 [1905]:112), and in the Standard Edition he warns those who would reject this conviction using a striking metaphor: 'No one who disdains the key will ever be able to unlock the door' (Freud, trans. Strachey 2001:115). This recalls an earlier use of the same metaphor in a different context. During the process of interpreting Dora's first dream in an analytic session, Dora comes to associate the presence of her father next to her bed in the dream with finding Herr K. standing next to her bed as she awoke from a nap in real life (Freud 2007 [1905]:66). Herr K. was able to enter Dora's bedroom because there was no key in the door. Freud connects Dora's use of the German word *Zimmer* (room) with a pejorative word used to denote women, *Frauenzimmer* (literally: women's room), and reads the locking and unlocking of Dora's room sexually, as symbolic of her own person. In the footnote to this section of the case study (ibid), Freud remarks with no little innuendo that 'The question of whether a woman is "open" or "shut" can naturally not be a matter of indifference. It is well known, too, what sort of "key" effects the opening in such a case' (Freud, trans. Strachey 2001:67). The use of exactly the same metaphor to describe the importance of sexuality for his theory of the psychoneuroses can surely not be 'a matter of indifference', to echo Freud's own words. In the Whiteside and Bell translations, however, the metaphor is absent: 'No one who scorns this idea will ever be in a position to solve this problem' (Freud, trans. Whiteside 2006:102–3) and 'Those who reject that idea will never be able to solve it' (Freud, trans. Bell 2013:98). The metaphor is, however, present in the German text.

One aspect of the source text neglected by all three of the translations discussed here is the 'charm, flexibility, and force of Freud's Viennese expression [which] differs markedly from the typical rigidity of his German counterparts' (Mahony 1987:18). Freud's 'Dora' is distinctly Austrian, which will not be apparent to the English reader. In the example of the key/door metaphor above, for instance, the German word rendered as 'disdain', 'scorn' and 'reject' by the various translators is 'verschmähen' (Freud 2007 [1905]:113), a verb which occurs with more frequency in Austrian, Swiss and Southern German varieties of German. In a statement where Freud remarks on women's pride in their genitals being characteristic of their vanity, in the German the women are 'our women' ('bei unseren Frauen', Freud 2007 [1905]:83), which not only suggests that Freud is primarily addressing a male audience of his peers, but also has a distinctly Austrian ring to it. This connotation is not present in any of the English translations, however; it might take a rendering into a regional variety of English to hint at some of the effect.

### How do we assess the success of a literary translation?

As this discussion of Freud shows, translations document their source texts idiosyncratically. Anglophone culture encounters the Stracheys' Freud, Whiteside's Freud and Bell's Freud, but not Freud himself in any unmediated fashion. Our picture of Freud, of his patients and of psychoanalysis will greatly depend on the translation or translations in which we encounter Freud's (and Jung's and Lacan's) work. The fewer the number of translations of a given text in the receiving culture and the longer the period of time during which a particular translation holds sway, the more likely it is that the reception of that text will be heavily influenced by those translations and that new translations will be seen as audacious challengers and/or as vehicles of great innovation. Neither of these claims must necessarily be true: the re-translation hypothesis, a teleological view of translation proposed as necessarily improving with each new version of a source text (Berman 1990), has certainly been widely criticized (see, for example, Gambier 1994; Susam-Sarjeva 2003). Translations can be 'wrong' in the sense that they contain errors, as we have seen. Whether or not one chooses to view these errors as motivated and worthy of analysis depends on one's knowledge of the material facts of the translation in question (was the translator pressed for time? did he or she have a sufficient grasp of the subject matter?) and on one's belief in the explanatory powers of psychoanalysis. It does seem fair to say, however, that a translation can have great literary merit and still contain errors, but that once the number and severity of errors reaches a critical mass, the literary merit of a text will suffer. We must assume, however, that the vast majority of professional literary translators have more than adequate competence in both source and target languages and will acquit their task well. Thus the 'success' of a translated text, rather than being a matter of accuracy – minor hiccups and miscomprehensions notwithstanding – has to do with its success as a particularly complex type of literary text rather than in terms of its relationship to its source. The relationship between source and target is in fact something that few people are qualified to assess, and despite Clive Scott's engaged plea for more parallel reading of source and target texts based on a concept of complementarity rather than replacement (2012a:179), the primacy of translations created to serve the needs of the monolingual reader is unlikely to be displaced any time soon. But if the relationship between a translation and its source text – and the history of translation thought has revolved around statements describing or prescribing the nature of this relationship – is not the best basis on which to judge the success of a translation, then why do translators, rather than allowing themselves to be loosely inspired by a source text and producing a work of art that is more akin to an adaptation, work their way line by line through a source text, creating something tied to another text, even if the nature of that tie still has the potential to vary enormously? The answer is that translators are trying to understand the unique literariness of the source text, 'being alert to its moods and directions, to the ways in which it *makes* its meanings' (Scott 2000:247), practising the stylistic sensitivity argued for by Boase-Beier (Boase-Beier 2006, 2011) in order to draw on the source text's literariness as the 'ground of an ethics of innovation in the translating culture' (Venuti 2013b:8). The translator is both a highly attentive reader and a writer who produces a text that ideally offers the reader the potential for cognitive gains. The complexity of the source text, which is the complexity inherent in all literary texts, combined with the unique context of the individual translator (biographical, temporal, geographical, readerly), the wider cultural framework in which the translation comes into being and is received and the unique context of the target-culture reader will affect the ways in which the translated text makes its meanings. So it is the translation's complex literariness to which we should be attentive rather than merely the equivalence of source and target (especially if we can conceive of equivalence only at the level of individual linguistic units or the sentence), and we should resist the temptation to rank translations in a hierarchy from best to worst. Breon Mitchell, who re-translated Günter Grass' seminal post-war novel *Die Blechtrommel* [*The Tin Drum*] (1959) forty-seven years after Ralph Manheim's contemporaneous translation, addresses this issue in his translator's afterword:

> The most common question I faced while working on the new *Tin Drum* was, 'What was wrong with the old one?' This question reveals a fundamental misunderstanding about the nature of literary translation. [. . .] We translate great works because they deserve it – because the power and depth of the text can never be fully revealed by a single translation, however inspired. A translation is a reading, and every reading is necessarily personal, perhaps even idiosyncratic. Each new version offers, not a better reading, but a different one, one that foregrounds new aspects of the text, that sees it through new eyes, that makes it new.
> 
> (Mitchell 2009:567)

In assessing a translation then, particularly in a situation where various versions of a source text are available for comparative analysis, we should not be asking 'Which is the best translation?' or even 'Is this a good translation?' but 'How does this translated literary text make its meanings?'.

## T(w)in drummers

The two English translations of Grass' text present a pertinent case study of how we might go about assessing the literary qualities of different translations. Ralph Manheim's translation was published in 1962, only three years after *Die Blechtrommel* first appeared in Germany. Breon Mitchell's translation appeared subsequent to Mitchell's participation in the 2005 Gdańsk translation workshop that was organized to mark the impending fiftieth anniversary of the novel's publication, a workshop led by Grass himself. Manheim's *Tin Drum* does not feature a translator's introduction or afterword, whereas Mitchell's includes a thirteen-page afterword in which he addresses the part played by Manheim's translation in 'catapult[ing] its young German author to the forefront of world literature' (Mitchell 2009:565) and outlines the differences between Manheim's translation and his own, many of which stem from the fifty-year interval between the production of the two texts.

*Die Blechtrommel* is a doorstopper of a novel which offers a magical realist portrayal of the Nazi and post-war eras. In common with the Latin American magical realist tradition, it offers an alternative, grass-roots perspective on historical events – here the coming and going of the Third Reich. It features as protagonist and highly unreliable narrator Oskar Matzerath, a child born into a grocer's family in Danzig, who at the age of three receives a tin drum for his birthday and takes the momentous decision to stop growing, thus becoming a dwarf. In Grass' own introduction to Mitchell's re-translation, he writes that the 'disgusting or blasphemous' parts of the book, which include Oskar's accounts of his sexual adventures and tales of the escapades of others, were frequently censored in contemporaneous translations (Grass 2009:viii); these have been restored in the Mitchell version. Mitchell himself points out that certain intertextual relationships have emerged in the years since 1959. Thus, for example, cooks have emerged as a theme in Grass' wider oeuvre and this has affected the way in which a figure referred to as the *schwarze Köchin* [black cook] appears in English. Whereas in Manheim's translation, the black cook 'was reduced to a generic "witch, black as pitch"' (Mitchell 2009:571), in Mitchell's version *schwarze Köchin* is translated literally as Black Cook. The main differences between Manheim's and Mitchell's translations are stylistic, however. Mitchell argues that Manheim's overall approach, although 'often against the grain of standard literature' (ibid:570), is generally smoothing and that the openness of modern readers to foreignness has allowed the new translation to emphasize the more challenging elements of Grass' style, particularly the syntactic complexity of the novel.

Let us compare Manheim and Mitchell's respective approaches in the chapter 'Glaube, Hoffnung, Liebe' (Grass 1993 [1959]:253–64) [Faith, Hope, Love]. This chapter depicts the events of *Kristallnacht*, including the suicide of the Jewish toymaker who supplies Oskar's drums. In keeping with the alternative history of Grass' magical realist approach, *Kristallnacht* is deliberately portrayed as the incidental backdrop to a number of dramas closer to home: the death and funeral of Oskar's friend Herbert Truczinksi and the reaction to this death of Herbert's alcoholic friend Meyn, a trumpet player who has joined the music corps of the SA and who batters his four cats almost to death in his alcohol-fuelled grief. The chapter displays the striking parallel syntax and repetition characteristic of fairytales, using the phrase 'Es war einmal', the German equivalent of 'Once upon a time' or 'There was once', to indicate when a character is being 'introduced' – the reader has in fact met all of these characters at earlier stages in the novel – or when new details are forthcoming about a character who has already featured in the chapter. Here is the opening example, taken from Manheim's translation:

> There was once a musician; his name was Meyn and he played the trumpet too beautifully for words. He lived on the fifth floor of an apartment house, just under the roof, he kept four cats, one of which was called Bismarck, and from morning to night he drank out of a gin bottle. This he did until sobered by disaster.
> (Grass, trans. Manheim 1998:181)

We are given exactly the same information in the seventh paragraph of the chapter, but with a slight variation: 'and from morning to night he drank out of a gin bottle until, late in '36 or early in '37 I think it was, he joined the Mounted SA' (ibid:182). The conventional language of fairytale is both at odds and – with the propensity of fairytales to evoke savage violence – in grotesque harmony with the events depicted within the chapter: the violent battering of four cats and attempts to cover up the deed; the discovery of the half-dead cats, in a stroke of irony, by another Nazi who happens to be an animal-lover and who reports Meyn to the authorities; and the coexistence of this animal-oriented aggression and sentimentality with the destruction wreaked during *Kristallnacht*, all told from Oskar's faux-naïve perspective. At its close, the chapter descends into linguistic and narrative chaos, calling into question the ability of language to remain untainted when faced with the burden of representing evil.

The Mitchell and Manheim translations do display significant syntactic differences that affect the order in which information is presented to the reader. When Oskar's friend Herbert is buried, Leo Schugger, or Crazy Leo in Mitchell's version, offers his condolences to the assembled mourners.

> When Herbert was buried in Langfuhr Cemetery, I once again saw Leo Schugger, whose acquaintance I had made at Brenntau. Slavering and holding out his white mildewed gloves, he tendered his sympathies, those sympathies of his which made little distinction between joy and sorrow, to all the assembled company, to Mother Truczinski, to Guste, Fritz and Maria Truczinski, to the corpulent Mrs. Kater, to old man Heilandt, who slaughtered Fritz' rabbits for Mother Truczinski on holidays, to my presumptive father Matzerath, who, generous as he could be at times, defrayed a good half of the funeral

expenses, even to Jan Bronski, who hardly knew Herbert and had only come to see Matzerath and perhaps myself on neutral cemetery ground.
(Grass, trans. Manheim 1998:181–2)

When Herbert was buried at Langfuhr Cemetery, I saw Crazy Leo again, whose acquaintance I'd made at Brentau Cemetery. To all of us – Mother Truczinski, Guste, Fritz and Maria Truczinski, the stout Frau Kater, old Heilandt, who slaughtered Fritz' rabbits for Mother Truczinski on holidays, to my presumptive father Matzerath, who, generous as he could be at times, was paying half the burial costs, and Jan Bronski, who scarcely knew Herbert and had only come to see Matzerath, and possibly me, on neutral burial ground – to all of us Crazy Leo, drooling and trembling, extended his white, mildewed glove, offering confused condolences in which joy and pain seemed indistinguishable.
(Grass, trans. Mitchell 2009:181)

In Manheim's version, Leo first holds out his hand in greeting then tenders his sympathies to the many mourners, who are listed only at the end of the very long sentence (Grass, trans. Manheim:181–2). In Mitchell's version, the mourners are listed first, and only then does Leo extend his hand to finally offer his condolences. The effect, in Manheim's translation, is to drive the narrative onwards, to give us further information about Leo Schugger following the reintroduction of his character at this juncture in the novel. In Mitchell's version, the wealth of detail given to the reader before he or she learns what Leo Schugger is doing in the cemetery contributes to the fairytale register and confounds the reader's curiosity by withholding information until the end of the sentence. This syntactic approach also foregrounds the 'obsession with detail' and the battle over the 'obscure constraints of chronology' which Grass has described as characteristic of his novel (Grass 2009:viii).

Later in the chapter, when Oskar enters the toy shop from which he procures his tin drums and finds Markus the toymaker sitting lifeless behind his desk, the sentence which implies that Markus has committed suicide in the face of Nazi thuggery receives markedly different treatments in the two translations:

Before him on the desk stood an empty water glass; the sound of his crashing shopwindow had made him thirsty no doubt.
(Grass, trans. Manheim 1998:187)

Before him on the desk-top stood a water glass that thirst must have urged him to empty at the very moment the splintering cry of a window in his shop turned his throat dry.
(Grass, trans. Mitchell 2009:187)

It is immediately apparent that Mitchell's sentence is much longer than Manheim's (thirty-four words to Manheim's twenty-two) and features no punctuation beyond the closing full stop. In Manheim's translation, cause and effect are very clear – the breaking of Markus' shop window made the toymaker thirsty – whereas in Mitchell's translation cause and effect are more confused – thirst appears to be the reason why Markus emptied his glass, and the shop window happened to break at exactly the same time his thirst struck. The ironic naïvety of Oskar's observation comes across in both versions, but Manheim's version relies on the flair of its rapid delivery for its effect and Mitchell's on the long drawn-out presentation of information and the terrible coincidence of thirst and thuggery. In both of these examples Mitchell's versions are much closer to Grass' own syntactic rhythms.

Humour, often very dark in tone, plays a significant part in the success of Grass' novel, and there are numerous instances in which Manheim's lexical and collocational choices, his brevity of syntax and sheer writerly skill achieves more of a humorous effect than Mitchell's version. For example, after Meyn has disposed of his four half-dead cats, he returns to his flat which, in Manheim's words, 'though catless still stank of cats' (Grass, trans. Manheim 1998:184), and in Mitchell's was 'a catless flat that still smelled of cats' (Grass, trans. Mitchell 2009:184). Manheim's separation of 'catless' from the noun that it qualifies and the alliteration of 'still stank' contrive to produce a more humorous rendering. Elsewhere in the chapter, in Manheim's more colloquial rendering the cats are described as 'tough customers, as cats tend to be' (Grass, trans. Manheim 1998:185), whereas in Mitchell's words they are 'tough, like most cats' (Grass, trans. Mitchell 2009:184). In a further example, after Meyn has fallen off the wagon, he finds himself ginless, but is too embarrassed to leave his flat to purchase another bottle for fear of what the neighbours might say, as he had publicly

> embarked on a new life of rigorous sobriety [...] away with the vapors of a botched and aimless youth
> (Grass, trans. Manheim 1998:183)

> start[ed] a new life of total sobriety [...] far removed from the drunken excesses of a wasted and unstable youth
> (Grass, trans. Mitchell 2009:183)

The unusual collocation of 'rigorous' and 'sobriety', the choice of the word 'vapors', which conjures up fumes of alcohol on a person's breath, and the colloquial term 'botched' all contribute to Manheim's foregrounding of the novel's comedic aspects.

Towards the end of the chapter, when narrative breaks down and Oskar's stream of consciousness disturbingly jumbles the Christian values of faith, hope and love with the coming Christmas season and a Hitleresque figure called the gasman (notably capitalized in Mitchell's version) who is the new saviour of the world, not to forget sausage stuffing and words in dictionaries, Manheim and Mitchell demonstrate markedly different approaches, as illustrated here:

> I know not wherewith they fill the dictionaries or sausage casings, I know not whose meat, I know not whose language: words communicate, butchers won't tell
> (Grass, trans. Manheim 1998:189)

> don't know what fills those dictionaries, fills those casings, don't know what flesh, don't know what tongue: a word has a meaning, a butcher is silent
> (Grass, trans. Mitchell 2009:189)

Mitchell's lexis is visceral, even more so than Grass', which uses the word *Sprache* [language] rather than *Zunge* [tongue]; it can be read as a reference to the horrors of the concentration camps and their reduction of the human being to his or her emaciated body. The elision of the subject pronoun 'I' brings an urgency to the statements and strengthens the rhythm, which is striking throughout this section of the chapter. Manheim's syntax and lexis are more formal ('I know not wherewith') and eerily reminiscent of the words of Jesus upon the cross in the King James version of Luke 23:34, as he asks God to forgive those who have put him to death: 'Forgive them, Father, for they know not what they do'. Here Manheim appears to be strengthening the theme of ignorance and guilt that permeates Grass' novel, the question of the extent to which ordinary Germans were ignorant or willing accomplices of the genocide committed under the Nazi regime. But in tapping into the language of English Bible translations and specifically the phrase used by Jesus at the moment of his crucifixion, Manheim also strengthens the association between Christianity and anti-Semitism that is forged in this chapter, which, after all, bears the three theological virtues in its title.

Read in isolation, the individual examples discussed above would hardly provide enough evidence to support a particular reading or impression of *The Tin Drum*, but perceived as individual instances of tendencies that recur throughout a translation of some 550 pages, they have the ability to dramatically shape our encounter with the novel. Although one can identify qualitative differences between the two translations – Manheim's translation may well be funnier, for example – overall the choices made by the two translators add up to different novels rather than to an inferior or a superior version. *The Tin Drum* is eminently translatable, in Walter Benjamin's sense of that term: it calls out for translation, its complex literariness can be mined and mined again and the translators who have done so show us that translation is a unique form of reading and writing and should be appreciated as such.

### Exercises

1. Write a review of a new translation. Consider any paratexts created by the translator or by other agents (publishers, scholarly experts, celebrities) that give the reader an indication of why this text was selected for translation or re-translation and what the translator's general approach might be. Look at the style of the translation and consider its success as an 'instrumental' text, bearing in mind its dual authorship. Investigate the context of the source text and the translation: to what extent is the text representative of its source literary culture; why is it being brought into the receiving culture at this particular moment?
2. Keep a reader's diary while reading a literary translation from a language with which you are not familiar, noting anything that comes to mind but particularly anything that strikes you as arising from the translated nature of the text. This might include elements of local colour, stylistic innovation, defamiliarization or hybridity, evidence of localization or domestication, genre alignment or misalignment etc. Are you able to identify whether foregrounded features arise from the source text, the author, the translator or the source language?
3. Choose a text that has been translated more than once and write a comparative analysis of a key paragraph or paragraphs in a selection of the translations available.
4. Collect a corpus of translation reviews from a particular publication, by a particular reviewer, of a particular book or of a selection of books from a specific source culture and analyse them for evidence of implicitly or explicitly held beliefs about translation. Describe their reviewing practice(s).

## Further reading: thinking more about how we read translations

In the Bibliography below see Allen 2014; Boase-Beier 2006, 2011; Damrosch 2009; Maier and Massardier-Kenney 2010; Venuti 2002, 2004, 2013b.

## Bibliography

Allen, E., 2014. Lost in the Book Review. *In Other Words* 44, pp. 26–33.
Authors' Licensing and Collecting Society, 2014. *What Are Words Worth Now? A Survey of Author's Earnings*. London: Authors' Licensing and Collecting Society. Available at: www.alcs.co.uk/Documents/what-are-words-worth-now.aspx [accessed 30 March 2015].

Bachmann, I., 2006. *Darkness Spoken. The Collected Poems*. Translated from German by P. Filkins. Brookline, MA: Zephyr Press.
Bachmann, I., 2011. *Enigma. Selected Poems*. Translated from German by M. Lyons and P. Drysdale. Riverside, CA: Ariadne Press.
BBC Radio 4, 2004. *Toast*, A Good Read. 21 December 2004. Available at: www.bbc.co.uk/programmes/p00d3wtq [accessed 1 April 2015].
Benjamin, W., 1991 [1923]. Die Aufgabe des Übersetzers. In: W. Benjamin, *Gesammelte Schriften Band IV. 1*. Frankfurt am Main: Suhrkamp. pp. 9–21.
Berman, A., 1990. La retraduction comme espace de la traduction. *Palimpsestes* 4, pp. 1–8.
Berman, A., 2008. *L'Âge de la Traduction*. Saint-Denis: Presses Universitaires de Vincennes.
Berman, A., 2012 [1985]. Translation and the Trials of the Foreign. Translated from French by L. Venuti. In: L. Venuti, ed. *The Translation Studies Reader*. 3rd ed. New York: Routledge. pp. 240–53.
Bernheimer, C. and Kahane, C., eds. 1990. *In Dora's Case: Freud – Hysteria – Feminism*. New York: Columbia University Press.
Bettelheim, B., 1984 [1982]. *Freud and Man's Soul*. New York: Vintage.
Bird, R., 2014. Forever Young. *The Times Literary Supplement*, 19 September 2014, pp. 4–5.
Boase-Beier, J., 2006. *Stylistic Approaches to Translation*. Manchester: St. Jerome.
Boase-Beier, J., 2011. *A Critical Introduction to Translation Studies*. London: Continuum.
Boase-Beier, J. and Holman, M., 1999. Introduction: Writing, Rewriting and Translation. In: J. Boase-Beier and M. Holman, eds. *The Practices of Literary Translation*. Manchester: St. Jerome. pp. 1–17.
Chesterman, A., 2009. The View from Memetics. *Paradigmi*, 27(2), pp. 75–88.
Christ, R., 2010. Translation Transvalued. In: C. Maier and F. Massardier-Kenney, eds. *Literature in Translation*. Kent, Ohio: Kent State University Press. pp. 85–96.
Damrosch, D., 2003. *What Is World Literature?* Princeton and Oxford: Princeton University Press.
Damrosch, D., ed. 2009. *How to Read World Literature*. Chichester: Wiley-Blackwell.
Dryden, J., 2012 [1680]. From the Preface to *Ovid's Epistles*. In: L. Venuti, ed. *The Translation Studies Reader*. 3rd ed. New York: Routledge. pp. 38–42.
Even-Zohar, I., 2012 [1978]. Translated Literature in the Polysystem. In: L. Venuti, ed. *The Translation Studies Reader*. 3rd ed. New York: Routledge. pp. 162–7.
Fauconnier, G. and Turner, M., 2002. *The Way We Think*. New York: Basic Books.
Filkins, P., 2006a. On the Border of Speech. In: I. Bachmann. *Darkness Spoken. The Collected Poems*. Translated from German by P. Filkins. Brookline, MA: Zephyr Press. pp. xx–xxxvii.
Filkins, P., 2006b. Translator's Note. In: I. Bachmann. *Darkness Spoken. The Collected Poems*. Translated from German by P. Filkins. Brookline, MA: Zephyr Press. pp. xxxviii–xxxix.
France, P., 2000. Dostoevsky. In: P. France, ed. *The Oxford Guide to Literature in English Translation*. Oxford: Oxford University Press. pp. 594–8.

Freely, M., 2013. Misreading Orhan Pamuk. In: E. Allen and S. Bernofsky, eds. *In Translation: Translators on Their Work and What It Means*. New York: Columbia University Press. pp. 117–26.
Freud, S., 2001 [1953]. Fragment of an Analysis of a Case of Hysteria (1905 [1901]). Translated from German by A. Strachey and J. Strachey. In: J. Strachey, ed. *The Standard Edition of the Complete Psychological Works of Sigmund Freud*. Vol. VII (1901–1905). London: Vintage. pp. 7–122.
Freud, S., 2006. Fragment of an Analysis of Hysteria (Dora). Translated from German by S. Whiteside. In: S. Freud, *The Psychology of Love*. London: Penguin. pp. 3–109.
Freud, S., 2007 [1905]. *Bruchstück einer Hysterie-Analyse*. Frankfurt am Main: Fischer.
Freud, S., 2013. *A Case of Hysteria (Dora)*. Translated from German by A. Bell. Oxford: Oxford University Press.
Freud, S. and Breuer, J. 2004. *Studies in Hysteria*. Translated from German by N. Luckhurst. London: Penguin.
Gambier, Y., 1994. La Retraduction, Retour et Détour. *Meta*, 39(3), pp. 413–17.
Grass, G., 1993 [1959]. *Die Blechtrommel*. München: Deutscher Taschenbuch Verlag.
Grass, G., 1998 [1962] [1959]. *The Tin Drum*. Translated from German by R. Manheim. London: Vintage.
Grass, G., 2010 [2009] [1959]. *The Tin Drum*. Translated from German by B. Mitchell. New York: Mariner.
Heaney, S., trans. 1999. *Beowulf*. London: Faber and Faber.
Henitiuk, V., 2012. Optical Illusions? In: R. Wilson and L. Gerber, eds. *Creative Constraints: Translation and Authorship*. Clayton, Victoria: Monash University Publishing. pp. 3–20.
Hermans, T., 2014. Positioning Translators: Voices, Views and Values in Translation. *Language and Literature*, 23(3), pp. 285–301.
Kundera, M., 2002 [2000]. *Ignorance*. Translated from French by L. Asher. London: Faber and Faber.
Mahony, P.J., 1987. *Freud as a Writer*. New Haven/London: Yale University Press.
Mahony, P.J., 1996. *Freud's Dora*. New Haven/London: Yale University Press.
Maier, C. and Massardier-Kenney, F. eds., 2010. *Literature in Translation: Teaching Issues and Reading Practices*. Kent, Ohio: Kent State University Press.
May, R., 1994. *The Translator in the Text*. Evanston, Illinois: Northwestern University Press.
Mitchell, B. 2009. Translator's Afterword. In: G. Grass. *The Tin Drum*. Translated from German by B. Mitchell. New York: Mariner. pp. 565–77.
Moi, T., 2002. While We Wait: The English Translation of 'The Second Sex'. *Signs*, 27(4), pp. 1005–35.
Moi, T., 2010. The Adulteress Wife. *London Review of Books*, 32(3), pp. 3–6.
Phillips, A., 2007. After Strachey. *London Review of Books*, 29(19), pp. 36–8.
Pym, A., 2012. *On Translator Ethics*. Translated from French by H. Walker. Amsterdam/Philadelphia: John Benjamins.
Schleiermacher, F., 2012 [2000] [1813]. On the Different Methods of Translating. Translated from German by S. Bernofsky. In: L. Venuti, ed. *The Translation Studies Reader*. 3rd ed. New York: Routledge. pp. 43–63.

Scott, C., 2000. *Translating Baudelaire*. Exeter: University of Exeter Press.
Scott, C., 2012a. *Translating the Perception of Text*. London: Legenda.
Scott, C., 2012b. *Literary Translation and the Rediscovery of Reading*. Cambridge: Cambridge University Press.
Spivak, G.C., 1993. The Politics of Translation. In: G.C. Spivak. *Outside in the Teaching Machine*. New York: Routledge. pp. 179–200.
Stockwell, P., 2002. *Cognitive Poetics: An Introduction*. London: Routledge.
Susam-Sarajeva, S., 2003. Multiple-Entry Visa to Travelling Theory. *Target*, 15(1), pp. 1–36.
*The Economist*, 2014. Get into Characters (New Chinese Fiction). 22 March. p. 88.
Venuti, L., 1995. *The Translator's Invisibility*. New York: Routledge.
Venuti, L., 1998. *The Scandals of Translation*. New York: Routledge.
Venuti, L., 2002. The Difference that Translation Makes: The Translator's Unconscious. In: A. Riccardi, ed. *Translation Studies: Perspectives on an Emerging Discipline*. Cambridge: Cambridge University Press. pp. 214–41.
Venuti, L., 2004. How to Read a Translation. *Words Without Borders*, July. Available at: http://wordswithoutborders.org/article/how-to-read-a-translation [accessed 8 April 2015].
Venuti, L., 2013a. The Difference that Translation Makes: The Translator's Unconscious. In: L. Venuti. *Translation Changes Everything*. New York: Routledge. pp. 32–56.
Venuti, L., 2013b. Introduction. In: L. Venuti. 2013. *Translation Changes Everything*. New York: Routledge. pp. 1–10.
Waisman, S., 2010. Between Reading and Writing. In: C. Maier and F. Massardier-Kenney, eds. *Literature in Translation*. Kent, Ohio, Kent State University Press. pp. 69–84.
Wang, H., 2014. *Name the Translator*. Personal communication, 27 October, 2014.
Whiteside, S., 2006. Translator's Preface. In: S. Freud. Fragment of an Analysis of Hysteria (Dora). Translated from German by S. Whiteside. In: Freud, S., *The Psychology of Love*. London: Penguin. pp. xxvii–xxxii.
Yun, S., 2014. Sniffle. *London Review of Books*, 36(17), pp. 40–1.

# 3 How do translators read?

Why begin a chapter that focuses on the actual process of translation with the question 'How do translators read?' rather than 'How do translators translate?'. As we saw in the first chapter of this book, the answer to the latter question has much to do with the answer to the question '*Why* do we translate?'. The type of target text created by a translator can be influenced ideologically, for instance, or may be the result of a creative, self-exploratory impulse or both of these things. But regardless of what a literary translator understands the purpose of literary translation to be, he or she must be an accomplished reader. Translators translate on the basis of their reading experience, and target texts are written reflections of those source-text encounters. This does not mean that a target text is necessarily a wildly idiosyncratic rendering of a literary text composed in another language, unless its translator explicitly wishes it to be so. Although the translator's context inevitably plays its part in the reading encounter – there is, after all, no such thing as a neutral reading of a text: we read both from our subjectivity and *for* our subjectivity, for the mind-altering effects of literature – there are textual constraints on subjective reading. These constraints include linguistic features such as metaphor, repetition, iconicity, register and ambiguity, but also stylistic features in the broader sense such as 'voice, otherness, foreignization, contextualization and culturally-bound and universal ways of conceptualizing and expressing meaning' (Boase-Beier 2006:2). From this cognitive linguistics perspective, style is more than simply the linguistic features of a text and is indicative of the author's choices, or 'mind-style', defined by Fowler as 'any distinctive presentation of an individual mental self' (Fowler 1977:103) as inferred or constructed by the reader from the text. Even if this definition of style is not embraced or is not part of the translator's theoretical toolkit, an attentive translator will nonetheless be extremely sensitive to the style of a literary text and to the poetic effects of this style.

In this chapter I will be drawing on my own experience as a literary translator who is also a student and teacher of the discipline we call Translation Studies. As case studies of how a translator reads, I will focus on the two text-types which have broadly formed the areas of specialization in my translation career thus far: literature for children and young adults, and German exophonic literature – that is, German literature written by 'migrants' in the German language. In each case study I will draw on texts that I have translated to show how I read and the textual decisions that I make on the basis of this reading. I will address the following issues:

- How do the translator's motivations affect her approach?
- How does the translator's understanding of genre, and hence also consideration of audience, affect the process of reading for translation?
- How does the translator interpret linguistic features of style in the source text and retextualize them in the target text?
- How important is knowledge of extratextual context (historical, socio-cultural and/or biographical background, but also relevant literary scholarship) when reading for translation?
- Do translators have to arrive at an interpretation of a text's 'meaning' in order to create a coherent translation? For example, when translating poetry does the translator need to develop a sense of what a poem is 'about' before beginning to translate?

It will become obvious in the discussion that follows that my translations are informed by a range of motivations and approaches, although above all my approach is sensitive to the workings of style in the source text and stresses respect for the poetic integrity of the translation. Most of my translations aim to afford readers of the target text a literary encounter in which they, like the readers of the source text, experience a range of specific poetic effects, although, as we shall see, the stylistic features that allow for these effects in the source text may be displaced into different features in the target text – a strategy known as compensation – because of the basic fact of the lack of equivalence between languages.

## Reading for translation (1): literature for children and young adults

> The skills demonstrated by the great translators of children's books, Anthea Bell and her Asterix is just one, far surpass anything that has ever been asked of me by an adult novel [...] discipline, freshness, inventiveness, dexterity.
> 
> Daniel Hahn, 'A World for Children' (*Four Thought*, BBC Radio 4, 2014)

In a talk for BBC Radio 4's *Four Thought* series, broadcast in September 2014, translator Daniel Hahn made an impassioned plea for more translated children's literature to be made available to an Anglophone readership (BBC Radio 4, 2014). Earlier generations of English-speaking readers, fed by earlier generations of translators, were fortunate enough to access works and characters that are now classics of the Anglophone children's canon: Asterix, Tintin, Heidi, the Moomins, Pippi Longstocking, Swiss Family Robinson, The Little Prince. But Hahn points out that the channels by which that literature reached us are now closed and that the numbers of translated children's books on the Anglo-American market have become statistically pitiful. Hahn's main argument for the translation of more children's literature is a humanist one: 'If the books our children read are one of the ways they learn to map the world, well, we do well to kit them out with the very best gear we can afford' (ibid). His words echo those of another translator, Patricia Crampton, who declares that 'children are entitled to works of genius', irrespective of the nationality or language of those works (cited in Lathey 2010:187). I cannot claim that my initial foray into translating for children and young adults had these humanist motives, even if I am in complete agreement with Daniel Hahn's arguments. I have always enjoyed reading books written for children and young adults and this is probably why the first two books that I pitched to publishers happened to be written for this audience. It was fortunate for me that my pitches coincided with the success of German writer Cornelia Funke's work in English translation and that I was able to ride that particular literary wave. Over the years my reader's enjoyment has deepened into a writer's enjoyment: translating for children and young adults – documenting anarchic, funny, moving texts from cultures with a different *Weltanschauung*, but also creating instrumental texts that often move quite far away from their sources – is a particularly challenging and rewarding form of writing.

Children's literature is a misnomer both in the sense that this 'genre' encompasses several text-types – unsurprisingly, since its readership undergoes monumental physical, cognitive and emotional changes over the span of its involvement with this literature – and that there is no 'single vision of childhood behind [it]' (Reynolds 2011:29). Children's literature translators can be called upon to translate picture storybooks, easy readers, chapter books, young adult novels, crossover titles and even texts for young learners of English, each of which carries its own set of challenges. Oittinen has argued that we should speak of 'translating for children instead of the translation of children's literature' (Oittinen 2000:69), thus placing the audience and its reading experience at the heart of the translational endeavour, and allowing for variations in age and background. Certain issues are common to the practice of translating for children, however, irrespective of the age and nature of the target audience (Oittinen 2000; Lathey 2006, 2010; Van Coillie and Verschueren 2006; Epstein 2012). These include the translation of sound, lexical issues (particularly neologism), censorship and cultural adaptation.

## Sound

The importance of sound in translating for children is most apparent in picture storybooks, which cater for pre-readers but also for the adult facilitators who read aloud and are responsible for purchasing or borrowing the books. Oittinen stresses that such texts should 'live, roll, taste good on the reading adult's tongue' (Oittinen 2000:32). The status of these books as texts for the pre-literate means that visual and aural elements play a crucial role. Alongside their aesthetic function, they are companions on the storytelling road, with images and sounds acting as mnemonic aids in the narrative. The translator will be creating a text that is accompanied by artwork and he or she must therefore be mindful of the need for cohesion between these two constituent elements. There will be a limited amount of page space for the text: the translation should approximate the source text in length to avoid graphic-design problems. Texts in picture storybooks are usually minimalist, but for this reason every word is significant – hence then by the margin for translational error is particularly small.

I have always begun the process of translating a picture storybook by reading the source text aloud to create awareness of rhyme and rhythm, repetition, alliteration, assonance and consonance, which do not jump off the page as easily when a text is read silently. The opening of Cornelia Funke and Kerstin Meyer's picture storybook *Käpten Knitterbart und seine Bande* (2003), known in English as *Pirate Girl* (2005), reveals a wealth of alliteration and sibilance. This is highlighted in bold below. The German text is followed by a gloss and then by the published version of the translation.

> Käpten Knitterbart war der **Sch**recken aller Meere. Sein **Sch**iff, der ‚Blutige Hering', **sch**oss **sch**neller als der **W**ind über die **W**ellen.
>
> Wenn Knitterbart am Horizont erschien, **sch**lotterten alle ehrlichen Seeleute vor Angst wie **W**ackelpudding.
>
> (Funke 2003, n.pag)

> Captain Crinkly-Beard was the terror of-all seas. His ship, the 'Bloody Herring', shot faster than the wind over the waves.
>
> [gloss] Whenever Crinkly-Beard on-the horizon appeared, shook all honest sea-people for fear like wobble-pudding [lit. jelly].

> Captain Firebeard was the terror of the **h**igh seas. His ship, the **H**orrible **H**addock, sailed faster than the **w**ind over the **w**aves.
>
> **W**henever the **H**orrible **H**addock appeared on the horizon, the knees of honest seafaring folk would shake like jelly.
>
> (Funke, trans. Wright 2005: n.pag)

With *Wind*/wind and *Wellen*/waves, the German and the English words conveniently align to allow for the 'w' sound, which happens to repeat in 'whenever', but the sibilance of the German has been replaced or compensated for by the alliteration of 'h' in English. The ship's name in English, the 'Horrible Haddock', prompted this decision: I avoided a literal translation of 'Blutige Herring' because English uses 'bloody' as a descriptive – and mildly offensive – term to express annoyance or anger, and it struck me that 'Horrible Haddock' was actually much funnier than 'Bloody Herring', potentially allowing for the dropping of the 'h' when reading aloud to evoke a more piratical voice. The publisher's decision to change the name of the head pirate from Captain Crinkly-Beard to Captain Firebeard (this change of name still aligned with artist Kerstin Meyer's depiction of the Captain, who sports a fiery red beard) meant that a 'c/k' sound was no longer at my disposal, but there was, coincidentally, an opportunity to introduce some 'k' consonance in 'folk', 'shake' and 'like'. The basic fact that there is no exact equivalence between any two given languages means that aural features such as alliteration, sibilance and consonance will almost certainly not translate one to one in any text. Whether it is possible to create aural patterns and eye rhymes will only become clear in the actual process of jotting down words on a notepad or typing various options onto a computer screen. It may be possible to introduce such features into other areas of a text if the translator considers this to be appropriate, i.e. to displace the stylistic feature. In the case of picture storybooks, where such stylistic features are often foregrounded and have a specific effect – that of making the text funny and hence enjoyable but also memorable for a pre-literate child – retextualizing these effects is clearly desirable.

In another of Cornelia Funke and Kerstin Meyer's picture story books, *Prinzessin Isabella* (1997), known in English as *Princess Pigsty* (2007), the opportunity to introduce alliteration presented itself at the following juncture, when Princess Isabella, who has declared that being a princess is boring, is banished to the kitchens to do menial tasks:

Da schälte sie Kartoffeln, polierte Töpfe, rupfte Hühner und rührte die Schlagsahne, die ihre Schwestern so gern zum Frühstück aßen.
(Funke 1997: n.pag)

[gloss] There peeled she potatoes, polished pans, plucked chickens and stirred the cream, which her sisters very like to-the breakfast ate.

and Isabella peeled potatoes, polished pans, plucked pheasants and whipped the cream that her sisters liked to eat for breakfast.
(Funke, trans. Wright 2007: n.pag)

The alliteration and repetition of the 'p' sound arises naturally here in English; the only departure from the propositional content of the German text is the decision to render 'Hühner' as 'pheasants', both to create an eye rhyme and because pheasants are game birds and therefore fit well within the story's royal context.

I generally complete the process of translating a picture storybook as I begin, by reading the target text aloud to ensure that it is successful aurally and as a performance, even if foregrounded features in the source text such as alliteration and sibilance do not align exactly with foregrounded features in the translation, for the reasons outlined above.

**Lexis and neologism**

Finding an appropriate lexis is of greater consideration in texts for young independent readers than it is in picture storybooks, since sounds and illustrations can carry a story or a poem for a pre-literate reader even where the 'meaning' is unclear. A.A. Milne's volumes of poetry *When We Were Very Young* (1924) and *Now We Are Six* (1927) are good examples of this: the early twentieth-century childhood of its protagonists, brought to life in E.H. Shephard's illustrations, has long vanished, but the poetry remains accessible to the contemporary child and even to the non-UK child because of poetic features such as rhyme and rhythm. A slightly more elevated lexis in a picture storybook also plays to the text's dual audience, making the reading experience more enjoyable for the adult or the older child who is doing the reading aloud. Older children may, of course, ask for explanations of words that are unfamiliar to them and in this manner come to share in a joke or appreciate the text on a different level. In Michael Bedard's picture storybook *Sitting Ducks* (1998), which depicts a world in which ducks are bred in factories for consumption by alligators, the idiom in the title, which is accompanied by a picture of a line of ducks sitting on a conveyor belt, fulfils this function of appealing to the adult reader. The name of the café visited by the little duck who has escaped the factory will also immediately warn the adult reader of the dangers that lie ahead: it is called the Decoy Café, and sure enough, the duck behind the counter turns out to be an alligator in disguise. Bedard cleverly marries this verbal clue to a visual element designed to appeal to adults: the Decoy Café is an homage to Hopper's 1942 painting *Nighthawks*. This is an example of what Wall (1991) identified as dual address, where both the adult and the child involved in the reading of a picture storybook are addressed 'simultaneously and equally, resulting in a satisfying reading experience for both' (Reynolds 2011:25).

In my experience, one of the reasons that translating books for the 8–11 age range is lexically challenging is because there is usually a key term, often a neologism coined by the juvenile protagonist, which recurs throughout the text, and it is crucial to render this term in a convincing, memorable and often humorous manner. In Andreas Steinhöfel's *Rico, Oskar und die Tieferschatten* (2008), known in English as *The Pasta Detectives* (2010, 2011a), the reader is introduced to Rico and Oskar, a pair of child sleuths with unusual gifts. Oscar is *hochbegabt* [literally, highly gifted], a child prodigy who sports a crash helmet at all times to protect him during his encounters with the outside world. Rico, in contrast, self-describes as *tiefbegabt* [lowly, or deeply gifted], which I chose to translate as 'child proddity'. A child proddity is, to quote Rico,

> a bit like being a child prodigy, but also like the opposite. I think an awful lot, but I need a lot of time to figure things out. (Some people find this odd.) There's nothing wrong with my brain, though. It's a perfectly normal size. Only sometimes a few things go missing, and unfortunately I never know when or where it's going to happen. And I can't always concentrate very well when I'm telling a story. I have a mind like a sieve – at least I think it's a sieve, it could be a cheese grater or a whisk . . . and now you see my problem.
>
> My head is sometimes as topsy-turvy as a barrel full of lottery balls.
> [Steinhöfel, trans. Wright 2010:10]

Whereas the word *hochbegabt* is in common use in German, the word *tiefbegabt* is Rico's invention. *Tiefbegabt* suggests the opposite of *hochbegabt*, but since *tief* means both 'deep' and 'low', suggesting profundity or breadth as well as lack or limitation, the term was ambiguous, and the fact that Oskar's giftedness is tempered by a certain amount of social incompetence and a fear of the outside world further confuses the boundaries between gifted and less gifted. 'Lowly gifted' did not sound right. It was not humorous enough, and it had none of the ambiguity of *tiefbegabt*, which implies that Rico has special needs but also special talents. 'Child proddity' suggested something on the opposite end of the scale from child prodigy but without being derogatory; the word 'oddity' hints at Rico's unique character. Hana Linhartová, who translated *Rico, Oskar und die Tieferschatten* into Czech, rendered *tiefbegabt* as 'mimoradne nenadane dite', which translates into English as 'extraordinarily ungifted child', an invention that parallels the commonly used Czech expression for 'extraordinarily gifted child' (Linhartová 2014a).

In Milena Baisch's book for the 8 to 11 age range, *Anton taucht ab* (2010), known as *Anton and Piranha* (2013) in English, Anton goes on holiday to a campsite with his grandparents, only to find that the much anticipated swimming pool fails to materialize and that in its stead there is a lake. The lake fills Anton with terror, and the book narrates the tenacity with which he avoids getting even so much as a toe wet for the entirety of his camping holiday until events finally force him to overcome his fear. Anton's imagination construes what lies beneath the lake's surface:

> Das musste alles voll sein von **Sch**lingpflanzen und dem Ekelsdreck. Glipschige Fische, die von allen Seiten ange**sch**ossen kommen und den Menschen an die Beine glip**sch**en. Mu**sch**eln, die auf und zugehen und einen dabei kneifen. **Sch**necken, die ihren **Sch**leim ausstoßen. Auch die Fi**sch**e stoßen was aus. Sie pinkeln ins Wasser und machen sonst was da rein.
> (Baisch 2010:15–16)

[gloss] That had-to everything full be of creepers and the horrible-dirt. [Glipschige – adj., neologism] fish, which from all sides up-shooting come and to-the people on the legs [glipschen – verb, neologism]. Mussels, which open and closed-go and one in-the-process pinch. Snails, which their slime out-let. Also the fish let something out. They wee into-the water and do other what there in.

Sibilance is much more available in German because of the frequency of the consonant cluster 'sch'. Nonetheless the prevalence of the 'sch' sound here points to a particular poetic effect at work, with Anton's disgust at the lake and its contents being expressed in this fashion. The adjective 'glipschig' and the morphologically related verb 'glipschen' are neologisms coined by Anton. They reference the adjective *glitschig*, which means 'slippery', and the colloquial noun *Klitsch*, which means 'a soggy mess'. I chose to translate these words using 'glibbery' and 'slibbering': 'glibbery' references 'glib' with its connotation of slickness, but is nonetheless a neologism in English, and 'slibbering', also a neologism, references 'slithering' and creates consonance, while also adding to the sibilant effect of the passage. Additionally, I endeavoured to make other sounds repeat where possible:

> It had to be full of creepers and filthy yuck. Glibbery fishes shooting along in all directions and slibbering against people's legs. Mussels opening and closing and pinching people. Snails secreting slime. Fish secrete stuff too. They wee into the water – and who knows what else comes out of them.
> (Baisch, trans. Wright 2013:11–12)

The centrality of word play and the fascination with sound in pre-teenage children's literature reflect the fact that child readers are actively building vocabulary in their daily lives and being socialized into and through language. In *Rico, Oskar und die Tieferschatten*, the issue of lexical development and its relationship to cognitive processes is highlighted in the figure of Rico the child proddity, whose unspecified learning disability means that he has difficulty remembering new words and understanding figurative language use. When Rico encounters a word he hasn't heard before, he looks it up in the dictionary and writes it down to help him remember it in future. These dictionary definitions of Rico's – of which there are twenty in the book – are foregrounded by being typographically distinct within the text, as though written in Rico's handwriting rather than in typescript. They are a crucial part of Rico's characterization and a not insubstantial part of the text's humour. Here is an example of one of Rico's dictionary definitions, taken from my translation:

> GRAVITY: When something is heavier than something else, it pulls the other thing towards it. For example, the earth is heavier than almost everything else, that's why nothing falls off it. A man called Isaac Newton discovered gravity. It is dangerous for apples. And possibly for other round things too.
> (Steinhöfel, trans. Wright 2010:17)

Much of the humour in Rico's definitions results from his tendency to understand words and statements literally, leading to confusion. The word play upon which these misunderstandings depend was rarely directly translatable from German into English, and it is when faced with a challenge such as this that the translator's task moves from documentary translation to a much freer retextualization. The rewriting that the translator is called upon to do is constrained by the following factors: Rico's dictionary definitions have to make sense within the context of the story and hence not disrupt the flow of the narrative; they must be funny; and they must make sense, cognitively and linguistically speaking, for Rico.

What follows is an illustration of a challenge thrown up by this source text and the solutions found by the English and Czech translators. By way of background, *Rico, Oskar und die Tieferschatten* is a mystery story: Oskar goes missing, kidnapped by the ALDI kidnapper – so-called because he demands ridiculously small ransoms – and Rico is hot on his trail. In this particular scene, Rico visits the flat where a little girl, Sophia, lives, in order to ask her some important questions about the case. Sophia's mum shows Rico in but is really only interested in watching television. The German text is followed by a literal translation.

> Zwei Nachbarn keiften sich in einer Talkshow an, weil der eine dem anderen betrunken über den Gartenzaun gepinkelt hatte und daraufhin dessen Rabatte eingegangen waren.

RABATT: Wenn man was einkauft und dafür eine kleine Gutschrift bekommt. Viele Einkäufe später ist es eine große Gutschrift und man kann sich was Tolles dafür kaufen. Keine Ahnung, warum jemand auf eine Rabatt draufpinkelt oder warum Leute ihn überhaupt im Garten liegenlassen.
(Steinhöfel 2008:153)

Two neighbours were shouting at each other in a talk show, because one of them had peed over the other's garden fence while drunk and subsequently his neighbour's border plants [*Rabatte*] had died.

[gloss] DISCOUNT [*Rabatt*]: When you buy something and you get a little voucher for it. Lots of shopping trips later it's a big voucher and you can buy yourself something great with it. No idea why somebody would pee on a discount [*Rabatt*] or why people would leave it lying around in the garden.

In English this makes little sense; clearly, literal translation will not work here. Rico has never encountered the noun 'Rabatte', which is a type of border plant for the garden, and confuses it with the noun 'Rabatt', meaning 'discount', which he has heard before but has also not entirely understood. The challenge in rewriting this in English is to find a homonym in English which, in one of its definitions, is something that would be found in a garden. I settled on the word 'squash'.

Two neighbours were arguing on a chat show. One of them had peed over the other one's garden fence and his neighbour's squash plant had died.

SQUASH: Juice in a bottle that you mix with water to make a drink. No idea why anybody would pee on a bottle of squash or why you would plant one in the garden.
(Steinhöfel, trans. Wright 2010:144–5)

A Canadian in the audience at a lecture I gave at City University London in December 2013 pointed out that squash – the drink – was unknown in Canada and hence my recreation of Rico's definition would not travel. This had not occurred to me as a speaker of British English and it prompted me to go to the North American edition and check to see if this had been localized by the editor. Squash had indeed metamorphosed into the ball game and the neighbour had therefore peed on a squash racket rather than a bottle of squash (Steinhöfel 2011a:115). This use of squash would also have worked in British English, of course, and 'squash' is certainly not the only solution, nor necessarily the best. Czech translator Hana Linhartová retextualized Rico's *Rabatt/Rabatte* definition in the following way (the English translation is my rendering of Hana Linhartová's own back-translation into German (Linhartová 2014b); I have not altered the Czech cases):

> Zrovna tam na sebe ječeli dva sousedi, poněvadž jeden se tomu druhému v opilosti vyčůral přes plot a zničil mu tak jeho rebarboru.
>
> REBARBORA je nejspíš socha jeho ženy Barbory, poněvadž *re-*vždycky znamená opakovat, jako třeba u počítače restartovat anebo ve škole dělat reparát. A když ho člověk neudělá, je z něj repetent. Nechápu, proč si Barboru postavil v dočůrací vzdálenosti u sousedova plotu. Já bych si ji dal hned vedle dveří, anebo nejspíš do obýváku.
>
> (Steinhöfel, trans. Linhartová 2012:149)

> Two neighbours were arguing because one of them had peed over the other's garden fence while drunk and ruined his neighbour's *rebarboru* [rhubarb].
>
> REBARBORA [RHUBARB] is probably a statue of his wife *Barbory* [Barbara], because 're-' always means 'repeat', like restart on the computer or a *reparát* [*a test that you have to take again*] at school. Which if you don't pass means you are a *repetent* [*a pupil who has to repeat a school year*]. I don't understand why he placed Barbara in peeing distance from his neighbour's fence. I would have put her right next to the door or, even better, in the living room.

Rico's word definitions were not the only transformations undergone by *Rico, Oskar und die Tieferschatten* in translation. In its passage over the Atlantic, the book's title metamorphosed from *The Pasta Detectives* into *The Spaghetti Detectives*. The publisher's decision to alter the German title in the first place was taken because of its ambiguity. The *Tieferschatten*, or 'deeper' shadows, mentioned in the title reference the fact that, unbeknownst to Rico, the deeper, scarier shadows he sees at night in the abandoned building that backs onto his apartment block are actually thrown by the ALDI kidnapper, who is using the empty building as his lair. Rico's compound noun *Tieferschatten* is morphologically acceptable in German but semantically vague until, in the course of the novel, Rico eventually describes the phenomenon of the 'deeper' shadows that he has observed. I chose to translate this term as 'shadowier shadows', using an almost successful grammatical construction in English, to hint at Rico's German neologism. One of the chapters in the translation bears this expression as its title, but the title of the book became *The Pasta Detectives* in reference to a piece of pasta that Rico finds on the pavement outside his building and which busies his mind as he investigates how it landed there. The decision to rename the book *The Spaghetti Detectives* in North America might have been taken because spaghetti is considered more of a children's dish than 'grown-up' pasta; it might also be a gesture towards the spaghetti western. Whatever the reason, it allowed the US publisher to emblazon the pun 'They've got to use their noodles!' on the front cover.

## Censorship and cultural adaptation in literature for children and young adults

A translator of literature for children and young adults is likely, at some point in his or her career, to face the issue of how to deal with source-text material that is considered age-inappropriate or that contravenes target-cultural norms. In the Anglophone world, bad language, descriptions of or allusions to teen or pre-teen sexual activity and implied or explicit acts of violence may all cause a problem for publishers who are concerned about public and parental opinion. In translating from German, it has been my experience that the socially liberal attitudes of the German-speaking world where teen sexuality is concerned are often perceived as unacceptable in the UK and even more so in the US. Before we consider how a translator might behave in a situation of potential censorship, rewriting or adaptation, it is important to remember that this phenomenon has a long tradition where children's literature is concerned, both in and out of translation. Reynolds points out that until the late twentieth century 'there was an unwritten agreement that children's books would not include sex, bad language, or gratuitous violence, on the grounds that writing for children is part of the socializing process and so ought to set good examples' (2011:27). In an interview given shortly before his death in 2012, US children's author Maurice Sendak expressed the opinion that contemporary children's literature was not 'truthful or faithful to what's going on with children' and that there was a trend of 'going back to childhood innocence that I never quite believed in' (Paul 2011). In this respect, the issue of what can be appropriately consumed by children appears not to be the consequence of culture clashes in translation but rather reflects differing concepts of childhood within the wider culture. If self-censorship on the part of the author or censorial measures at the editorial level fail then censorship can also occur at the reading-aloud stage, as Oittinen reminds us (2000:52–3). On the one hand, the translator may justifiably feel that any form of censorship is reprehensible and that the experience of reading foreign children's literature is an encounter with difference, which should encompass different social mores; on the other, translators are in a disempowered position *vis-à-vis* publishers. When faced with problematic passages in a text and an anxious editor, the translator should not necessarily feel an obligation to single-handedly attempt to reverse a long-standing tradition. Oittinen even argues, disagreeing with the views of Shavit (1986) and Klingberg (1986), both of whom view adaptation as 'a negative issue in itself, a sign of disrespect for children' (Oittinen 2000:99), that a certain degree of adaptation is an intrinsic part of translation and that 'adaptations have validity as works of literature' and 'can also reflect love and respect for the reading child' (ibid:160). The translator may also take the view that it is more important for the text to appear in English in a censored form than for the text to remain untranslated. This is not to say that translators should identify and pre-censor any areas of a text they feel might cause offence. Translation contracts typically contain a clause which states that the translator 'will not introduce into the Translation any matter of an objectionable or libellous character which was not present in the Work' (Society of Authors 2013) or that the translator 'will translate the Underlying Work accurately, without omissions, additions or other changes except as necessary to produce a translation that is idiomatic and faithful to the Underlying Work in spirit and content' (Literary Translators' Association of Canada 2007). Generally, translators have a contractual obligation to make sure the translation fulfils a documentary function or conforms to a 'relation norm' (Chesterman 1997:149), i.e. that it shows the publisher what is in the source text, which means that the translator must deliver a complete rendition of the source text, with no omissions. It may, however, be advisable for the translator to pre-empt potential problems, particularly in a situation where the publisher has purchased the rights to a book on the translator's recommendation rather than on its own initiative. Alerting the publisher to potential problems is best done in the early stages of a translation project, when providing a synopsis of the title and/or a reader's report. This may require translators to empathize with a conservatism that is not naturally their own and to anticipate publishers' commercial and parents' pedagogical concerns. In situations where the translator expects the author to be involved in the translation process to a greater or lesser degree and anticipates conflict between author, publisher and perhaps even translator, the translator may request a right-of-final-review clause to be written into the translation contract. Overwhelmingly, the right of final review will lie with the publisher, but this contractual clarity is a means of avoiding deadlock. There is no simple answer to the issue of censorship in translation, but a confident translator will anticipate potential areas of sensitivity and have the confidence to argue his or her case. For translators of children's books, the act of reading for translation thus includes identifying issues that may cause cultural offence or scare the publisher away from the project.

In practical terms, what happens to words and passages in a text that are considered inappropriate for the target audience and have the potential to cause offence? There are two basic approaches: the offending passages can simply be removed – censored – with small measures being taken to ensure the necessary textual cohesion; alternatively, passages can be rewritten to tone down existing material or substitute it for something less offensive. The latter strategy was employed in a book for teens which I translated from German. With this approach, the rewriting can be done by the publisher as part of its editorial purview, or the publisher can request that the author rewrite the text to conform to its demands, with the rewritten text subsequently being (re-)translated – this may cause offence on the part of the author and may place the translator in the unfortunate situation of smoothing ruffled writerly feathers – or the publisher and/or author might request that the translator make the necessary alterations. When faced with a situation of this kind, I have generally felt a moral responsibility to apprise the author of the situation and the action being taken, even if not all authors take an active interest in the translation process. The translator may or may not agree with the proposed editorial interventions and may feel moved to advocate against censorship, rewriting or adaptation. The situation is complex: of the three agents in the process, the translator has the least power and must bear in mind the need to maintain a healthy long-term working relationship with the publisher, who will hopefully be a source of future work. The translator must balance the need to make his or her voice heard with the need for diplomacy and good business sense. Having said this, it is not always easy to predict what will cause offence, perhaps proving the point that the translator cannot be expected to anticipate the entire spectrum of readers' responses to a book. I expected conservative resistance to *The Pasta Detectives*' inclusion of a homosexual character but did not foresee that some reviewers and bloggers would object to the theme of kidnapping itself and its implied threat of violence against children (see, for example, Word Candy 2011; Library of Clean Reads 2011) as well as to the fact that, contrary to middle-class norms, Rico was allowed to run around the city of Berlin unsupervised (Cothern 2012). Happily, however, the title won the 2011 NASEN Inclusive Children's Book Award for its portrayal of child proddity Rico.

Beyond an awareness of culturally sensitive themes, the translator also reads a source text with an eye to the prominence of cultural markers. Depending on how one wishes to translate, one can view culturally specific items such as food, place names and national holidays and traditions as an opportunity to introduce younger readers to the 'other' or as textual elements that need to be localized. Books for children and young adults typically also contain references to the school and examination systems of the source culture; these rarely align with the systems of the target culture. Award-winning translator Sarah Ardizzone argues that 'the issue of cultural adaptation has to be addressed head-on in a children's book, since children do not deliberately choose the difference of a translation' (cited in Lathey 2010:190). When deciding whether to maintain or domesticate cultural specifics, the translator will be guided in part by editorial policy at the publishing house. An independent publisher such as Milet, which specializes in bilingual and multicultural titles, will be more likely to preserve the foreignness of the source text than a more commercial publisher. The translator's decision-making will also be influenced by their reading of the text and their sense of audience: in the case of a horror thriller for teenagers, culturally specific items are perhaps less important than they are in a book for early teen learners of English in Germany who are reading an English translation of a contemporary German children's classic with which they are very familiar.

Zoran Drvenkar's Gothic thriller *Sag mir was du siehst* (2002), known as *Tell Me What You See* (2005) in English, offers a good example of a culturally specific detail for which the translator had to judge the appropriate translation strategy. The novel begins atmospherically in the early hours of 25 December, when its protagonist Alissa declares 'Weihnachten ist vorbei' [Christmas is over] (Drvenkar 2002:11) and leaves the warmth of her bed to pay her annual Christmas-night visit to her father's grave. For an Anglophone reader, Christmas would only really be over on the evening of the 25th, but in much of continental Europe, of course, Christmas is celebrated on the evening of the 24th, with the 25th being more akin to Boxing Day in the UK. The decision to translate 'sechs Uhr am Weihnachtsabend' [literally, 6 o'clock on Christmas evening, i.e. 24 December in Germany] as 'six o'clock on Christmas Day' was made because it was important in narrative terms that Christmas be over in order for Alissa's adventures to begin. One could argue, of course, that since the book is clearly set in Berlin – a prefatory paratext explains where the events of the novel are taking place, and German street names have been preserved and italicized for emphasis – this tweaking of a cultural detail is inappropriate and the reader should be trusted to understand that Christmas in Germany takes places on the 24 December. But since German and English have different ways of referring to 24 December – in German Christmas Eve is referred to as Holy Evening [*Heiligabend*] or Christmas Evening [*Weihnachtsabend*] – and since these variations in terminology clearly delineate the fact that for Germans 24 December is Christmas, whereas for Anglophones 24 December is the night before Christmas, it would be confusing to use the term Christmas Eve and expect the reader to understand that Christmas is over in Germany at midnight on the 24th. Other strategies might include retaining the German term *Weihnachtsabend* and italicizing it, incorporating an explanation about differing Christmas traditions into the prefatory paratext or incorporating a paratextual explanation into the translation itself.

Some foreign-language publishers, such as Carlsen in Germany, have begun commissioning English translations of contemporary classics for young domestic learners of English. The source text is already familiar to the audience, who can read it alongside the translation if they wish. This is an interesting situation for a translator, as the target audience is the same as the original audience, hence there is no shift in cultural background. In Andreas Steinhöfel's *Dirk und ich* (2008 [1991]) [literally, Dirk and I], translated into English as *My Brother and I* (2011b), a group of children go on a school trip to Ulm in Baden-Württemberg where, they are told, they will eat the local food specialities *Spätzle* and *Maultaschen*. If the book were being translated for an Anglophone audience, a variety of strategies might be employed, from wholesale domestication of the book, with its setting being moved to a different country entirely, to replacing certain elements with local equivalents or simply giving additional information to aid the reader's understanding. In Germany there is no need or indeed rationale for doing this, but the translator must remember that the purpose of the translation is to give young Germans the opportunity to read something that is age-appropriate and culturally familiar to them through the medium of English, with the aim of extending their English vocabulary. When the children finally get to eat *Maultaschen* – and one must remember that *Maultaschen* are a regional speciality from Baden-Württemberg and hence as strange to Northern German children as they would be to non-German children – they comment on the fact that the food's appearance does not match its description:

> Ich wusste nicht, warum die so hießen, weil, ein Maul hatten sie nicht und wie Taschen sahen sie auch nicht aus, jedenfalls nicht so richtig. Eigentlich waren sie wie große Ravioli, nur nicht so lecker.
> (Steinhöfel 2008 [1991]:131)

> [gloss] I knew not, why they so were-called, because, a snout had they not and like pockets looked they also not like, at-least not so rightly. Actually were they like large ravioli, only not so tasty.

There is no reason why this cannot be translated literally, but first the German reader needs to be told the English words for 'Maul' and 'Tasche[n]': snout and pocket[s]:

> *Maultaschen* means snoutpockets in German. I didn't know why they were called that because they didn't have a snout and they didn't look like pockets either, at least not properly. They were actually like giant ravioli, only not as tasty.
> (Steinhöfel, trans. Wright 2011b:134)

Imagining how the parameters of a translation project might shift if the target text were destined for the same audience as the source text is a useful exercise, and the above example also serves as a reminder that the nation remains an 'imagined community' (Anderson 2006 [1983]): in other words, within any nation, and certainly within linguistic communities operating at a supra-national level such as those that use English or Spanish, there exist significant cultural and linguistic differences. Children may be more 'local' than adults, too, embedded in their school environment and local community. For all of these reasons, one might argue, it is foolish to attempt to appeal to a standardized child reader, and healthy to expand a child's horizons through exposure to difference.

### Reading for translation (2): German exophonic literature

> The containers where we store our happiness/ are not without significance.
> Tzveta Sofronieva, 'On Happiness after reading Schopenhauer, in California', trans. Chantal Wright (2014:272)

I have written elsewhere about exophony – the phenomenon of writers adopting a literary language other than their mother tongue – and the issues that this raises for the literary translator (Wright 2010, 2013), but here I would like to focus on one particular exophonic writer whose work I have translated from German into English: Tzveta Sofronieva. I will return to the question posed by the first chapter of the book and first scrutinize my motivations for translating Sofronieva's work in order to consider how these motivations interact with my reading and translation of her texts. I met Tzveta Sofronieva by chance, on a train travelling from Berlin to the Frankfurt Book Fair. The poet happened to take the seat next to mine and we began talking. I have since been told that there is no such thing as a coincidental literary meeting on the trains travelling to Frankfurt in fair season, but at the time it did seem to me to be a stroke of luck that I, at that time engaged in writing a PhD on exophonic writers in Germany, found myself sitting next to a bona fide exemplar of the species. This fortuitous meeting was the beginning of a friendship and of a working relationship, as I made my first forays into poetry translation with Tzveta Sofronieva's nascent German exophonic poetry. Tzveta Sofronieva was born in Sofia, Bulgaria, in 1963, studied physics and history of science, left Bulgaria shortly before the fall of the Iron Curtain and has been resident in Berlin since 1992; she learned German as an adult, subsequent to her arrival in Germany and in addition to her knowledge of English, Russian and Serbian. Her first German poems were published in the journal *Akzente* in 2007, and in 2009 she was awarded the Adelbert-von-Chamisso-Förderpreis, a prize which at that time was given to emerging writers whose cultural background and/or mother tongue were not Germanic/German. Tzveta Sofronieva's work has since been published in Hanser's prestigious Lyrik Kabinett poetry series.

The intellectual fascination with exophony that predated my meeting with Tzveta Sofronieva was predicated on a number of grounds. First, from a Translation Studies perspective, exophonic texts complicate conventional notions of source and target text. The exophonic source text is not entirely at one with the culture in whose language it was written, but nor is it simply a foreign import into that language, i.e. it is not an essentially Bulgarian text that just happens to have been composed in German or literally translated into that language, nor it is necessarily the hybrid product of (only) two languages and cultures. As I translated Sofronieva's German-language poetry I realized that there were aspects of the 'source' text, both linguistic and cultural, that remained out of my reach. What, for example, was I to do in the wittily named poem 'Das Schließen der Fakultät für Südslawistik' ['The Closure of the Faculty for South East European Studies'] (Sofronieva 2012: 58–61) when I came across the Bulgarian phrase *бялото саламурено сирене*. I do not speak Bulgarian and hence I did not know what the phrase meant. The Cyrillic alphabet meant that I was unable even to attempt a pronunciation of the three words; this, in the context of a poem, where sound and rhythm are so important, was problematic. Similarly, in the poem 'Rutschuk, Russe, an der Donau' ['Ruschuk, Rousse, by the Danube'] (ibid:84–7) I encountered an unfamiliar concept – *Ökoglasnost* – and references to the geographical details of the Bulgarian–Romanian border. It goes without saying that translators encounter unfamiliar words in the texts they translate all the time, regardless of whether the writer is a native speaker of his or her literary language or not, and sometimes these unknown words are in a language of which they have no knowledge. Translators are also frequently confronted with gaps in their historical, geographical and cultural knowledge, but the exophonic source text has perhaps a greater capacity to take translators out of their comfort zone and make them less sure of their footing.

Translating Sofronieva's poetry undermined the notion of the source text in another important fashion: there were often several source texts for a given poem, written in any one of three languages – Bulgarian, German or English – at different time periods. Although one of these poems was, technically speaking, the source in the sense that it had been written first, the poet often could not remember which 'source' version took precedence and even when she did, that version was frequently unavailable to me because it was in Bulgarian. But this did not mean that the German source text from which I was working was necessarily a self-translation from another language: Sofronieva explained that her texts were 'thought' differently in different languages, using the possibilities that the language in question had to offer. If the exophonic source text complicates the very notion of a 'source' text in this fashion, how then is the simple label 'Translated from the German' an adequate description of a translation based on such a text? If one deems it important to attempt to convey the complexity of the exophonic text – an issue to which I will return presently – how is the translator to create a text that does not flatten or reduce or deny?

Beyond this interrogation of source and target, exophonic literature is attractive to the translator because it foregrounds how all literary texts function. The German exophonic literature with which I have engaged – and this includes texts by Franco Biondi, Emine Sevgi Özdamar and Yoko Tawada – is striking for its lack of complacency towards language, for its ability to be self-conscious and innovative in its style, not so much by drawing on the resources of another language, although this does feature in these texts, but by ceaselessly interrogating the possibilities of the adopted language and the conventions of the adopted culture. This interrogation is prompted by an awareness of the fact of linguistic and cultural difference. This poses a writerly challenge for the translator, particularly the native-speaker translator, if he or she wishes to interrogate the possibilities of English in the same way and recreate the sense of cultural defamiliarization.

The socio-political dimension of exophonic literature in Germany also appealed to the activist translator in me. Many German exophonic writers arrived in West Germany as skilled or unskilled labour migrants, *Gastarbeiter*, in the 1960s and 1970s, recruited to fill the needs of the Federal Republic's booming economy. They began to write in response to the experience of migration, many of them eventually adopting German as a literary language. Exophony as a phenomenon is not, of course, confined to Germany, nor to the modern era. In the classical world and indeed in the pre-nation-state era, exophony was the norm rather than the exception, but in the era of the nation-state, monolingualism has become the dominant paradigm. Yildiz (2012) has identified the modern emergence of exophony in Germany as part of the response to this monolingual paradigm; exophony is one of several 'linguascapes' (ibid:109) of resistance to or uneasy coexistence with the monolingual.

In Germany, *Gastarbeiterliteratur* – guest-worker literature – emerged in the late 1970s: it was programmatic, angry; it called for socio-political change, for acknowledgement of the fact that Germany had become an immigrant nation, for changes to the laws governing the right to residence and citizenship (see, for example, Biondi and Schami 1981). The writers who belonged to this literary movement struggled to be recognized by the German literary establishment, found it difficult to obtain publishing opportunities and saw their attempts at self-representation challenged by the establishment's need to take ownership of the phenomenon of exophony and to depoliticize non-native-speaker writing by framing it primarily as a linguistic feat worthy of praise (Wright 2014). Tzveta Sofronieva arrived in Germany in the early 1990s and hence does not belong to this generation of writers, but the history of post-war immigration to Germany, its relationship to German exophonic writing and the struggle to redefine German national identity, predicated for so long on ethnic belonging, are her inheritance. Sofronieva's career too has been marked by the struggle for acceptance by the literary establishment and characterized, until her recent appearance in Hanser's Lyrik Kabinett series, by publication with small presses. She has had to fight against what writer Franco Biondi has described as *Obrigkeitsdeutsch* (literally, authority-German) (Biondi 1995; von Saalfeld 1998:151–4), a phenomenon whereby German native speakers insist on their ownership of and authority over the German language *vis-à-vis* non-native speakers. The editorial pen's drive to normalization is something with which many writers are familiar, of course, but the balance of power between the exophonic writer and the native-speaker editor has the potential to make the editorial process more fraught. The frustrated outburst in Sofronieva's lyrical poem 'Eine Hand voll Wasser' [A Hand Full of Water] (Sofronieva 2012:42–5), a poem that references German and Bulgarian folk songs, is a symptom of this situation: 'und lass mich endlich/ Worte und Grammatik schreiben,/ wie ich empfinde' (ibid:42); 'and please let me/ use words and grammar/ as I see fit' (ibid:43). The translator too has to fight against the unconscious drive to normalize the text, and here Berman's 'negative analytic' (Berman 2012) serves as a useful reminder of the ways in which a text can be deformed. The decision to translate a text for reasons other than the likelihood of its commercial success is a statement of the translator's belief in its literary worth. In the case of exophonic texts, the decision to translate is a political act, just as exophony itself is a political act: it is an affirmation of the value of the writer's work and of her struggle. Arguably, though, all translation is a political act, particularly so in cultures where a monolingual paradigm holds sway and where the cultural attitude to difference is one of aggressive assimilation. Here, as elsewhere, exophonic texts exemplify or condense important issues relating to monolingualism, translation and literature.

Finally, beyond the fact that exophonic texts challenge conventional notions of source and target in Translation Studies, that they highlight the essential nature of literature and that the translation of these texts can be a highly political act, exophonic literary texts bring with them the same challenges and pleasures as all other literary texts. Sofronieva's poems share in the elliptical nature of poetry, requiring the reader to construct a narrative, to be attentive to signifying networks, both intra- and intertextually, and to carefully consider the relationship of form and content.

### Translating Tzveta Sofronieva's poetry (1): 'Attaining Citizenship on Valentine's Day'

In the discussion that follows, I will focus on the decision-making processes involved in the translation of two of Sofronieva's poems that explicitly or implicitly engage with the theme of national identity and belonging, and particularly with political and cultural definitions of European-ness, beginning with the poem 'Einbürgerung am Valentinstag' ['Attaining Citizenship on Valentine's Day'] (Sofronieva 2012:74–9). The complete German-language source texts for the two poems under discussion can be found in the appendix to this book (note that for the first poem, the line numbers given for the German and English texts do not align because of the line shifts that have occurred in translation). My understanding of exophony and of the translation of exophonic literature as political acts guided my approach from the outset. 'Einbürgerung am Valentinstag' is about the process of becoming a German citizen – *Einbürgerung* is the German term for becoming a *Bürger*, or 'citizen', of Germany – on the basis of marriage to a German, something that Sofronieva herself has experienced. The title of the poem neatly ties together the bureaucratic and the romantic, legal necessity and personal circumstance. Throughout, the poem refuses to use upper case and – with the exception of en-dashes and question marks – punctuation, which strikes the reader as a form of resistance to the dominant order, both legal and linguistic. In German, a language which capitalizes nouns, the eschewing of upper case has a pronounced effect on the physiognomy of the poem.

**Attaining Citizenship on Valentine's Day**

*Tzveta Sofronieva*
*Trans. Chantal Wright*

| | |
|---|---:|
| things are different, simply | 1 |
| different | 2 |
| things i would need, first i would need | 3 |
| first i would have to, i needed | 4 |
| to love you long enough | 5 |
| my word | 6 |
| your city | 7 |
| to turn your world into a word in me | 8 |
| a bed for three years | 9 |
| and proof of the nationality | 10 |
|     of one's spouse | 11 |
| no passport; the requirements are: the number | 12 |
| of the unit in which his/her father | 13 |
|     served in the german army | 14 |
| (with intent to kill my father) | 15 |
| and the unit in which his/her grandfather | 16 |
|     served in the german army | 17 |

| | |
|---|---|
| (against my grandfather) | *18* |
| nothing else will prove the european citizenship of the german | *19* |
| bed | *20* |
| the idea | *21* |
| mastering everything by oneself: 10 years of | *22* |
| earning well | *23* |
| paying rent with no arrears | *24* |
| means you are german | *25* |
| that's it | *26* |
| wordwitnesses have no role to play | *27* |
| and giving birth to a german child is absolutely not enough | *28* |
| there's nothing german about being a woman | *29* |
| having a mother is not proof of citizenship | *30* |
| mothers only give birth | *31* |
| they beget nothing | *32* |
| they cannot bear witness | *33* |
| my word | *34* |
| your city | *35* |
| to turn your world into a word in me | *36* |
| how long is long enough for love? | *37* |
| let's start with 13 | *38* |
| for superstition's sake | *39* |
| no bed and no money | *40* |
| just the country of my chance wanderings | *41* |
| of my last love | *42* |
| i've said so often | *43* |
| china, let's move to china | *44* |
| it's so exciting there | *45* |
| berlin was yesterday | *46* |
| new york the day before yesterday | *47* |
| and sofia the day before that | *48* |
| your world – my word | *49* |
| different things | *50* |
| accidentally | *51* |
| words | *52* |
| made me | *53* |
| more german than the germans | *54* |
| more chinese than the chinese | *55* |
| more american than the americans | *56* |
| more bulgarian than the bulgarians | *57* |

| | |
|---|---|
| and so on | 58 |
| i like to push nonsense into the grotesque | 59 |
| and anyway – | 60 |
| we've been here long enough | 61 |
| even if long enough isn't considered long enough | 62 |
| it's time | 63 |
| my word – your world | 64 |
| before it's too late | 65 |
| before i grow less german | 66 |
| less bulgarian, american, chinese etc. | 67 |
| let's move | 68 |
| beyond | 69 |

The first five lines of the poem have several marked stylistic features. First, they display a heightened awareness of the morphological possibilities of the German language, playing with the morpheme *brauch*, which forms the noun meaning 'custom' or 'tradition' (*der Brauch*; plural: *die Bräuche*), but which is also in the verbs *brauchen*, meaning 'to need', and *gebrauchen*, which will appear later in the poem (line 27 in the German version), meaning 'to use/make use of'.

| | |
|---|---|
| die bräuche sind andere,   einfach andere<br>*the customs are   different, simply   different* | 1 |
| bräuche<br>*customs* | 2 |
| bräuchte,   erst brauchte ich,<br>*would-need, first needed   i* | 3 |
| hätte         ich, habe ich gebraucht,<br>*would-have i,   have i   needed* | 4 |
| dich lange genug   zu lieben<br>*you  long   enough  to love* | 5 |

The narrative voice is showing off its facility with German by playing with the morpheme *brauch* but simultaneously and deliberately occupying the role of a language learner by conjugating the verb *brauchen*, working its way through the tenses. This is a movement that is iconic of a journey through and into language, from the classroom to exophonic writerly competence. Conjugating the verb and endlessly deferring its object also creates a sense of frustration, of bureaucratic hurdles that must be overcome. The connection forged between *Brauch* and *brauchen* reflects the list of requirements for citizenship, i.e. one of the things that is needed (*brauchen*) is a familiarity with German law and tradition (*Brauch*). Later in the poem (line 50 in the German version), *Brauch* will also take on the sense of 'habit', describing the manner in which the couple depicted has become used to living their lives. The morphological relationship between *Brauch* and *brauchen* has no equivalent in English; there is no link between 'need' and the English words typically used to translate *Brauch* – words such as 'habit', 'tradition' and 'custom'. Nonetheless, it is important to maintain something of the link between *brauchen* and *Brauch* and with it the idea that a familiarity with German custom is one of the requirements for citizenship, even if this connection no longer exists on the morphological level. My solution to this was to use the prosaic word 'things':

| | |
|---|---|
| things are different, simply | 1 |
| different | 2 |
| things i would need, first i would need | 3 |
| first i would have to, i needed | 4 |
| to love you long enough | 5 |

The repetition of 'i would need' in line 3 of the translation, where the German offers two different tenses – first the conditional (*bräuchte*) and then the simple past tense (*brauchte*) – occurs because German and English verb tenses do not align exactly. In the source text, lines 3 and 4 end in a different past tense in German (the simple past *brauchte* and the perfect *ich habe gebraucht*), but since both of these past tenses most naturally translate into English as 'needed' (one can of course translate *ich habe gebraucht* as 'I have needed', but this calls much more attention to itself in English than it does in German and it cannot be used interchangeably with the simple past as is the case in German), it seemed preferable to repeat 'would need' in line 3 and to soften the repetition by inserting the object 'things' and then using the adverb 'first', rather than ending lines 3 and 4 with the same word. This upholds the sense of the poetic voice moving through a verb conjugation.

In line 8 the poem introduces a play on the morphological relationship between the nouns *Wort* [word] and *Ort* [place], a pairing that will be repeated four times in the poem (in lines 8, 34, 48 and 63 of the German text): 'aus deinem ort ein wort in mir zu machen' [literally, out-of your place a word in me to make]. The man's country must become the woman's language; this is one of the requirements for feeling at home, a requirement also governed by the verb *brauchen*, but one imposed by the woman rather than the state. To create this link in English, I used the word 'world' instead of 'place', so that the reader has the sense of the woman selecting letters from 'world' to make her 'word', just as she does from *Wort* to make *Ort*: 'to turn your world into a word in me'. The list of bureaucratic requirements that follows on from this is staccato and impersonal:

| | |
|---|---|
| das bett drei jahre<br>*the bed three years* | 9 |
| und beweise über die herkunft<br>*and proofs about the origin* | 10 |
| des ehegatten oder der ehegattin<br>*of-the husband or of-the wife* | 11 |
| kein pass, benötigt werden: die nummer<br>*no passport, required are: the number* | 12 |
| der einheit, in der sein bzw. ihr vater<br>*of-the unit, in which his or her father* | 13 |
| in der deutschen armee gedient hat<br>*in the german army served has* | 14 |
| (mit der absicht, meinen vater zu töten)<br>*(with the intention, my father to kill)* | 15 |
| und der einheit, in der sein bzw. ihr großvater<br>*and the unit, in which his or her grandfather* | 16 |
| in der deutschen armee gedient hat<br>*in the german army served has* | 17 |
| (gegen meinen großvater)<br>*(against my grandfather)* | 18 |

The move from personal to bureaucratic conditions that have to be fulfilled in order to obtain citizenship is signalled by a shift from the first and the second person of the first six lines (*ich, dich, mein, deine, deinem, mir*) to the third person and the definite article (e.g. *sein bzw. ihr vater; die herkunft des ehegatten*), with the narrative voice interjecting in parentheses. The German half of the couple must prove his (or her) German-ness in order to extend this German-ness to his (or her) spouse. The characteristic features of German bureaucratic language are present: the formal word for 'spouse' is used in both its gender declensions – *Ehegatte* (male) and *Ehegattin* (female) – and since English has no formal gendered equivalents, I opted for the word 'spouse' and the formal, impersonal possessive pronoun 'one's'; the bureaucratic abbreviation *bzw.*, which stands for *beziehungsweise* and can mean simply 'or' but also 'or more specifically', I mimicked with a forward slash: 'his/her grandfather'. There is no sense of agency in this list, of who is doing the requiring, and verbs are also largely absent. So, for example, the person applying for citizenship needs to have cohabited with their partner for three years but is not asked to produce a passport – this is reduced to the minimalist *das bett drei jahre* and indicated by the curt *kein pass*. The English translation upholds this elliptical feel:

| | |
|---|---:|
| a bed for three years | 9 |
| and proof of the nationality | 10 |
|     of one's spouse | 11 |
| no passport: the requirements are: the number | 12 |
| of the unit in which his/her father | 13 |
|     served in the german army | 14 |
| (with intent to kill my father) | 15 |
| and the unit in which his/her grandfather | 16 |
|     served in the german army | 17 |
| (against my grandfather) | 18 |

These are the proofs that are required to show 'die europäische zugehörigkeit/ des deutschen/ bettes' [literally, the european belonging/ of-the german/ bed]. I elected to translate *Zugehörigkeit* as 'citizenship', deliberately indulging in what Berman would have labelled 'clarification', an 'impos[ition] [of] the definite' (2012:289). The German noun *Zugehörigkeit*, like many abstract German nouns, can be used in a very general, abstract way or in a concrete, even bureaucratic sense. The English noun 'belonging' felt too abstract and sentimental for the context, and I wanted to highlight the irony implicit in defining Europe only in a political sense – as the European Union – rather than as the land mass of Europe, to which Bulgaria has of course always belonged.

The list of requirements for citizenship ends in the statement 'wortzeugen sind nicht zu gebrauchen' [literally, word-witnesses are not to make-use-of]. *Wortzeugen* is a neologism that plays on *Augenzeugen* [eye-witnesses]. *Wortzeugen* can be read as 'word-witnesses', suggesting witnesses who could speak to the applicant's facility with German (facility with the German language has now become a requirement for obtaining German citizenship in most cases, although this was not always the case), but it hints too at 'producers of words', even though grammatically speaking this would have to be *Wortzeugende*. *Zeuge* [witness] is morphologically related to the verb *zeugen* [to produce, beget], and the poetic voice will go on to tell the reader that giving birth to a German child does not entitle you to German citizenship since 'mütter gebären nur/ sie zeugen nichts/ sie können keine zeugen sein' [literally, mothers give-birth only/ they produce nothing/ they can no witnesses be]. *Zeugen* and *zeugen* would normally be typographically distinct, and here we can see that the poem's decision to eschew the upper case eradicates the boundaries between nouns, which are capitalized in German, and other parts of speech. The verb *zeugen* also contrasts with *gebären*: men actively 'beget' and woman passively 'give birth'. The connection between *Zeugen* and *zeugen* has to be forged differently in English. I translated this as 'mothers only give birth/ they beget nothing/ they cannot bear witness' using the alliteration of 'birth', 'beget' and 'bear' to suggest a connection, but if I were to revise the translation now, I would be tempted to translate 'mütter gebären nur' as 'mothers only bear children' to allow for the repetition of 'bear' in 'they cannot bear witness'.

*Auswandern*, like *Zugehörigkeit*, is an example of a German word that has a very specific meaning – 'emigrate' – but can also be used in its literal sense of *wandern + aus* [walk/wander + out/from]. The poem uses the verb twice. On the first occasion, the poetic voice argues 'china, wandern wir nach china aus' [literally, china, walk we to china out], and on the second occasion, at the very end of the poem, the suggestion comes again, 'wandern wir aus', and is followed by the enigmatic noun/ preposition 'jenseits'. On this occasion I chose not to clarify and translate *auswandern* as 'emigrate' but rather as 'move': 'china, let's move to china' and 'let's move/ beyond'. The poem expresses a desire to escape from national categories and legal requirements and ends with 'jenseits', a word which has religious connotations and suggests a transcendental space of freedom in which all modes of being, irrespective of nation and culture, can be embraced. 'Emigrate' seemed too legalistic a term to capture this meaning and loses the commonplaceness of the German *wandern* inherent to *auswandern*. I translated *jenseits* as 'beyond' to capture this notion of escape. The process of reading for translation, as modelled in this discussion of Sofronieva's poem, thus demonstrates how complex the concept of equivalence really is and how foolish any attempt to view it as a matter of mere lexical fidelity.

### Translating Tzveta Sofronieva's poetry (2): 'Landschaften, Ufer'

The poem 'Landschaften, Ufer' ['Landscapes, Shore'] features imagery that recurs throughout Sofronieva's collection *Eine Hand voll Wasser*: water as de-territorialized space, often a feminist space, a space of exploration (Wright 2010b). Three different types of water are mentioned in the poem: *Meer* [sea/ocean], *Seen* [seas/oceans, but also, if the noun is masculine rather than feminine, lakes] and *Fluss* [river]. For German readers, and perhaps others, too, the geographic location given in the first line of the poem and the reference to fences [*Zäunen*] in the final line will invoke the memory of the 2007 G8 summit which was held in the former East German coastal resort of Heiligendamm and at which protestors were prevented from coming too close to the leaders of the world's strongest economies by a 7.5-mile-long, 8-foot-high steel fence.

## Landscapes, shore

*Tzveta Sofronieva*
*Trans. Chantal Wright*

| | |
|---|---:|
| By the sea in Heiligendamm | 1 |
| in June, the water, gigantic, | 2 |
| silver, eats up skin and | 3 |
| spits out naked bodies. | 4 |
| | |
| Between the lakes, to the north, | 5 |
| the sun yields of its own volition, | 6 |
| the way only the south can yield, | 7 |
| the birches darken in amazement. | 8 |
| | |
| By the river, to the east, | 9 |
| pearls ripen in fig hearts, | 10 |
| amber-coloured resignation, | 11 |
| and the pebbles shine. | 12 |
| | |
| With hope | 13 |
| – that dirty word – | 14 |
| here, between | 15 |
| fences and shores. | 16 |

Though the poem does not explicitly reference the summit, it functions nonetheless as political commentary. There are references to three points of the compass – north, south and east – with the west foregrounded through its absence. The submissive position of the south in relation to the political and economic hegemony of the (largely northern) West is emphasized through the use of the reflexive verb *sich hingeben* (line 7) to describe the behaviour of both sun and south. I chose to translate this verb as 'yield'.

| | |
|---|---:|
| Am    Meer in Heiligendamm | 1 |
| *By-the sea    in Heiligendamm* | |
| im Juni, das Wasser, riesig, | 2 |
| *in June, the water,  gigantic,* | |
| silbern, schluckt  Haut und | 3 |
| *silver,  swallows skin  and* | |
| spuckt nackte Menschen aus. | 4 |
| *spits    naked  people    out.* | |
| | |
| Zwischen den Seen, nördlich davon, | 5 |
| *Between  the lakes, north    of-there* | |

| | |
|---|---|
| gibt sich die Sonne von alleine hin, | 6 |
| *gives itself the sun from alone to/there,* | |
| wie nur der Süden sich hingeben kann, | 7 |
| *as only the south itself there-give can,* | |
| erstaunt dunkeln die Birken. | 8 |
| *astounded darken the birches.* | |

*Sich hingeben* can mean 'to sacrifice oneself' but also 'to engage or commit oneself' or 'to make a present of oneself'. Given the range of potential meanings expressed by this verb, an alternative translation could have sent the English poem in a very different direction. But the mood of 'Landschaften, Ufer' is one of gracious, inevitable capitulation or resignation in the face of forces larger than the individual, and this pointed in the direction of 'yield'. In the first verse, for example, the sea is described as being *riesig* [gigantic], an usual choice of adjective, and one from which I made the associative leap to *Wirtschaftsriesen* [economic giants]. This gigantic sea 'schluckt Haut und/ spuckt nackte Menschen aus' [swallows skin and/ spits naked people out]; the rhyme of *schluckt* and *spuckt* and the threefold repetition of the diphthong 'ck' create an image of a monster swallowing and spitting out bodies. I could not re-recreate this rhyme and sound in English, so I opted for verb phrases to create some sort of parallelism, 'eats up skin and/ spits out naked bodies'.

| | |
|---|---|
| Am Fluss, östlich, | 9 |
| *at-the river, easterly,* | |
| im Feigenherz reifen Perlen | 10 |
| *in-the fig-heart ripen pearls* | |
| bernsteinfarbenes Abfinden, | 11 |
| *amber-coloured resignation* | |
| und der Kiesel erstrahlt. | 12 |
| *and the pebble shines.* | |
| | |
| Von der Hoffnung | 13 |
| *On/About the hope* | |
| – dieses schmutzige Wort – | 14 |
| *– this dirty word –* | |
| hier, zwischen | 15 |
| *here, between* | |
| Zäunen und Ufern. | 16 |
| *fences and shores.* | |

In the third verse, the compound noun *Feigenherz* [fig heart] is an echo of the contradiction inherent in the sun yielding 'von alleine', 'of its own volition'. *Feige* is both a fig but is morphologically related to *feige*, an adjective meaning 'cowardly'. The heart of the fig contains both bravery and cowardice, and the fig comes from the south and the east; it does not grow in the north and the west. The dual meaning of *Feige* cannot be conveyed in English, of course, but it does strengthen the translator's sense of the poem's overall intention and thus aids the decision-making process elsewhere, with *sich hingeben*, for example. Within the fig heart, pearls are not merely ripening themselves but something else, too: the noun *Abfinden*, a noun that means 'coming to terms with', 'acceptance', 'resignation' or 'agreement'. In light of the poem's overall mood and in keeping with 'yield', I opted to translate *Abfinden* as 'resignation'.

Throughout the poem, the south and the east are portrayed using the imagery of colour and light. The *Ostsee* is 'silver'; when the sun yields, the birch trees of the north 'darken in amazement'; the resignation ripening inside the fig hearts is 'amber-coloured'; and the pebbles in the river to the east 'shine'. The beauty of the natural world described in the poem allows the reader to forget the troubled political backdrop that is gestured towards but not made explicit. For this reason, I decided to translate the seemingly innocuous yet troublesome little word *von* in the phrase 'von der Hoffnung' as 'with' because for me, the natural world is a source of comfort here. I later discovered that the poet finds the concept of hope deeply problematic; if I had known this and if I had felt it was important to incorporate this extratextual knowledge into my translation rather than to follow my own reading, I might have chosen to omit the preposition altogether and translated as follows:

Hope
– that dirty word –
here
between fences and shores.

We can see here how the translator traces the development of signifying networks through the text and how translation is an interpretative process. The next and final example will highlight the need for contextual research and the importance of placing the text into the hermeneutic circle it inhabits.

### Translating Tzveta Sofronieva's poetry (3): 'Korrespondenz mit Kappus'

Sofronieva's cycle 'Korrespondenz with Kappus' ['Correspondence with Kappus'] consists of eight poems bookended by a prologue and an epilogue. The Kappus referred to in the title, Franz Xaver Kappus, was a budding poet and a young military cadet at the Wiener Neustadt Military Academy in Austria. Between 1903 and 1908 he corresponded, at sporadic but sometimes more intense intervals, with the poet Rilke, seeking Rilke's advice on his poetry and on the conduct of his life more generally. Kappus published Rilke's letters in 1929 and they have been translated into English numerous times. Sofronieva's cycle takes up Kappus' questions to Rilke more than one hundred years later, recontextualizing them and creating a complex intertextual weave. By focusing here on several challenges that face the translator of this cycle in the prologue and the first poem, I will model how translators read, leaving the 'solutions' to these challenges open for the reader to contemplate (the two poems are reproduced in German below and glossed). Its close relationship with another set of texts means that 'Correspondence with Kappus' functions particularly well as an illustration of the importance of contextual knowledge and intertextual reading for the translator.

**From 'Korrespondenz mit Kappus'**

*Tzveta Sofronieva*
*Trans. Chantal Wright*

*Prolog*

| | |
|---|---|
| Glücklich waren Sie, Weihnachten 1908 | 1 |
| *Happy were you, Christmas 1908* | |
| irgendwo außer Gefahr, | 2 |
| *somewhere out-of danger,* | |
| mutig und allein in Ihrer rauen Wirklichkeit. | 3 |
| *brave and alone in your raw reality.* | |
| Ich kenne nur wenige Ihrer Gedichte, | 4 |
| *I know only few of-your poems,* | |
| bin sehr dankbar für Ihre Briefe an Rilke. | 5 |
| *am very grateful for your letters to Rilke.* | |
| Schön ist es weder Ergänzung noch Grenzen zu denken. | 6 |
| *Lovely is it neither addition/completion nor borders to think.* | |
| Ist es von Bedeutung, ob meine Fragen | 7 |
| *Is it of significance, whether my questions* | |
| ein Jahrhundert später Ihren ähnlich sind? | 8 |
| *one century later to-yours similar are?* | |

| | |
|---|---|
| Die Biene wird sterben, nur weil meine Haut dünn ist, | 9 |
| *The bee will die, only because my skin thin is* | |

| | |
|---|---|
| Menschenhaut. | *10* |
| *human-skin.* | |
| Ihr Stachel ist Bärenmäuler gewöhnt | *11* |
| *Her sting is bear-muzzles used-to* | |
| und pelzige Körper. | *12* |
| *and furry bodies.* | |
| | |
| Die Gefahr, dass ich ersticke | *13* |
| *The danger, that I suffocate* | |
| wegen der Unverträglichkeit gegenüber dem Stich | *14* |
| *because-of the intolerance towards the sting* | |
| – diese meine alte Schwäche – | *15* |
| *– this my old weakness –* | |
| hat nichts mit der Biene zu tun. | *16* |
| *has nothing with the bee to do.* | |
| | |
| Ist alles Grausame in unseren Träumen wirklich nur | *17* |
| *Is everything terrible in our dreams really only* | |
| das Zerbrechliche, was uns zu Hilfe ruft? | *18* |
| *the fragile, which us to help calls?* | |

The opening lines of the prologue to the cycle address Kappus, referencing Rilke's final letter to him from Christmas 1908, in which he wrote: 'Ich freu mich, mit einem Wort, daß Sie die Gefahr, dahinein zu geraten, überstanden haben und irgendwo in einer rauhen Realität einsam und mutig sind' (Rilke 2006:71) [I am happy, in a word, that you have withstood the danger of slipping into that and that you are lonely and courageous, somewhere in a raw reality (my translation)]. The danger from which Kappus has been saved is not a mortal danger, such as one might expect a soldier to face, but the danger of pursuing 'a half-artistic profession' (ibid) such as journalism or literary criticism. The 'raw reality' of Kappus' military career is infinitely preferable to this, Rilke writes, although under such circumstances a poetic soul will undoubtedly be lonely; courage will be required. Only one of Kappus' poems is included in the published correspondence, a sonnet that Rilke copied out by hand and sent back to Kappus 'because I know how important and what a new experience it is to find your own work in a foreign hand' (Rilke 2006:48); this is why the poetic voice in the prologue is unfamiliar with Kappus' poetry. When the voice thanks Kappus for his letters, her gratitude is both for the fact that Kappus committed his questions and doubts to paper and for the responses provoked in Rilke by Kappus' questions.

The questions asked by Sofronieva's cycle one hundred years later are very similar; these questions punctuate the cycle, interrogating the existence and purpose of fear, anxiety and trauma, especially within the artistic life. It would appear that both Kappus and Rilke are being addressed by a poet – a fledging poet, perhaps – a poet who shares in the doubts and insecurities expressed by Kappus a century earlier.

The sixth line of the prologue, *Schön ist es weder Ergänzung noch Grenzen zu denken*, is ambiguous. The poetic voice remarks that it is lovely not to have think in terms of *Ergänzung* or *Grenzen*. Possible English equivalents of *Ergänzung* include 'addition', 'completion' – the adjective *ganz* means 'whole' – 'supplement' or 'complement'; *Grenzen* means 'borders' or 'limits'. The two words are further foregrounded by the fact that they rhyme internally. To what might this ambiguous statement, which occurs within an otherwise straightforwardly narrative verse, refer? Drawing on a familiarity with Rilke's letters to Kappus – the cycle's intertextuality makes these indispensable reading for the translator – and on a wider contextual knowledge of Sofronieva's status as an exophonic poet and her poetry's preoccupations with exophony, several readings of this line seem plausible. The first, taking its cue from the immediate textual context, is that the poet who speaks in this cycle is expressing something about her relationship to the Rilke–Kappus correspondence. The cycle has, after all, reopened this correspondence and its questions almost a century on. Is it of any consequence that the poet who speaks here is troubled by the same questions that plagued Kappus, the prologue goes on to ask? Perhaps this statement, that it is good not to have to think in terms of *Ergänzung* or *Grenzen*, implies contentment that the poet does not need to differentiate herself from Kappus, that the poetic soul may indeed continue to be troubled by the same questions, even across the span of a hundred years. The second possible reading of this statement is that it is a reference to something Rilke wrote in one of his letters. The phrase *Ergänzung und Grenzen* is indeed a direct quotation from Rilke's 14 May 1904 letter, in which he discusses the changing identity and role of women in European society of the period, expressing the hope that women will eventually come to be seen and to see themselves as something more than simply the binary opposite of the masculine, but rather as 'etwas für sich' [an entity in their own right] (Rilke 2006:55). The inclusion of this phrase in the cycle would appear to identify the poetic voice as female and suggests that although the poem is voicing the same questions about life and suffering formulated by Kappus, they are now being voiced by a female poet, whose life experience is very different. The third reading, and this is a reading that stems from a familiarity with the context in which exophonic writers work in Germany, is that the words refer to the manner in which exophonic writers are often received: as a cultural enrichment of the German literary scene (*Ergänzung*), but an enrichment that is fenced off, kept behind borders (*Grenzen*), separated from the main body of German literature. The poet is pleased not to be forced to occupy either of these positions and instead to be simply a poet. The translator will not 'solve' the ambiguity of this phrase, nor is it desirable for him or her to do so, since all of these readings can happily coexist alongside each other and other potential readings, but by reading with sensitivity and an awareness of context it should be possible to translate this line in a way that gestures towards its polysemous ambiguity and allows the English reader to puzzle over it in a similar manner to the German reader. As the translator works his or her way through the cycle, these initial readings of the statement may shift, coming to seem more or less plausible in light of subsequent textual evidence, as signifying networks emerge. When, in the third poem of the cycle, for example, we encounter the lines *und wenn ich glaube an das, was in mir entspringt/ behaupte ich nicht, es verschaffe mir einen Platz unter den anderen/ nur, dass es einen Platz selber hat* (Sofronieva 2013:113) [literally, and if I believe in that, what in me leaps-out/ maintain I not, it creates for-me a place among the others/ only, that it a place itself has], we return to the notion of the poet carving out a place for herself, with the poetic voice once again suggesting that she is content to think and to exist outside the binary of *Ergänzung/Grenzen*. If poetry is a part of your being, Rilke wrote to Kappus on 17 February 1903, then any poem is 'a piece and a voicing of your life' (Rilke 2006:16) and this is the only criteria against which it should be judged; there is no need to seek external affirmation since works of art have a 'secret existence' and 'criticism is worst placed to reach them' (ibid: 13). This is surely also significant for the exophonic poet, whose place in the adopted national canon is frequently fraught and uncertain.

The first poem in the cycle abandons the grammatical punctuation and capital letters of the prologue, thus signalling a shift from formal correspondence, from the poetic voice's dialogue with Kappus, to internal monologue. The poem borrows from Rilke's August 1904 letter to Kappus, in which Rilke writes that periods of sadness, pain and difficulty are not caused so much by external events but by 'Momente der Spannung' (Rilke 2006:58) [moments of tension] in which a person experiences feelings that are alien to him or her and undergoes a painful process of change as these feelings are gradually assimilated, 'wie ein Haus sich verwandelt, in welches ein Gast eingetreten ist' (ibid) [translation: just as a house that has been entered by a guest is transformed/transforms itself].

1.

diese anstrengenden Momente der verlassenen   *1*
*these tiring   moments of abandoned*

vertrauten Gerüche und Gesten   *2*
*familiar smells and gestures*

|   |   |
|---|---|
| das Übertreten dieser Schwelle<br>*the crossing      of-this threshold* | 3 |
| unser Zuhause ändert  sich,  wenn ein Gast  eintritt<br>*our    house       changes itself, when a      guest enters* | 4 |
| höflich, mit  Schwertlilien der      besten Sorte<br>*politely, with  sword-lilies of-the best     kind* | 5 |
| sein Kommen ändert   uns bevor  wir ihn   treffen<br>*his  coming    changes us  before we  him meet* | 6 |
| der Besucher ist schon   im       Garten<br>*the visitor     is already in-the garden* | 7 |
| gleich wird es klingeln<br>*soon    will  it   ring* | 8 |
| immer seltener      lassen wir die Türen offen<br>*always more-rarely leave   we  the doors open* | 9 |
| die Geduld  des     Trauernden     schwindet<br>*the patience of the grieving-person dwindles* | 10 |
| allein und horchend<br>*alone and attentive* | 11 |
| leise, und doch geduldig mit  den Schwertern der     Lilien<br>*quiet, and yet    patient   with the swords      of-the lilies* | 12 |

This first poem rewrites Rilke's letter of August 1904 in verse form, with references to the sounds and lexis of the original. Thus where Rilke says that all our sadnesses are moments of tension 'weil uns alles Vertraute und Gewohnte für einen Augenblick fortgenommen ist; weil wir mitten in einem Übergang stehen, wo wir nicht stehen bleiben können' [because everything that is familiar and that we are used to has been taken away for a moment, because we are in the middle of a transition where we cannot remain] (ibid), the poem expresses this as

|   |   |
|---|---|
| diese anstrengenden Momente der verlassenen<br>*these tiring           moments of  abandoned* | 1 |
| vertrauten Gerüche und Gesten<br>*familiar    smells    and gestures* | 2 |
| das Übertreten dieser Schwelle<br>*the crossing     of-this threshold* | 3 |

The poem borrows the adjective *vertraut* [familiar] from Rilke's letter and references his *Gewohnte* [that which we are used to] with the alliteration of *Gerüche* [smells] and *Gesten* [gestures], and then later in the poem with *Gast* [guest], *Garten* [garden] and *Geduld* [patience]. The repetition of the 'v' (*verlassen, vertraut*) and 'g' sounds conjures up the comfort of the familiar, that which recurs. The word *Schwelle* [threshold] references Rilke's *Übergang* [transition] and is part of the poem's extension of Rilke's metaphor of a house being visited by a guest. Later in the poem, in place of Rilke's *Stille* [silence] and *schweigen* [being silent] (Rilke 2006:58), the poem uses *leise* [quiet]; where he speaks of being 'einsam und aufmerksam' (ibid:59) [lonely and attentive], the poem uses *allein und horchend* [alone and obedient]. The translator will have to find a way to gesture towards the absent familiar created by the 'v' and 'g' sounds using English resources, and to sustain the intertextual web that stretches from the Kappus correspondence to Sofronieva's cycle.

Another kind of challenge is posed by the metaphor inherent to the compound noun *Schwertlilien*, a word that literally means 'sword lilies': the German word for the genus of plants known as irises in English. These are the flowers borne by the guest who enters the house and transforms it. In English the term 'sword lily' also exists, but it designates a different plant: the genus gladiolus, which belongs to the iris family but is very different in appearance. When translating this term into English, the translator must consider whether it is more important that the guest be holding the same flower (in the truth-conditional sense) in the English translation, i.e. an iris, or whether the strong imagery represented by the term *Schwertlilien* be conveyed. The choice of such an unusual signifier must be motivated by the desire to create a particular image. Since the guest belongs to the source domain in a metaphor exploring the target domain of change and painful feelings, it makes sense that the flowers he or she is bearing will have a threatening aspect: sword-like qualities that can penetrate and cause harm. The plant signified by the signifier *Schwertlilien*, the iris, is in fact benign in appearance, but the real-world referentiality of the flower is less important than the symbolism of its signifier. In its final line, this first poem will once again refer to the *Schwertern der Lilien* [swords of the lilies], underlying the importance of the sword image. The grieving person referenced in the poem, presumably the person who has suffered the loss of familiar smells and gestures, learns to be patient with the swords of the lilies, and hence with the pain caused by the alienation of new feeling and experience, yet patience remains a challenge – the appearance of *Geduld* [patience] and its adjectival form *geduldig* within the same three lines foregrounds this. While one may be patient with the painful feelings caused by the loss of the familiar, there may still be an unwillingness to open the doors of one's house to new experience, to face what is new in a truth-conditional sense: a new country; new surroundings, a new language.

Thus each line, stanza and poem delivers new challenges, which may be lexical, rhythmic or hermeneutic, or arise through imagery and allusion. Reading for translation means identifying these challenges and weighing the translational possibilities. Reading for translation also means reading beyond the text that is to be translated: reading texts directly referenced by the source text; reading texts that explore or will explain concepts or images central to the source text; reading texts that provide points of comparison and contrast; reading biographically; reading other works by the same author that deepen the translator's understanding of the writer's 'mind-style'. It is for the latter reason that I chose to discuss three poems by the same writer in this final section of the chapter, to afford the reader the opportunity to engage with themes and patterns in Sofronieva's texts. Once the translator has done all of this, has read the source text well and read around it, all that remains is for her to follow Gregory Rabassa's already cited advice and 'write (*her*) ass off' (2005:8).

> Since I translated Sofronieva's poetry for the bilingual collection *A Hand Full of Water*, which was published by White Pine Press in 2012, German publisher Hanser has issued a collection of her texts in their Lyrik Kabinett series. This collection, entitled *Landschaften, Ufer*, includes new poems but also many of the poems from her earlier collection *Eine Hand voll Wasser*, upon which my translation *A Hand Full of Water* was based, although in revised forms. This is not the place to speculate on the editorial process for *Landschaften, Ufer*, but I would like to note that many of the stylistic features of Sofronieva's poems discussed here and that seem to me to be so significant to a political reading of her work have been eradicated in the Hanser versions. In 'Einbürgerung am Valentinstag', for example, the punctuation and capitalization have been reintroduced and the ambiguous final line, 'jenseits', has been replaced by the more definite and conventional 'in eine andere Welt' [into another world]. In the poem 'Landschaften, Ufer', the narrative setting has been clarified by the addition of a tagline that reads 'Heiligendamm, G8-Gipfel 2007' [Heiligendamm, G8 summit, 2007], the grammar has been 'corrected' and the imagery weakened by the deletion of several adjectives.

## Exercises

1. If you were asked to translate the names of the pirates in *Käpten Knitterbart und seine Bande* [*Pirate Girl*] into English or any other language, which factors might you bear in mind? Here are the names in German with a gloss:

Fieser Freddy [Mean Freddy]
Säbel-Tom [Sabre Tom]
Kahler Knud [Bald Knud]
Harald die Holzhand [Harald the Woodhand]
Buckliger Bill [Hunchbacked Bill]
Blauer Hein [Blue Hein]
Wilde Berta [Wild Berta]

Even for those who do not speak German, the alliteration in many of the names will be striking. The artwork in the book and the translator's culturally acquired knowledge of piratical stereotypes will also be of help. Direct translation may not be the right approach here.

2. The title of the French translation (translator not credited) of Michael Bedard's picture storybook *Sitting Ducks* is *Croque canards* (2001), a play on *croque-monsieur*, a grilled ham and cheese sandwich sold as a snack in France. Would it be possible to maintain the pun when translating into other languages? Which other strategies might one adopt when faced with the translation of this title? Would reading the story for other angles of approach be helpful?

3. Roald Dahl is the master of the humorous neologism. In *The BFG*, words such as 'whizzpopping' and 'frobscottle' (Dahl 2007a [1982]:64–9) are essential to the characterization of the giant and to the overall humour of the narrative. These words cannot be translated in any straightforward sense of the term. The translator will look to the resources of their own language to invent portmanteaus or neologisms that perhaps reference words in that language, but that are above all humorous, and even euphemistic, as is the case with 'whizzpopping', a joyously sneaky way of talking about the risqué subject of farting. In German, the noun 'whizzpopping' becomes 'Furzelbäume', a play on 'Purzelbaum', which means 'somersault', and 'Furz', which means fart. The drink 'frobscottle' turns into 'Blubberwasser' [bubble water] (Dahl, trans. Quidam 1990:70–7). In French, these neologisms become 'crépitage' and 'frambouille' (Dahl, trans. Fabien 2007b:75–82). The verb 'crépiter' means 'to crackle/sizzle', but 'crépitage' also contains something of the sound of 'péter', meaning 'to fart'. 'Frambouille' references 'framboise', the word for 'raspberry', and 'la bouille' is an informal word for 'face', particularly in the sense of pulling or making a face. How might these terms be retextualized in other languages? And if you are a fan of Roald Dahl, have you ever stopped to consider what Dahl's translators did, for example, with the taxonomy of giants from *The BFG*? In Japanese, does the Bonecrunching Giant still gallop off to Turkey to gobble Turks who taste of turkey? In Polish, do human beans from Jersey still have 'a most disgustable woolly tickle on the tongue' (Dahl 2007a [1982]:28) and taste of cardigans?

4. At a workshop for translators of German children's literature held in 2011, entitled Kein Kinderspiel!, I had the opportunity of discussing censorship with a group of fellow translators from all around the world. A translator from one of the Scandinavian countries noted that a German book in which a child's mother was a housewife was

> altered so that the mother went out to work, to reflect local norms of gender equality. Translators from Eastern European countries that had suffered Nazi occupation spoke of the need for sensitivity when translating children's books dealing with the Second World War and relations between Germany and their countries. Can you anticipate areas of cultural sensitivity that might arise when translating children's literature from 'your' source culture?

## Further reading: learning more about the translation of different genres

Prose translation: Berman 2012 [1985]; Weaver 1989; Wright 2013.
Poetry translation: Lefevere 1975; Loffredo and Perteghella 2009; Weinberger and Paz 1987.
Theatre translation: Aaltonen 2000; Baines *et al.* 2010; Johnston 1996.
Translation of children's literature: Epstein 2012; Lathey 2006; Oittinen 2000.
Translation of sacred texts: Abdul 2010; Everett 2008; Luther 1530.

## Bibliography

Aaltonen, S., 2000. *Time-Sharing on Stage: Drama Translation in Theatre and Society*. Clevedon: Multilingual Matters.
Abdul Raof, H., 2010. *Qur'an Translation*. New York: Routledge.
Anderson, B., 2006 [1983]. *Imagined Communities*. London: Verso.
Baines, R., Marinetti, C. and Perteghella, M., eds. 2010. *Staging and Performing Translation*. Basingstoke: Palgrave Macmillan.
Baisch, M., 2010. *Anton taucht ab*. Weinheim: Beltz & Gelberg.
Baisch, M., 2013. *Anton and Piranha*. Translated from German by C. Wright. London: Andersen Press.
BBC Radio 4, 2014. *A World for Children*, Four Thought Series 4. [podcast] 24 September 2004. Available at: www.bbc.co.uk/programmes/b04hyyr0 [accessed 13 April 2015].
Bedard, M., 1998. *Sitting Ducks*. London: Walker Books.
Bedard, M., 2001. *Croque canards*. Translator not credited. Paris: Nathan.
Berman, A., 2012 [2000] [1985]. Translation and the trials of the foreign. Translated from French by L. Venuti. In: L. Venuti, ed. *The Translation Studies Reader*. 3rd ed. New York: Routledge. pp. 240–53.
Biondi, F., 1995. Über Obrigkeitsdeutsch und Pluralität in der Sprache. *Tagungsprotokoll der Evangelischen Akademie Iserloh*, 6. pp. 18–23.
Biondi, F. and Schami, R., 1981. Literatur der Betroffenheit. In: C. Schaffernicht, ed. *Zu Hause in der Fremde: Ein bundesdeutsches Ausländer-Lesebuch*. Fischerhude: Atelier im Bauernhaus. pp. 84–93.
Boase-Beier, J., 2006. *Stylistic Approaches to Translation*. Manchester: St. Jerome.

Chesterman, A., 1997. Ethics of Translation. In: M. Snell-Hornby, Z. Jettmarová and K. Kaindl, eds. *Translation as Intercultural Communication*. Amsterdam/Philadelphia: John Benjamins.
Cothern, B., 2012. Review: The Spaghetti Detectives. *Portland Book Review*, 13 April. Available at: http://portlandbookreview.com/2012/04/the-spaghetti-detectives/ [accessed 7 May 2015].
Dahl, R., 1990 [1982]. *Sophiechen und der Riese*. Translated from German by A. Quidam. Reinbek bei Hamburg: Rowohlt.
Dahl, R., 2007a [1982]. *The BFG*. New York: Puffin.
Dahl, R., 2007b [1982]. *Le Bon Gros Géant*. Translated from English by C. Fabien. Paris: Gallimard Jeunesse.
Drvenkar, Z., 2002. *Sag mir was du siehst*. Hamburg: Carlsen.
Drvenkar, Z., 2005. *Tell Me What You See*. Translated from German by C. Wright. Frome: Chicken House.
Epstein, B.J., 2012. *Translating Expressive Language in Children's Literature*. Bern: Peter Lang.
Everett, D., 2008. *Don't Sleep, There Are Snakes: Life and Language in the Amazonian Jungle*. New York: Pantheon.
Fowler, R., 1977. *Linguistics and the Novel*. London: Methuen.
Funke, C., 1997. *Prinzessin Isabella*. Hamburg: Oetinger.
Funke, C., 2003. *Käpten Knitterbart und seine Bande*. Hamburg: Oetinger.
Funke, C., 2004. *The Princess Knight*. Translated from German by A. Bell. Frome: Chicken House.
Funke, C., 2005. *Pirate Girl*. Translated from German by C. Wright. Frome: Chicken House.
Funke, C., 2007. *Princess Pigsty*. Translated from German by C. Wright. Frome: Chicken House.
Johnston, D., 1996. *Stages of Translation*. Bath: Absolute Classics.
Klingberg, G., 1986. *Children's Fiction in the Hands of the Translators*. Lund: C.W.K. Gleerup.
Lathey, G., ed. 2006. *The Translation of Children's Literature. A Reader*. Clevedon: Multilingual Matters.
Lathey, G., 2010. *The Role of Translators in Children's Literature*. Abingdon: Routledge.
Lefevere, A., 1975. *Translating Poetry: Seven Strategies and a Blueprint*. Assen: Van Gorcum.
Library of Clean Reads, 2011. *Kid Konnection: The Spaghetti Detectives by Andreas Steinhofel*. Available at: http://libraryofcleanreads.blogspot.co.uk/2011/06/kid-konnection-spaghetti-detectives-by.html [accessed 7 May 2015].
Linhartová, H., 2014a. *Rico, Oskar und die Tieferschatten – tiefbegabt*. Personal communication, 5 March 2014.
Linhartová, H., 2014b. *Rico, Oskar und die Tieferschatten – Rabatt/Rabatte*. Personal communication, 11 March 2014.
Literary Translators' Association of Canada/Association des traducteurs et des traductrices littéraires du Canada, 2007. Trade Book Model Contract. Available at: http://www.attlc-ltac.org/model-translation-contract [accessed 22 October 2015].
Loffredo, E. and Perteghella, M., eds. 2009. *One Poem in Search of a Translator*. New York/Bern: Peter Lang.

Luther, M., 1530. *An Open Letter on Translating* [Sendbrief vom Dolmetschen]. Project Gutenberg. Available at: www.gutenberg.org/cache/epub/272/pg272.html [accessed 3 May 2015].
Milne, A.A., 1924. *When We Were Very Young*. London: Methuen.
Milne, A.A., 1927. *Now We Are Six*. London: Methuen.
Oittinen, R., 2000. *Translating for Children*. London: Garland.
Paul, P., 2011. On the Phone with Maurice Sendak. *The New York Times*. Available at: http://artsbeat.blogs.nytimes.com/2011/09/16/on-the-phone-with-maurice-sendak/?_r=0#more-229911 [accessed 7 May 2015].
Rabassa, G., 2005. *If This Be Treason: Translation and Its Discontents*. New York: New Directions.
Reynolds, K., 2011. *Children's Literature: A Very Short Introduction*. Oxford: Oxford University Press.
Rilke, R.M., 2006. *Briefe an einen jungen Dichter. Briefe an eine junge Frau*. Zürich: Diogenes.
Shavit, Z., 1981. Translation of Children's Literature as a Function of its Position in the Literary Polysystem. *Poetics Today*, 2(4), pp. 171–9.
Shavit, Z., 1986. *The Poetics of Children's Literature*. Athens: University of Georgia Press.
Society of Authors, 2013. *Basic Translator/Publisher Contract and Commentary*. London: Society of Authors.
Sofronieva, T., 2012. *A Hand Full of Water*. Translated from German by C. Wright. Buffalo, NY: White Pine Press.
Sofronieva, T., 2013. *Landschaften, Ufer*. München: Carl Hanser Verlag.
Steinhöfel, A., 2008 [1991]. *Dirk und ich*. Hamburg: Carlsen.
Steinhöfel, A., 2008. *Rico, Oskar und die Tieferschatten*. Hamburg: Carlsen.
Steinhöfel, A., 2010 [2008]. *The Pasta Detectives*. Translated from German by C. Wright. Frome: Chicken House.
Steinhöfel, A., 2011a [2008]. *The Spaghetti Detectives*. Translated from German by C. Wright. New York: Scholastic.
Steinhöfel, A., 2011b [1991]. *My Brother and I*. Hamburg: Carlsen.
Steinhöfel, A., 2012 [2008]. *Rico, Oskar a přízraky*. Translated from German by H. Linhartová. Prague: Nakladatelství Mladá fronta.
Van Coillie, J. and Verschueren, W.P., eds. 2006. *Children's Literature in Translation: Challenges and Strategies*. Amsterdam/Philadelphia: John Benjamins.
von Saalfeld, L., ed. 1998. *Ich habe eine fremde Sprache gewählt*. Gerlingen: Bleicher.
Wall, B., 1991. *The Narrator's Voice: The Dilemma of Children's Fiction*. Basingstoke: Macmillan.
Weaver, W., 1989. The Process of Translation. In: J. Biguenet and R. Schulte, eds. *The Craft of Translation*. Chicago: University of Chicago Press. pp. 117–24.
Weinberger, E. and Paz, O., eds. 1987. *19 Ways of Looking at Wang Wei*. Kingston, RI: Asphodel Press.
Word Candy, 2011. Review: The Spaghetti Detectives by Andreas Steinhöfel. Available at: www.wordcandy.net/7-13-2011-the-spaghetti-detectives-by-andreas-steinhofel [accessed 7 May 2015].
Wright, C., 2010a. Exophony and Literary Translation. What It Means for the Translator When a Writer Adopts a New Language. *Target*, 22(1), pp. 22–39.

Wright, C., 2010b. The Water under the Bridge: Tzveta Sofronieva's 'Der alte Mann, das Meer, die Frau'. In: E. Agoston-Nikolova, ed. *Shoreless Bridges*. South East European Writing in Diaspora. Amsterdam: Rodopi.

Wright, C., 2013. *Yoko Tawada's 'Portrait of a Tongue': An Experimental Translation*. Ottawa: University of Ottawa Press.

Wright, C., 2014. Tzveta Sofronieva's 'Über das Glück nach der Lektüre von Schopenhauer, in Kalifornien'. In: R. McFarland and M. Stott James, eds. *Sophie Discovers America: German-Speaking Women Write the New World*. Rochester, NY: Camden House. pp. 261–74.

Yildiz, Y., 2012. *Beyond the Mother Tongue: The Postmonolingual Condition*. New York: Fordham University Press.

# Conclusion

> Well said, old mole! Canst work i' th' earth so fast?
> A worthy pioner! Once more remove, good friends.
> William Shakespeare, Hamlet, Act 1 Scene 5

One of the panels run by the Literary Translation Centre at the 2015 London Book Fair carried the intriguing title 'What Not to Translate'. It attracted a particularly large audience, and a surprising pocket of quiet established itself within the substantial background noise of the hall at Kensington Olympia as three translators who work from languages at the heart of the geo-political tensions of our age spoke about their work. The panel turned out to be less about what not to translate than why to translate in the first place. Arch Tait, who has translated many books on contemporary and twentieth-century Russian history, including *Putin's Russia*, by the murdered journalist Anna Politkovskaya, applied the concept of *glasnost* to literary translation, arguing that translation should be about shining light into dark places. Tenzin Dickie spoke about her decision to translate from Tibetan in terms of an act of resistance. Translating Tibetan literature champions a language whose use the Chinese government is actively trying to suppress; it is also an important means of connecting Tibetans in exile and Tibetans who live under occupation. Alice Guthrie, who translates from Arabic, talked of her ethical dilemma in deciding whether or not to translate a piece of satire on the war in Syria for a London stage event. Guthrie was uncomfortable with the reactionary nature of some of the text's satirical elements and reflected on how the translating act might shape the West's view of the Syrian conflict and the Arab world more broadly.

Listening to these three translators, whose areas of linguistic and cultural expertise in the current geo-political climate confers upon them a particular burden of responsibility, I was reminded that translators are not unmotivated agents, but rather 'participate in very decisive ways in promoting and circulating narratives and discourses of various types' (Baker 2005:12). All three translators possessed 'a tough sense of the specific terrain of the original' (Spivak 1993:320) and were keenly aware of the 'cultural conditions of the translating' (Venuti 2013 [2011]:247). They had a strong ethical sense of what they would not translate and were attuned to the effects of the translating act for their specific source culture and language, for themselves and for the receiving culture. The panel underlined the fact that a translator's work not only moves away from the page, but that what leads us to the page in the first place is a complex set of motivations that will influence whether we translate, what we translate and how we translate. The extent to which our textual endeavours are successful, however, will ultimately depend on our skills as readers and writers, and these skills will in turn influence the extent to which we are able to make our voices heard as public intellectuals. The ability to critically reflect on all aspects of the practice of literary translation, contextual and textual, and to develop an appreciation of literary translation as a unique genre of writing can only improve our practice and the texts that we create. Formal education has a very important role to play in this – I announced in the introduction to this book that I was an unashamed advocate of theorization and argued that Translation Studies' consolidation of its position within academia had contributed to improving the fortunes of the real-world practice. But the nature of translation is such that its practitioners are lifelong learners by necessity, and the informal training and peer exchange in which all translators participate are also vital for critical engagement. The theorization that forms part of formal study promotes reflection and increases knowledge – not necessarily of facts or methods but of questions and issues. It should create confident practitioners with the ability to interrogate the framework(s) within which they produce translations for consumption by readers, if indeed they do produce translations intended for reading by others. This ongoing interrogation may result in very subtle shifts in practice or lead down avenues of radical experimentation. Since neither language nor the world are static, the translation of literary texts and the textual products that emerge from this process will always be in a contingent state of flux. The task of the translator is therefore as endless as that of the reader. Once more remove, good friends, there is work to be done.

## Bibliography

Baker, M., 2005. Narratives in and of Translation. *SKASE Journal of Translation and Interpretation*, 1(1), pp. 4–13.

Spivak, G.C., 1993. The Politics of Translation. In: G.C. Spivak. *Outside in the Teaching Machine*. New York: Routledge. pp. 179–200.

Venuti, L., 2013 [2011]. Towards a Translation Culture. In: L. Venuti. *Translation Changes Everything*. New York: Routledge. pp. 231–48.

# Appendix
## Tzveta Sofronieva's German-language poems

**Einbürgerung am Valentinstag**

| | |
|---|---:|
| die bräuche sind andere, einfach andere | *1* |
| bräuche | *2* |
| bräuchte, erst brauchte ich, | *3* |
| hätte ich, habe ich gebraucht, | *4* |
| dich lange genug zu lieben | *5* |
| mein wort | *6* |
| deine stadt | *7* |
| aus deinem ort ein wort in mir zu machen | *8* |
| das bett drei jahre | *9* |
| und beweise über die herkunft | *10* |
|     des ehegatten oder der ehegattin | *11* |
| kein pass, benötigt werden: die nummer | *12* |
| der einheit, in der sein bzw. ihr vater | *13* |
|     in der deutschen armee gedient hat | *14* |
| (mit der absicht, meinen vater zu töten) | *15* |
| und der einheit, in der sein bzw. ihr großvater | *16* |
|     in der deutschen armee gedient hat | *17* |
| (gegen meinen großvater) | *18* |
| nichts anderes beweist die europäische zugehörigkeit | *19* |
| des deutschen | *20* |
| bettes | *21* |
| die idee alles allein zu meistern: 10 jahre lang | *22* |
| gut verdienen, | *23* |
| miete ohne rückstände bezahlen | *24* |
| bedeutet deutsch zu sein | *25* |
| das ist alles | *26* |
| wortzeugen sind nicht zu gebrauchen | *27* |
| und keinesfalls reicht es, ein deutsches kind geboren zu haben | *28* |
| frau sein ist sowieso nicht deutsch, | *29* |
| eine mutter zu haben beweist keine zugehörigkeit, | *30* |
| mütter gebären nur, | *31* |
| sie zeugen nichts, | *32* |

| | |
|---|---|
| sie können keine zeugen sein | *33* |
| aus deinem wort einen ort in mir zu machen | *34* |
| wie lange ist lange genug für die liebe? | *35* |
| fangen wir mit 13 an | *36* |
| weil es seit jeher abergläubisch klingt | *37* |
| ohne bett und ohne geld, | *38* |
| nur das land meines zufälligen umherirrens | *39* |
| meiner letzten liebe | *40* |
| ich sagte schon so oft | *41* |
| china, wandern wir nach china aus | *42* |
| es ist dort spannend | *43* |
| spannender als hier | *44* |
| berlin war gestern | *45* |
| new york vorgestern | *46* |
| und sofia davor | *47* |
| dein ort – mein wort | *48* |
| der brauch | *49* |
| aus versehen | *50* |
| durch worte | *51* |
| wurde ich | *52* |
| deutscher als die deutschen | *53* |
| chinesischer als die chinesen | *54* |
| amerikanischer als die amerikaner | *55* |
| bulgarischer als die bulgaren | *56* |
| und so weiter | *57* |
| ich mag den unsinn ins groteske übertreiben | *58* |
| und vor allem – | *59* |
| wir sind lange genug hier gewesen | *60* |
| sogar wenn es nicht als lange genug gelten mag | *61* |
| es wird zeit | *62* |
| mein wort – dein ort | *63* |
| bevor es zu spät wird | *64* |
| bevor ich weniger deutsch werde | *65* |
| weniger bulgarisch, amerikanisch, chinesisch u.s.w. | *66* |
| wandern wir aus | *67* |
| jenseits | *68* |

**Landschaften, Ufer**

| | |
|---|---|
| Am Meer in Heiligendamm | *1* |
| im Juni, das Wasser, riesig, | *2* |

silbern, schluckt Haut und *3*
spuckt nackte Menschen aus. *4*

Zwischen den Seen, nördlich davon, *5*
gibt sich die Sonne von alleine hin, *6*
wie nur der Süden sich hingeben kann, *7*
erstaunt dunkeln die Birken. *8*

Am Fluss, östlich, *9*
im Feigenherz reifen Perlen *10*
bernsteinfarbenes Abfinden, *11*
und der Kiesel erstrahlt. *12*

Von der Hoffnung *13*
– dieses schmutzige Wort – *14*
hier, zwischen *15*
Zäunen und Ufern. *16*

# Glossary

### Domestication and foreignization

The two approaches to translation represented by these binary terms are generally understood to represent opposite ends of a particular spectrum of translation methods, although this need not in fact be the case. The domestication/foreignization binary was most recently brought to prominence by Lawrence Venuti in his monographs *The Translator's Invisibility* (1995) and *The Scandals of Translation* (1998) as part of a broader postcolonial sensibility within Translation Studies. For Venuti and much of modern Anglophone Translation Studies, domestication is a descriptive term that summarizes the practice of translating in such a way as to 'domesticate' a translated text, making it appear as though it had originally been written in English rather than a foreign language. This approach to translation might involve erasing or toning down elements of the text that are culturally specific such as food items or national holidays and/or not allowing the grammatical peculiarities of the source language, e.g. its syntactic rules, to affect the target language in any way. This, Venuti argues, is the dominant mode of translation in the Anglo-American world today. For Venuti, foreignization is a prescriptive translation method designed to make the reader of a translation aware of the translated text's foreign origins. This involves using the resources of the English language (rather than the foreignness of the source text) to create a text that in its lexical choices and mix of registers, for example, refuses to offer a smooth reading experience so that it cannot be easily assimilated. Foreignization may also, however, involve translating in a manner that conforms to target-culture norms in order to smuggle in important texts that might otherwise remain untranslated and inaccessible. Earlier modern views of foreignization (Schleiermacher 2012; Berman 2012) are more focused on a foreignization that derives from the foreignness of the source text and language. The political charge of Venuti's arguments has meant that they have dominated Translation Studies since the 1990s and are often erroneously assumed to have global relevance even though they are specifically and explicitly predicated on the situation in the Anglo-American publishing world – and even here one might argue that there are significant differences between the UK, Ireland, the US, Canada, Australia and New Zealand. Domestication and foreignization are often seen as an either/or scenario, when in fact each of the two methods encompasses a range of possible strategies and may in fact coexist within a given text.

Key texts: Berman 2012; Schleiermacher 2012; Venuti 1995, 1998.

## Equivalence

Equivalence describes the nature of the relationship between source and target text and can be defined in many different ways, from equivalence at the level of lexical units or grammatical categories to equivalence at the textual level or at the level of a text's message, function or effects. The term also exists in mathematics, where it describes the idea that two entities, though different, are interchangeable. The concept of equivalence is problematic because no two languages are identical, but in 'Linguistic Aspects of Translation' (2012 [1959]) Prague School linguist Roman Jakobson argues nonetheless that 'equivalence in difference' (2012 [1959]:127) is possible and that 'all cognitive experience and its classification is conveyable in any existing language' (ibid:128). Bible translator Eugene Nida moves away from linguistic definitions of the concept to differentiate between 'formal' and 'dynamic' equivalence, arguing that when translating Christian scripture, a dynamic method that ensures the text has the same effect on its readership as the source text had on its original readership, i.e. the early Christians, is preferable to a method that preserves the text in its cultural and historical moment of origin, potentially obscuring its message.

Key texts: Jakobson 2012 [1959]; Nida 2003 [1964]; and, for an overview, Pym 2014.

## Gloss

A gloss is the most literal form of translation and is used as an explicatory tool within the classroom and in scholarly texts to allow those who have no knowledge of the source language under discussion to understand something of the structure of the language and the decisions involved in the translation process. It generally involves accompanying the words given in the source language with a word-by-word translation, either in parentheses or on a separate line or lines. A gloss translation adheres to the syntax and literal meaning of the original text. It may also give full or partial details of parts of speech, number, case, tense and gender, as in the following example of a sentence taken from Freud's *Die Traumdeutung* [*The Interpretation of Dreams*]:

| Es | wird niemand | erwarten | dürfen, |
|---|---|---|---|
| it (object) | will nobody (subject) | to expect | allow/be able, |

| daß ihm | die | Deutung | | seiner | Träume |
|---|---|---|---|---|---|
| that him (dat.) | the (f.) | meaning/interpretation | | his (gen.) | dreams (m. pl.) |

| mühelos | in | den | Schoß (m.) | falle. |
|---|---|---|---|---|
| effortlessly | into | the (acc.) | lap | fall (subjunctive). |

Glossing is also a strategy used in postcolonial literary texts and translations when the writer or translator deems it important to retain a particular term in its original language either to respect its cultural specificity or because the foreign word is crucial for a broader understanding of the text. If a term is glossed in this sense, an approximate English translation will follow the foreign word either in parentheses or in a foot- or endnote. Alternatively, the translator might choose to translate the term into English and include the foreign word in parentheses or in a note. On the practice of glossing in postcolonial texts see *The Empire Writes Back* by Ashcroft *et al.* 2002 [1989]). See also *Literal translation*.

### Interlingual, intralingual and intersemiotic translation

Roman Jakobson differentiates between three different kinds of translation (2012 [1959]:127). Interlingual translation ('translation proper'), which is the focus of this book, is translation between distinct natural languages such as translation from Russian into English or from Spanish into Japanese. Intralingual translation ('rewording') is translation between different variants of the same language. This can include translation between historical variants of the same language, e.g. between Old or Middle English into modern-day English, but also translation between different dialects or sociolects. Finally, intersemiotic translation ('transmutation') is the movement of a written text into another type of sign system. Examples might include a dramatic or cinematic adaptation of a novel, or a painting that purports to translate a poem. Clive Scott (2012:13) argues for a refinement of Jakobson's division by replacing the term 'intersemiotic' with 'intermedial' to include translation between non-verbal sign systems.

Key text: Jakobson 2012 [1959].

### Literal translation

A literal translation is more readable than a gloss and functions in complete sentences, but it adheres closely to the source text formally (in terms of lexis, syntax, etc.) and/or in terms of meaning, which might involve sacrificing certain formal features of the original. Vladimir Nabokov's *Eugene Onegin* (1964a, 1964b, 1964c, 1964d), which refused to recreate the rhyme scheme of the original Russian text for fear of pushing it into absurdity, is perhaps the best-known example of a literal translation. Literal translations are more 'documentary' than 'instrumental', to borrow Christiane Nord's (1997) terms, i.e. they offer a documentary record of the source text rather than functioning as literary texts in their own right. Translators typically use literal translations as an explicatory tool when they wish to provide a more functional guide to a source text than a gloss is able to offer. So for the sentence glossed under 'Gloss' above, a literal translation that adheres to the lexis of the original (rather than to the syntax) might read as follows:

Es wird niemand erwarten dürfen, daß ihm die Deutung seiner Träume mühelos in den Schoß falle.

Nobody should be able to expect that the interpretation of his dreams falls effortlessly into his lap.

Literal translations are typically not idiomatic and are generally characterized by their translationese, an awkwardness that results from their over-fidelity to particular features of the source text.
Key text: Nabokov 1955.

## Process and product

These two terms are used to differentiate between the process of translating and the text that results from that process, each of which can be theorized and analysed. The process of translation is precisely what it suggests: the work that takes place before a translation is completed, delivered or published, i.e. the reading, decisions and actions (of the translator and other agents) that result in a finished translation product. The translation product is, of course, more easily accessible for unfiltered scrutiny than the process, but from Roman times translators have presented and defended their decision-making, thereby opening up the translation process for the interested reader. The branch of Translation Studies known as Descriptive Translation Studies focuses its attention on translation products and through them the process of translating, conducting 'carefully performed studies into well-defined corpuses, or sets of problems' (Toury 1995:1).
Key text: Toury 1995.

## Source and target

One frequently encounters the abbreviations SL, ST, TL and TT in the Translation Studies literature. These abbreviations stand for *source language* and *source text* – the original language and the original text – and *target language* and *target text* – the language of the translation and the translation itself. The terms *source culture* and *target culture* are also commonly used, as are the terms *target reader*, *target audience* and *target readership*. The terms *source* and *target* can mistakenly suggest that a text arises within, or is delivered to, a monoculture, whereas a text may well be the product of a blend of cultures – national, subnational, sociological – and be received by multiple readerships in different ways.

## Style and stylistics

The *Dictionary of Stylistics* defines style as 'the perceived distinctive manner of expression in writing or speaking' (2011:397). Literary style is understood to encompass the use of linguistic features such as metaphor, repetition and iconicity, but the definition has widened in recent years to include much broader issues of text and context. Writers, texts, genres and time periods all have distinctive or characteristic styles.

Stylistics, the study of style, began to gain momentum in the UK and the US in the 1960s, although its application to Translation Studies has been much more recent. Jean Boase-Beier has been a pioneer in theorizing how translators take style into account when reading source texts and creating target texts, arguing that style is the outcome of choices made by the author and to which the translator will therefore necessarily be attentive. The translator will also make choices in the process of translating and his or her style becomes part of the target text.

Key texts: Boase-Beier 2006, 2011.

## Translatability and untranslatability

The terms *translatability* and *untranslatability* can have linguistic, ideological and philosophical inflections and cover issues such as whether translation is actually possible, given the non-equivalence of languages, but also whether translation furthers or disrupts the humanist cause of greater understanding between peoples, encouraging linguistic laziness instead of curiosity and promoting assimilation rather than acknowledging and respecting difference. In Walter Benjamin's more esoteric definition of translatability (*Übersetzbarkeit*), it is seen on the one hand as an essential property of certain literary works, and on the other as a condition that might depend upon a text finding its ideal translator. See also *Equivalence*.

Key texts: Apter 2013; Benjamin 2012; Jakobson 2012 [1959].

## Translation

The definition of translation from which this book proceeds is that of the movement/transfer of a written (and in this context, a literary) text from one language into another, this transfer being carried out by a human agent or agents, i.e. the translator(s). But even such a simple definition gives rise to a welter of questions and qualifying statements. For example, a text that moves from one language into another surely also moves from one culture into another. Stieg Larsson's *Millennium* trilogy (*The Girl with the Dragon Tattoo*, *The Girl Who Played with Fire* and *The Girl Who Kicked the Hornet's Nest*) was translated into English from the Swedish by Reg Keeland. The English translation provides footnotes and endnotes to explain references to real-life figures such as the assassinated Swedish Prime Minister Olof Palme, whose name would be instantaneously recognizable to a Swedish readership but less familiar to Anglophone readers. In other words, translators translate more than simply words on a page: they are required to mediate the source culture for its new audience, explaining or finding equivalents for cultural references. Defining translation as the movement of a text from one language into another is also problematic (see *Interlingual, intralingual* and *intersemiotic translation*). My definition of translation also makes no reference as to how the written text is transferred from one language to another, nor to how we might go about judging if the transfer has been successful, yet questions of methodology and quality assessment have been central to translators' pronouncements on translation since Cicero and are a main focus of Translation Studies. The definition also excludes the translation of texts for performance, and indeed theatre translation is a thriving field that straddles Translation Studies and Theatre/Performance Studies. Elsewhere, the term translation is frequently used in a metaphorical sense to describe processes of movement across linguistic, cultural and social boundaries.

## Translation Studies

Modern Translation Studies is typically traced back to James S. Holmes' essay 'The Name and Nature of Translation Studies' (1998 [1972]), a metatext concerned with categorizing types of translation and delineating areas of study. Translation Studies is an academic discipline devoted to the study of the theory and practice of translation of all types of texts and to broader translational processes in texts, cultures and societies. Translation Studies is sometimes accused of not being a discipline in its own right and there has been discussion within the field as to whether it should more properly be known as an 'interdiscipline' (Snell-Hornby 2006:70–2). In universities it may be housed within its own department or within Modern Languages, English, World or Comparative Literature, Creative Writing or Applied Linguistics. Linguistics, literary studies and cultural studies have certainly all made their contributions to the discipline, and methodological approaches within Translation Studies can vary dramatically depending on the background of the scholar. Translation Studies scholars can specialize in corpus studies, stylistics, translation theory and translation history, but may also be interested in migration studies, travel writing or performance studies; they can be classical scholars, medievalists or modernists. Pronouncements on translation that precede the advent of Translation Studies are sometimes referred to as 'pre-scientific' and were typically penned by practitioners as an accompaniment to their products.

Key texts: Gentzler 2001; Holmes 1998 [1972]; Snell-Hornby 2006.

## Translation theory

Theories of translation attempt to account for how translation operates and may look at everything from what motivates translation to how the process is carried out and how translation products are perceived. It is often erroneously assumed that theories of translation can straightforwardly be applied or put into practice, i.e. that a theory essentially equates to a strategy or a method. Theories are hypotheses: tentative accounts of how processes work that are in a continual process of refinement on the basis of observation of phenomena. They are, in other words, descriptive but not prescriptive, although they can certainly influence methodology. Translation theory draws primarily upon the insights of linguistics, stylistics and literary studies, but other fields such as cultural studies, sociology and anthropology are also influential.

Key texts: Boase-Beier 2010; Munday 2012; Tyulenev 2014.

## Bibliography

Apter, E., 2013. *Against World Literature: On the Politics of Untranslatability*. London: Verso.

Ashcroft, B., Griffiths, G. and Tiffin, H., 2002 [1989]. *The Empire Writes Back*. 2nd ed. London: Routledge.

Benjamin, W., 2012 [1923]. The Task of the Translator. Translated from German by S. Rendall. In: L. Venuti, ed. *The Translation Studies Reader*. 3rd ed. New York: Routledge. pp. 75–83.

Berman, A., 2012 [2000] [1985]. Translation and the Trials of the Foreign. Translated from French by L. Venuti. In: L. Venuti, ed. *The Translation Studies Reader*. 3rd ed. New York: Routledge. pp. 240–53.

Boase-Beier, J., 2006. *Stylistic Approaches to Translation*. Manchester: St. Jerome.

Boase-Beier, J., 2010. Who Needs Theory? In: A. Fawcett, K.L. Guadarrama García and R. Hyde Parker, eds. *Translation: Theory and Practice in Dialogue*. London: Continuum. pp. 25–38.

Boase-Beier, J., 2011. *A Critical Introduction to Translation Studies*. London: Continuum.

Gentzler, E., 2001. *Contemporary Translation Theories*. 2nd ed. Clevedon: Multilingual Matters.

Holmes, J., 1998 [1972]. The Name and Nature of Translation Studies. In: J. Holmes, ed. *Translated: Papers on Literary Translation and Translation Studies*. 2nd ed. Amsterdam: Rodopi. pp. 67–80.

Jakobson, R., 2012 [1959]. On Linguistic Aspects of Translation. In: L. Venuti. *The Translation Studies Reader*. 3rd ed. New York: Routledge. pp. 126–31.

Munday, J., 2012. *Introducing Translation Studies*. 3rd ed. New York: Routledge.

Nabokov, V., trans. 1964a. Aleksandr Pushkin's *Eugene Onegin*. Volume 1. New York: Pantheon.

Nabokov, V., trans. 1964b. Aleksandr Pushkin's *Eugene Onegin*. Volume 2. New York: Pantheon.

Nabokov, V., trans. 1964c. Aleksandr Pushkin's *Eugene Onegin*. Volume 3. New York: Pantheon.

Nabokov, V., trans. 1964d. Aleksandr Pushkin's *Eugene Onegin*. Volume 4. New York: Pantheon.

Nabokov, V., 2012 [1955]. Problems of Translation. *Onegin* in English. In: L. Venuti, ed. *The Translation Studies Reader*. 3rd ed. New York: Routledge. pp. 113–25.

Nida, E., 2003 [1964]. *Toward a Science of Translating*. Leiden/Boston: Brill.

Nord, C., 1997. *Translating as a Purposeful Activity*. Manchester: St. Jerome.

Pym, A., 2014. *Exploring Translation Theories*. London: Routledge.

Schleiermacher, F., 2012 [2000] [1813]. On the Different Methods of Translating. Translated from German by S. Bernofsky. In: L. Venuti, ed. *The Translation Studies Reader*. 3rd ed. New York: Routledge. pp. 43–63.

Scott, C., 2012. *Literary Translation and the Rediscovery of Reading*. Cambridge: Cambridge University Press.

Snell-Hornby, M., 2006. *The Turns of Translation Studies*. Amsterdam/Philadelphia: John Benjamins.

Toury, G., 1995. *Descriptive Translation Studies and Beyond*. Amsterdam/Philadelphia: John Benjamins.

Tyulenev, S., 2014. *Translation and Society: An Introduction*. New York: Routledge.

Venuti, L., 1995. *The Translator's Invisibility*. New York: Routledge.

Venuti, L., 1998. *The Scandals of Translation*. New York: Routledge.

Wales, K., 2011. *The Dictionary of Stylistics*. 3rd ed. Harlow: Pearson.

# Index

*A Critical Introduction to Translation Studies* (book) 53
*A Good Read* (radio programme) 88–90
*A Grain of Truth* (novel) 45
'A Hand Full of Water' (poem) 139
*A Hand Full of Water* (poetry collection) 14–16, 149, 156
'A Kind of Loss' (poem) 96
*À la recherche du temps perdu* (novel) 67–8
Adelbert-von-Chamisso-Förderpreis (literary prize) 136
Adler, H.G. 27–8, 51, 70
Adorno, Theodor W. 27
Akunin, Boris 20
*Akzente* (literary journal) 136
ALCS (Authors' Licensing and Collecting Society) 82
*Alf Laylah wa-Laylah* (story collection) 33–4
Allen, Esther 3, 7–8, 82, 86–7, 91
alliteration 57, 114, 123–5, 146, 155
ALTA (American Literary Translators Association) 81
Althusser, Louis 31
Anderson, Sam 25
*Anton and Piranha* (children's book) 126–7
Apter, Emily 28
Ardizzone, Sarah 133
Armitage, Simon 65–6
Asher, Linda 88–90
assessing success (of literary translation) 108–10, 115–16
*Asymptote* (online literary journal) 3
'Attaining Citizenship on Valentine's Day' (poem) 139–46

*Austerlitz* (novel) 27–8
Avila, Consuelo 50–1

Babel (Biblical story) 68–9
Bachmann, Heinz 97
Bachmann, Ingeborg 88, 94–8
Baisch, Milena 126–7
*Bajo mis pies no florecen amapolas* (poetry collection) 50–1
Baker, Mona 28–9
Balding, Clare 88–90
Batchelor, Kathryn 38, 41, 43
Baudelaire, Charles Pierre 7
BCLT (British Centre for Literary Translation) 3, 8
Bedard, Michael 125
Bell, Anthea 45, 101, 102–8
Benjamin, Walter 7, 26, 53, 54, 60–2, 64, 99, 115, 171
*Beowulf* (epic poem) 65–6, 81
Berman, Antoine 2, 4, 20, 37–8, 40–1, 42, 59, 60–1, 81, 139
Bernofsky, Susan 3, 16
Bettelheim, Bruno 106
Bible translation 29–30, 168
Biondi, Franco 15, 138, 139
Bird, Robert 90–1
Blasim, Hassan 27
'blends' 83–4
Boase-Beier, Jean 1–2, 4, 53, 54–5, 58, 63, 83–4, 109, 171
'Bohemia Lies on Sea' (poem) 97
Borde, Constance 35
Breuer, Josef 102
Translators Association 66
*Bruchstück einer Hysterie-Analyse* (book) 88, 100–108
Bulgakov, Mikhail 52

# Index

Burgin, Diana 52
Burton, Sir Richard Francis 33–4

Calvino, Italo 45
Carcelen-Estrada, Antonia 34
Carson, Ciaran 66
censorship 131–3
Cervantes 19
Chandler, Raymond 24
Chesterman, Andrew 66, 85
children's and YA literature, translation of 5, 8, 17, 121–2, 127, 131, 133, 157–8
Cleeves, Ann 45
Coates, Jennifer 58
Collins, Andrew 88, 89
colonialism 6, 20, 33–4
Conrad, Joseph 68
'Correspondence with Kappus' (poetry cycle) 149–56
*Cosmicomics* (short story collection) 45
Crampton, Patricia 122
*Crime and Punishment* (novel) 90–1
Cunningham, Barry 43–5

Damrosch, David 7–8, 20, 21, 23, 85, 87
Dante 66
*Darkness Spoken* (poetry collection) 95
de Beauvoir, Simone 32, 34–5, 98, 99
de Gandillac, Maurice 60–1
Dead Sea Scrolls 29
*Decoded: A Novel* 91–4
*Der geheimnisvolle Ritter Namenlos* (children's book) 44
*Der verwaltete Mensch* (book) 27
*Der Zauberberg* (novel) 25, 46–8
Destutt de Tracy, Antoine 31
Deutsche Übersetzerfonds (German Translators' Fund) 3
Dickie, Tenzin 162–3
'Die Aufgabe des Übersetzers' (essay) 53, 60–2
*Die Blechtrommel* (novel) 88, 110–16
*Die Traumdeutung* (book) 168–9
*Dirk und ich* (children's book) 135

documentary translation 58–63
domestication 41–8, 52–3, 67–8, 82, 116, 135, 167–8
'Dora' (*Bruchstück einer Hysterie-Analyse*) 88, 100–108
Dostoevsky, Fyodor 38–40, 90–1, 99
Drvenkar, Zoran 134
Dryden, John 82
Drysdale, Patrick 88, 94–8
'dual address' 125
dynamic equivalence 29–30, 168

Eckermann, J.P. 24
'Einbürgerung am Valentinstag' (poem) 139–46
*Eine Hand voll Wasser* (poetry collection) 14–16, 149, 156
*Eine Reise* (novel) 27, 28
Engels, Friedrich 31
*Enigma* (poetry collection) 88, 94–8
*Epic of Gilgamesh* (poem) 23
equivalence 16, 29–30, 52, 57, 63–4, 110, 124, 146, 168
*Escrito para no morir: Bitácora de una militancia* (memoir) 50, 51–2
'Estrangement' (poem) 95
*Eugene Onegin* (verse novel) 58–9, 169–70
'Every Day' (poem) 96
existentialism 35, 64
exophony 8, 15–16, 121, 136–40, 142, 152
'Explain to Me, Love' (poem) 96
*Explanatory Notes on the Manners and Customs of Moslem Men* (notes) 34

*Faust* (play) 24
feminism 32, 34–5, 44, 50, 52, 104, 146
Filkins, Peter 27–8, 51, 70, 95, 97–8
Findlay, Jean 67
Fitzgerald, F. Scott 24
foreignization 37–8, 40–1, 42, 43, 48–53, 85, 167–8
Forshaw, Barry 23
*Four Thought* (radio programme) 121–2
Fowler, Roger 120

Freeden, Michael 31
Freely, Maureen 16, 70
Freud, Anna 36
Freud, Sigmund 5, 34, 35–7, 88, 99, 100–108, 168–9
Frisch, Max 96
Funke, Cornelia 44, 122, 123–4

Gaddis Rose, Marilyn 2, 13, 60, 62
García Márquez, Gabriel 1, 19, 92
Garnett, Constance 38, 39–40, 91, 99
*Gastarbeiterliteratur* (guest-worker literature) 138
Gauck, Joachim 3
'Germans' (poem) 55–7
gloss/glossing 168–9, 170
Goethe, Johann Wolfgang 6–7, 20, 21, 24
Grass, Günter 88, 110–16
Grossman, Edith 19–20, 24, 26, 58
Guthrie, Alice 162–3
Gutt, Ernst-August 54

Hahn, Daniel 2–3, 121–2
Hamburger, Michael 97
'Harlem' (poem) 98
Heaney, Seamus 65–6, 81
Heim, Michael Henry 16
Heim, Priscilla 16
Hemon, Aleksandar 25
Hermans, Theo 84
*Hinterland* (television series) 23–4
Høeg, Peter 23
Höller, Hans 97
Holmes, James S. 172
Hopper, Edward 125
Horton, David 47–8, 62
'How to Read a Translation' (article) 87
*How to Read World Literature* (book) 87
humanist motivations 19–30

ideological agendas/motivations 19, 30, 32–3; and colonialism 33–4; defining 'ideology' 31; and 'domestication' 41, 42, 43–8, 52–3; and 'foreignization' 37–8, 40–1, 42, 43, 48–53; and remuneration of translators 31–2; systems of thought 34–7; textual decision-making 37–43
*If This Be Treason* (book) 1, 53
*Ignorance* (novel) 88–90, 91
*In Other Words* (journal) 3
Independent Foreign Fiction Prize 27
*Inferno* (epic poem) 66
Institute of Psychoanalysis 36
instrumental translation 63–9
interlingual translation 64, 81, 169
intersemiotic translation 64, 169
intralingual translation 64, 81, 169

Jakobson, Roman 64, 168, 169
Jia, Mai 91–4

*Kafka Translated* (book) 62
Kappus, Franz Xaver 150–5
*Käpten Knitterbart und seine Bande* (children's book) 44, 123–4
Keeland, Reg 172
Klingberg, Göte 132
'Korrespondenz with Kappus' (poetry cycle) 149–56
Kundera, Milan 88–90, 91

*L'Âge de la Traduction* (commentary) 60–1, 81
'La traduction comme épreuve de l'étranger' (essay) 37–8
'Lab Coats' (short story) 49
'Landscapes, Shore' (poem) 146–9, 156
'Landschaften, Ufer' (poem) 146–9, 156
*Landschaften, Ufer* (poetry collection) 156
Larsson, Stieg 23, 24, 172
*Le Deuxième Sexe* (book) 34–5, 98, 99
Leigh, Mike 94–5
Leo Baeck Prize 27
Lewis, Philip 42
lexis 125–31
Linhartová, Hana 126, 129–30
Link, Perry 93

# Index

literal translation 58, 124, 128–9, 169–70
literariness 5, 38, 63
Llosa, Mario Vargas 1
Lloyd-Jones, Antonia 45
'Lost in the Book Review' (article) 86–7
Lowe-Porter, Helen 46–8
Lyons, Mike 88, 94–8

MacGregor, Sue 88–9, 90, 91
Mafouz, Naguib 21
Maier, Carol 7–8, 87
Malovany-Chevallier, Sheila 35
Mankell, Henning 23
Mann, Thomas 25, 46–8
Mannheim, Ralph 88, 110–15
Manning, Chelsea 96
Marx, Karl/Marxism 31–2, 68
Massardier-Kenney, Françoise 7–8, 87
McGowan, Gerard 21–2
'Message' (poem) 96
Meyer, Kerstin 123–4
Milburn, Olivia 92, 94
Milne, A.A. 125
Miłoszewski, Zygmunt 45
Mishra, Pankaj 25–6
*Miss Smilla's Feeling for Snow* (novel) 23
Mitchell, Breon 88, 110–15
Mitsutani, Margaret 16
mode of reading/writing, translation as 19, 53–4; documentary translation 58–63; instrumental translation 63–9; and response to reading 54–7
Modi, Narendra 25, 26
Moi, Toril 35, 99
Moncrieff, C.K. Scott 67–8
*Mr Turner* (film) 94–5
Murakami, Haruki 24–5, 26
Musil, Robert 25, 26
*My Brother and I* (children's book) 135
*My Life as a Colombian Revolutionary: Reflections of a Former Guerrillera* (memoir) 50, 51–2

Nabokov, Vladimir 58–9, 169–70
NASEN (National Association for Special Educational Needs) 17, 133
'negative analytic' 37–8, 61, 139
neologism 36, 125–31
Newmark, Peter 28
Nida, Eugene 29–30, 168
*Nighthawks* (painting) 125
Nord, Christiane 58, 170
*Norwegian Wood* (novel) 24
*Notes for a Rescue Narrative* (poetry collection) 55
*Now We Are Six* (poetry collection) 125

O'Connor, Katherine Tiernan 52
*Obrigkeitsdeutsch* (authority-German) 139
Ogawa, Yoko 48–9
Oittinen, Riitta 123, 131–2
'On Happiness after reading Schopenhauer, in California' (poem) 136
'On Reviewing Translations' (series of articles) 8
'On the Different Methods of Translating' (lecture) 20–1
*On Translator Ethics* (book) 13
Orientalism 31, 32, 33–4
*Orientalism* (book) 22, 30–1
Özdamar, Emine Sevgi 138

Pamuk, Orhan 16, 70
Pappenheim, Bertha 102
Parshley, H.M. 32, 34–5
Payne, Christopher 92
Payne, John 33
Pelevin, Victor 20
PEN/Heim Translation Fund 15, 16, 26–7
Pevear, Richard 38–40, 81, 90–1
Phillips, Adam 36–7, 99
*Pirate Girl* (children's book) 44, 123–4
Politkovskaya, Anna 162
'Portrait of a Tongue' (prose text) 14–16, 18, 65
Prenderghast, Christopher 67–8

*Princess Pigsty* (children's book) 124
*Prinzessin Isabella* (children's book) 124
process, defining 170
product, defining 170
*Projet d'éléments d'idéologie* (book) 31
Proust, Marcel 67–8
psychoanalysis 32, 34, 36–7, 102, 108–9
Pushkin, Alexander 58–9
*Putin's Russia* (book) 162
Pym, Anthony 13, 21, 22, 30, 32, 38, 42, 63–4, 66–7, 70

Rabassa, Gregory 1, 53, 156
*Reading in Translation: Teaching Issues and Reading Practices* (book) 87
reading of translations: assessing success of literary translation 108–10, 115–16; 'Dora' study 100–108; *Tin Drum* study 110–16; and 'translated textuality' 98–100
Ready, Oliver 90–1
Rebanks, James 5
relevance, theory of 54
*Remembrance of Things Past* (novel) 67–8
remuneration of translators 1, 14–18, 31–2
*Revenge* (short story collection) 48–9
reviewing translations 86–7, 88–98
Reynolds, Kimberley 131
*Rico, Oskar und die Tieferschatten* (children's book) 16–17, 126, 127–31, 133
Rilke, Rainer Maria 150–5
Robinson, Douglas 42
Rowling, J.K. 43
'Ruschuk, Rousse, by the Danube' (poem) 137

*Sag mir was du siehst* (YA novel) 134
Said, Edward 22, 30–1, 34
Salinger, J.D. 25

Sartre, Jean-Paul 35
Schleiermacher, Friedrich 20–1, 22, 38, 42, 85
Schmidt, Arthur 51
Schulz, Bruno 98
Scott, Clive 32, 53, 63–5, 66–7, 69, 83, 84, 94, 109, 169
Scott Moncrieff Prize 88
Sebald, W.G. 27
Selden, Yumi 16
Sendak, Maurice 131
Shavit, Zohar 132
Shephard, E.H. 125
Simons, Margaret 35
*Sir Gawain and the Green Knight* (Middle English text) 65–6
*Sitting Ducks* (children's book) 125
SL (source language) 170–1
Smith, J. Mark 55–6
'Sniffle' (review article) 91–2, 93–4
Snowden, Edward 96
Snyder, Stephen 48–9
Society of Authors 66
Sofronieva, Tzveta 8, 14–16, 136–7, 138–56, 164–6
Soljan, Maja 26
sound 123–5
Sperber, Dan 54
ST (source text) 170–1
Standard Edition of Freud (collection of works) 35–7, 99, 101, 102–8
Steiner, George 69
Steinhöfel, Andreas 16–17, 126, 128–30, 135
Strachey, Alix 36
Strachey, James 36–7, 99, 101, 102–8
stylistics 10, 171, 173

TA (Translators Association) 81–2
Taber, Charles 29
Tait, Arch 162–3
Taiwan Cultural and Creative Platform Foundation 3
Taiwan Literary Translation Center 3
Tawada, Yoko 15–16, 18, 65, 138

# Index

*Tell Me What You See* (YA novel) 134
Terando, Lorena 50–2, 70
testimonies/*testimonios* 50–1, 52
*The Book of the Thousand Nights and a Night* (story collection) 33–4
*The Brothers Karamazov* (novel) 24
*The Catcher in the Rye* (novel) 25
'The Closure of the Faculty for South East European Studies' (poem) 137
*The German Ideology* (book) 31
*The Girl with the Dragon Tattoo* (film) 24
*The Great Gatsby* (novel) 24
*The Interpretation of Dreams* (book) 168–9
*The Iraqi Christ* (short-story collection) 27
*The Killing* (television series) 23, 24
*The Long Goodbye* (novel) 24
*The Magic Mountain* (novel) 25, 46–8
*The Man Without Qualities* (novel) 25–6
*The Master and Margarita* (novel) 52
'The New Face of India' (article) 25–6
'The Name and Nature of Translation Studies' (essay) 172
*The Pasta Detectives* (children's book) 16–17, 126, 127–31, 133
*The Possessed/Demons/The Devils* (novel) 39–40
*The Scandals of Translation* (book) 41, 82, 167–8
*The Second Sex* (book) 34–5, 98, 99
*The Shepherd's Life* (book) 5
'The Task of the Translator' (essay) 7
*The Tiananmen Papers* (book) 93
*The Tin Drum* (novel) 88, 110–16
*The Translator's Invisibility* (book) 41–2, 82, 167–8
*The Wind-Up Bird Chronicle* (novel) 24
*The Winter's Tale* (play) 97

*Theresienstadt 1941–1945* (book) 27, 28
*Thomas Mann in English* (book) 62
Thomas, Ed 24
'Time on Loan' (poem) 96
TL (target language) 170–1
Tolstaya, Tatyana 20
translatability 28, 99, 115–16, 171
*Translated Poe* (book) 62
'translated textuality' 83, 98–100
*Translating Baudelaire* (book) 63–4
*translatio studii* (transferal of classical learning) 28
'translation', defining 2, 171–2
Translation Across Frontiers forum (Taiwan) 3
*Translation and Literary Criticism* (book) 13
'Translation and the Trials of the Foreign' (essay) 61
translation theory 2–4, 173
Translation Studies: and academia 2, 163; Canadian tradition 6; and colonialism 33; defining 172–3; domestication and foreignization 167–8; and exophonic texts 137, 139; and ideological agendas/motivations 37, 41, 52–3; and non-financial rewards 14; and 'specialness' of translated literary text 84, 85; and subjectivity of the translator 64; and translation products 170; and undervaluation of translators 83
*Translation Studies Reader* (book) 41
Translators in Schools project 3
Treaty of Waitangi (1840) 33
TT (target text) 170–1
Tyson, Alan 36

United Bible Societies 29
untranslatability 28–9, 32, 171

Valéry, Paul 39
Vásquez Perdomo, María Eugenia 50, 51–2
Venuti, Lawrence 7–8, 30, 32, 37–8, 41–3, 45, 49–50, 52–3, 61, 82–3, 85–7, 102, 167–8

Volokhonsky, Larissa 38–40, 81, 90–1
von Flotow, Luise 32

Waisman, Sergio 86
Wall, Barbara 125
*Wallander* (series of novels, television series) 23, 24
Wang, Helen 82
*War and Peace* (novel) 25
Weaver, William 45
*Weltliteratur* (World Literature) 6–7, 20–1, 24
West Point (US military academy) 21–2
*What I Talk about When I Talk about Running* (memoir) 24
'What We Talk about When We Talk about Love' (short story) 24
*When We Were Very Young* (poetry collection) 125
Whiteside, Shaun 101–8
*Why Translation Matters* (book) 19
'William Turner: Backlight' (poem) 95
Williams, Henry 33
Wilson, A.N. 67–8
Wilson, Deirdre 54
Woods, John E. 46–8
Woods, Michelle 62
Word Wave Festival (Taiwan) 3
*Words Without Borders* (literary journal) 3, 8
World Copyright Convention 92
'world literature' 6–8, 16, 20–2, 26, 85–7
Wright, Chantal 81, 126, 127, 128, 135, 136, 140–2, 147–8, 150–1
Wright, Jonathan 27

*Y Gwyll* (television series) 23–4
Yildiz, Yasemin 138
Yun, Sheng 91–4

# eBooks
## from Taylor & Francis

Helping you to choose the right eBooks for your Library

Add to your library's digital collection today with Taylor & Francis eBooks. We have over 50,000 eBooks in the Humanities, Social Sciences, Behavioural Sciences, Built Environment and Law, from leading imprints, including Routledge, Focal Press and Psychology Press.

**Choose from a range of subject packages or create your own!**

**Benefits for you**
- Free MARC records
- COUNTER-compliant usage statistics
- Flexible purchase and pricing options
- All titles DRM-free.

**Benefits for your user**
- Off-site, anytime access via Athens or referring URL
- Print or copy pages or chapters
- Full content search
- Bookmark, highlight and annotate text
- Access to thousands of pages of quality research at the click of a button.

**Free Trials Available**
We offer free trials to qualifying academic, corporate and government customers.

## eCollections

Choose from over 30 subject eCollections, including:

| | |
|---|---|
| Archaeology | Language Learning |
| Architecture | Law |
| Asian Studies | Literature |
| Business & Management | Media & Communication |
| Classical Studies | Middle East Studies |
| Construction | Music |
| Creative & Media Arts | Philosophy |
| Criminology & Criminal Justice | Planning |
| Economics | Politics |
| Education | Psychology & Mental Health |
| Energy | Religion |
| Engineering | Security |
| English Language & Linguistics | Social Work |
| Environment & Sustainability | Sociology |
| Geography | Sport |
| Health Studies | Theatre & Performance |
| History | Tourism, Hospitality & Events |

For more information, pricing enquiries or to order a free trial, please contact your local sales team: www.tandfebooks.com/page/sales

**www.tandfebooks.com**